Down the Horizon Line: The Working Adventures of
Hayes Perkins 1878-1964

John M. Martin

ISBN: 979-8-9921256-0-3 paperback;
        979-8-9921256-1-0 digital online

Library of Congress Control Number: 2024925797

Cover by Joyce Krieg
Back cover photograph by David Laws
Maps by Brian Timoney

First edition

For Ruth in memory.
For Kayann in love.

Table of Contents

Introduction

In October of 1964, an administrator at Forest Hills Manor retirement home addressed a letter on behalf of Henry Hayes Perkins to John Donaldson. Would Mr. Donaldson please come to Pacific Grove, California, at his earliest convenience? Mr. Perkins, who suffered diabetes, had fallen while walking on the coastline and subsequently developed pneumonia. Knowing he was gravely ill, Mr. Perkins had requested Mr. Donaldson drive from his home in Langlois, Oregon, to Pacific Grove to receive an important document from Mr. Perkins. The administrator closed with a certain note of urgency.

The letter could only have arrived as something of a surprise. John Donaldson, my maternal grandfather, knew Hayes only slightly. John had memories of Hayes passing through the family farm when John was a boy in the 1900s and 1910s. With little advance warning, on no particular schedule, this itinerant cousin would show up to work a few days, perhaps a couple of weeks, for John's father, James, and mother, Minnie. Minnie Perkins (Donaldson) and Hayes Perkins were first cousins, which makes me first cousin thrice removed to Hayes.

By chance, John had reconnected with Hayes shortly before receiving the letter from Forest Hills. John and his wife Rae had been touring Northern California in 1963 when they stopped at Pacific Grove very much surprised to discover Hayes still living. They spent a pleasant day with the 85-year-old traveler, undoubtedly sitting in rapt attention to at least a few of Hayes' stories of his times in Alaska, Australia, New

Guinea, Africa, and elsewhere, stories that John would have remembered from his youth.

After that visit, John and Hayes exchanged a few letters in 1963 and 1964. In one of the letters, Hayes mentioned that he had written an account of his seven years working for William Randolph Hearst at San Simeon and Wyntoon in the 1930s. Hayes would be willing to give John his Hearst papers. John could read them, as could perhaps John's son, and John's sister Mary, whom Hayes knew, but Hayes cautioned they were pretty "strong meat" and not suitable for general circulation, on pain of libel allegations.

The day after receiving the administrator's letter, John and Rae drove ten hours south to Pacific Grove, arriving late in the day. They spent a pleasant evening conversing with an obviously very ill, though still alert, Hayes Perkins. No, Hayes had not called John to receive the Hearst manuscript. Better! Hayes had recently received three bound copies of his travel diaries. Frank Preston, the same friend who had compiled Hayes' Hearst papers, had arranged for Hayes' two-thousand-page diary detailing Hayes' world travels between 1893 and 1955 to be typed in quintuplicate on onion skin, with each copy bound into three sturdy volumes. Preston retained two copies and had sent three to Hayes. The library at Pacific Grove had gladly accepted one; would John take the other two, one for himself and one for his sister Mary?

Hayes died quietly the following morning. John and Rae returned north with two copies of Hayes' diary, *Here and There*. As requested, John delivered one copy to his sister. After reading through the travel diaries, John shared volumes between his son and his two daughters. I first encountered volume one of Hayes' diary in the early 1970s where it sat neglected, seemingly always there, on a shelf in my boyhood home. In high school, I dipped in and out of the first volume of *Here and There*, captivated by the adventures, though mystified and almost completely ignorant of the geography and history Hayes so casually assumed. Nothing in my small-town Oregon education had prepared me to distinguish Lagos, Nigeria from Niangara, Belgian Congo from Ujiji, Tanganyika. And who was Chinese Gordon? The Mahdi? The Khedive of Egypt? It appeared the world might be broader than my small agricultural and logging town in Oregon presupposed.

Unlike my mother, my Aunt Ruth became fascinated with *Here and There*. Much as I would do later, Ruth poured over the diaries, mapping Hayes' routes and struggling to understand the context of his adventures. Sometime in the 1980s, Ruth contracted to have *Here and There* photocopied and bound, offering copies to anyone in the family who wanted one. Ruth's copies are clunky compared to the five original three-volume copies Preston had made for Hayes on onion skin paper. Still one-sided, but printed on much thicker paper, the pages in my copy of *Here and There* required binding in five volumes. At the end of Hayes' diary Ruth included copies of a number of letters to and from Hayes Perkins and a few photographs of Hayes.

Those five very thick volumes mostly sat on shelves in apartments and houses where I lived for the next 25 years. I had read through them completely more than once, even tried to make a list of all the place names, but ran out of steam, faced with the enormous extent of Hayes' travels. In those years, Hayes' barely believable, exotic adventures swirled all jumbled in my head, too many adventures to keep straight, in places varied and extended beyond my imagination. At various times, over more than 60 years wandering the globe, this distant cousin of mine had walked from San Antonio to Los Angeles; rowed 900 miles down the Yukon River in a dory; steamed the entire length of the Nile River; crisscrossed the African continent seven times; and worked at every manual labor imaginable – millwright, sailor, mining engineer, carpenter, prospector, quarry man, logger, ranch hand, farmer, cowpuncher, forester – and those were just the jobs and a few of the adventures that stuck in my memory.

By 2011, technology had made identifying the places Hayes had traveled a little easier. I launched a blog titled *Hayes Here and There,* complete with Google Earth maps, describing where Hayes had travelled and what his diary said he had done or seen in each place: dodged an elephant in Uganda; pushed bulls workaway in the hold of a steamship across the Atlantic; brokered a land deal in Papua New Guinea, or whatnot. After five years of fairly sustained work on the blog, I got through three-and-a-half of my thick volumes. The very impressive maps of Hayes' travels looked like colored spaghetti thrown at a globe. The maps were luminous, but I stalled out this time because the blog entries contained too many mysteries for me. I vaguely knew the famous names like Henry Morton Stanley, King Leopold of Belgium, Cecil Rhodes, and William Randolph Hearst. But who were CT Studd, Tippoo Tib, John Hanning Speke, Mustafa Kemal, and on and on, the minor characters flickering in and out of my blog?

The blog just didn't do Hayes or his times and places justice. Telling Hayes' story properly would require considerably more research. Thus, Hayes' diaries became for me an unconventional study guide to understanding the first half of the twentieth century as seen through the eyes of a unique, peripatetic, working-class traveler. Hayes' diaries became a workingman's *Where's Waldo?* of his time, inviting me to pick him out in scene after scene from among riots of other colorful characters along his path through gold rushes, suffrage marches, a great battle of World War I, and an astonishing range of colonial worksites all across Africa.

As is probably already clear, I am neither a historian nor a geographer, just a cousin thrice removed deeply interested in this man Hayes Perkins and his unique perspective on the rough and tumble world of his time. The more I read Hayes' diaries, the more convinced I became that his was not only an astonishing travel adventure story but also an important firsthand historical account detailing working conditions around the world in his time – particularly regarding colonial Africa.

Late in his life, Hayes wrote that he regretted missing only Russia in his travels. While it is an exaggeration to say he went everywhere else, he certainly tried his best. In order to make writing a partially informed synopsis of Hayes' travels even conceivable, I had to make a difficult decision early on. I would focus on Hayes' seven African adventures, giving short shrift to his travels elsewhere. In this book, years when Hayes traveled "everywhere else" are compressed into chapters titled "In the Meantime." Most of the highlights of his travels "in the meantime" get mentioned but, for pragmatic reasons, I simply could not develop these equally fascinating adventures. If his diaries were to be pared, Hayes probably would have agreed with my decision; he found his African adventures his most interesting, always writing more frequently and at greater length when on that continent.

Consequently, what follows does not aspire to history, nor even to a comprehensive biography of Hayes' travels. I think of it more in terms of storytelling, with a bit of historical context included, hopefully enough to make it accessible and engaging for a contemporary reader.

By Hayes' tenth birthday, the impressionable young boy, under the stern hand of an increasingly abusive father, had resolved to escape Oregon to join his hero Henry Morton Stanley adventuring in Africa, afraid only that "all the elephants and cannibals would be killed off before I might be old enough to assist in the game."

Stanley died in 1904, two years before Hayes first made it to Africa. By 1906, at the age of 28, Hayes had already been adventuring for nearly half his life. Having fled home at 15, he traipsed all about North America before escaping the continent of his birth, working as a deckhand on sailing ships: barques and schooners chased by the winds around the horn from the West Coast of the United States to European ports and back again.

"Adventuring" could be considered something of a vocation when Hayes was young. Lots of adventurous European and American men, and some women, went out to Africa, India, Australia, or the gold fields of Alaska, to places that still seemed wild, well into the first decades of the twentieth century. Some followed religious callings and many sought quick riches in a stultified economic time, but only a very few would be considered adventurers in the way Hayes understood the term.

For one thing, very few stayed the course for a lifetime. One here or there, but not many, returned to society with quick riches; many broke down and returned home; some settled into regular employment as the mines, plantations, and towns formerly undomesticated became so. Hayes never found quick riches. His health broke, but never so severely that he couldn't fall into a bed somewhere long enough to recover sufficiently for his return to "the long trail." At a couple of points in his life he thought about putting down roots in one place or another, but frontier towns beginning to settle, mining operations coming under the control of large corporations, plantations planted and producing, never caught his fancy – even when he might have grasped one of several opportunities to enrich himself by staying put. No, "other lands down the horizon line that need exploring…" sang the siren song to Hayes Perkins for his entire life, "…and to these I must go."

To appreciate the value of Hayes' independent, working class perspective on events in colonial Africa, the tone and content of his diaries can be compared to that of two other writers who documented events at two sites at which Hayes worked in the Congo.

Norman Grubb, English missionary successor to CT Studd, who founded the Heart of Africa Mission, published *Christ in Congo Forests* (1945), a history of the first twenty-five years of the evangelical mission in Northern Congo. (Grubb briefly mentions Hayes as the first labor assistant to Studd.) Where Grubb peopled the earliest days at the Heart of Africa in 1920 with stalwart British colossi of faith striding into a vast untamed wilderness of African souls in desperate need of Christian salvation, Hayes described working alongside courageous but frail men and women dropped into a foreign place with little preparation for their work and grave doubts about the character of their flamboyant leader. From conversations in Bangala, a trade language common to Azande and Mangbettu workmen of the region, Hayes learned much of Azande and Mangbettu lives. He also learned more than one sordid truth behind the scenes of missionary zeal: that the charismatic and aristocratic founder of the Heart of Africa mission was complicit in Belgian tax fraud – that indentured local workmen – in order to preserve British missionary welcome in the Belgian colony, and that the world famous evangelist purchased his welcome into unevangelized tribal regions by plying local chiefs with liquor.

Some years before Grubb published *Christ in Congo Forests*, Isaac F. Marcosson, American author and magazine editor, had published *An African Adventure* (1921), recounting his corporate-financed trip up through South Africa and down the Congo River. Marcosson's trip included a closely curated tour through the diamond mines of the joint Belgian/American Forminiere corporation in the southern Congo. Hayes was working for the Forminiere at that time and speculates that the Forminiere purposely scheduled Marcosson's itinerary to avoid Hayes, who had become increasingly outspoken concerning labor conditions that he likened to enslavement, for African men in Forminiere mines. Where Marcosson saw Belgian and American titans of industry utilizing contented, prosperous African labor to develop the vast resources of an uncivilized continent for the betterment of all humanity, Hayes saw American, Belgian, and African overseers murderously whipping African workmen who received little or no pay as both overseers and overseen were pressed to meet inhuman diamond quotas. While Marcosson was shown only snatches of actual mining practices, Hayes was working as an advance prospector surrounded only by African workmen where he witnessed and heard firsthand accounts of Forminiere treatment of its African workers.

In contrast to Grubb and Marcosson, Hayes traveled free from any obligation to aggrandize a missionary society or whitewash a multinational corporation, so he often turned his gaze away from the powerful men colonizing Africa to those he found more interesting: the common workers, often indigenous Africans, alongside whom he toiled. Furthermore, because Hayes wrote in a private diary not intended for publication, when his attention did turn to the high and mighty, Hayes could write with forthright candor concerning their misdeeds. This is not to say that Hayes' accounts didn't suffer his own biases, as will be discussed below, only that his were not those of an institutionally constrained missionary or journalist. This difference makes Hayes' account uniquely valuable among documentarians of his time.

Following a sincere conversion experience at a Salvation Army tent in Cripple Creek, Colorado, Hayes quite faithfully followed a rigid code of conduct for the rest of his life. Starting at age 22, the young, newly-redeemed man worked assiduously for several years at a mill in Eureka, California, doggedly sending his paychecks off at the end of every week to repay any man he remembered cheating or swindling in the previous years when he had "gone a little bit bad." With his conscience thus cleared, Hayes never again cheated, stole, lied, drank coffee, tea or alcohol, and had virtually no relations beyond passing conversation with any woman.

In several passages of his diaries, Hayes explained his austere lifestyle in practical terms. An adventurer with the genuine objective of seeing the entire world simply could not practice the various vices he so regularly witnessed other men indulging in and hope to survive. In many regards, Hayes' various abstinences served him well as a colonial adventurer: honesty and hard work gained him the high regard of most other men on various worksites; sobriety endeared him to employers; and sexual abstinence kept him clear of the marriage obligations he believed were required of honorable men of his class.

However, in more troubling passages, Hayes writes unmistakably that his morality was motivated by his belief in superiorities conferred on White, Christian men by God. This reprehensible view necessitates an explanation about the particularity of Hayes' beliefs, not to defend or promote them – just the opposite – but to explain my decision to publish a biography of an "African Adventurer" with White supremacist beliefs.

Hayes espoused a strain of White supremacy that Henry Louis Gates Jr. identifies as "dreadfully paternalistic" as opposed to the "Negro-as-separate-species" teaching also popularly wielded in Hayes' time. The racist ideology Hayes followed begins with the familiar trope used to justify slavery: the physical superiority of Black humans, suiting them to labor, and the mental superiority of White men, suiting them to administration. However, in addition to the physical and mental differences between races, Hayes also believed in a moral difference. Following the prevailing attitude of his time, Hayes understood White, Christian men to have moral capacities superior to all others.

To understand the deep irony of Hayes' life and writing, his moral reasoning can be traced one step further to its "dreadfully paternalistic" conclusion. Because he understood White, Christian men to be morally superior, Hayes believed that *all* White, Christian men bear a special charge from God to act with moral rectitude. And this rectitude includes treating children, women, and non-White people justly, with a level-but-firm hand that promotes development to their fullest potential – even if that potential is biologically less than that of

White, Christian men. As a result, Hayes rejected slavery as an institution, deplored the use of the whip on both the men and the animals with whom he worked, and rigorously upheld the rest of his moral code – sometimes at great personal risk, as when he spoke out to various authorities concerning the misdeeds of powerful missionaries, mining bosses, and purveyors of alcohol.

The doctrine of White supremacy, as Hayes understood it, taught him that all humans deserve fair and just treatment not because all are equal, but because the superior should not abuse the inferior.

However, to his great dismay, in all his travels, with the possible exception of a couple of itinerant missionaries, Hayes never met another White, Christian man who lived up to Hayes' moral standard. In every corner of the world where Hayes looked, he found White, Christian men who he believed enjoyed every capacity to live the exemplary lives into which they had been born, but men who nevertheless failed to live even decently. All those men with superior mental capacities, all the benefits of what Hayes thought of as advanced civilization, and the revelations of the one true Protestant Christian religion, nevertheless persisted in licentiousness, thievery, and brutality. They lied, cheated, and swindled one another and, worse, used their superior capacities to subjugate and exploit those men and women they believed inferior to themselves.

Hayes' outrage at the individual moral failings of White, Christian men burned so brightly his entire life that it blinded Hayes to the idea that some injustices might not be merely individual. He was always so mad at individual colonialists failing to implement colonialism *properly* that it never entered his mind that a worldwide economic system of resource appropriation buttressed by an ideology of White, Christian, male superiority would operate in much this same way regardless of the personal beliefs of its mechanics. Hayes never conceptualized structural injustice: the idea that *colonialism* was the problem rather than individual *colonialists*. Instead, the constant failures of individuals led Hayes to a generalized misanthropy. Rather than descry an unjust *economic system* or question his own racist beliefs, Hayes retreated to condemning the wickedness of humanity. He often remarked how much better the otherwise sublime natural world would exist absent the human species.

The moral outrage that flared within Hayes at each new job prompted lengthy accounts of the failings of each successive boss: the directors of the Scottish timber company in Nigeria that turned a blind eye to the harvest of mahogany trees smaller than permitted by forestry regulation; the aforementioned missionaries at the Heart of Africa mission in the northern Belgian Congo with the tax fraud and liquor; the diamond mining executives at the Forminiere who cooperated with the Belgian military in a laundry list of crimes – including murder, rape, torture, kidnapping for ransom, and false imprisonment – on top of using the whip so savagely on African mineworkers that Hayes vomited the first time he witnessed it; an English mining consortium chasing rumors of silver mines abandoned by the Germans following WWI in what was then Tanganyika revealed as a front for a land swindle; even rough-and-tumble elephant hunters who extravagantly exceeded all legal quotas.

Hayes' critique of individual *colonialists* is so forceful it could be mistaken for a critique of *colonialism*. But only by a reader who rejects the ideology of White, Christian, male superiority. As unfortunately Hayes did not.

Thus the biography of Hayes Perkins portrays a disturbingly complex man who lived according to a moral code exemplary in many regards – but, nevertheless, a code based on a morally reprehensible assumption of the superiority of those of his race, gender, and religion. Following his own logic forward from that reprehensible assumption, Hayes wrote a scathing exposé of colonialism *as practiced* – but an exposé that Hayes himself intended as an apology for colonialism *as theorized*. In Hayes' mind, if only individual men had acted faithfully to their birthrights, a colonial structure of greatest benefit for all, according to their supposed superiorities and inferiorities, could have been achieved.

Some propose that the time for voicing the views of White supremacists is past. That it is time to move forward, putting evils of the past behind us. At the current political moment, some are even calling for the abolition of teaching about slavery, colonialism, and other "critical race theoretical" subjects in US schools. In response to these suggestions, both Gates and Donald Yacovone, in his *Teaching White Supremacy* (2022), caution that false narratives concerning slavery and colonialism have, over the past 150 years, taken root in the fertile ground of intentional ignorance. Such writers argue that the truth about our histories is a better antidote to its evils than silent forgetfulness.

Hayes Perkins, a humble man from Oregon, wrote a lengthy diary from a uniquely valuable working class perspective detailing the actual conditions of Colonial Africa as witnessed firsthand on worksites across the continent. Despite the tragic irony that Hayes wrote from a moral stance vitiated by a White supremacist ideology, his seems an important story to tell at a time when intentional ignorance of history is being employed as a tool by those once again championing the virulent anti-democratic poison of that very ideology.

By a quirk of inheritance, Hayes' diary came to me – first cousin thrice removed – and got stuck under my skin for some fifty years. Much as the naïve, ten-year-old Hayes Perkins had been drawn to Africa for its "elephants and cannibals," I had been drawn to his diary as a young man for the astonishing feats of adventure so casually recounted from wherever in the world Hayes happened to land. As he aged through the first half of the twentieth century, the entries in Hayes' diary increasingly reflect a loneliness that shaded eventually toward bitterness at the perfidy of humankind. As I aged through the second half of the twentieth century, the more I traced Hayes' unconventional tutorial on world history and geography, the more I came to appreciate his diary as something beyond the (admittedly still astonishing) adventure chronicle. Intentionally or not, Hayes wrote a profoundly important document recording the working conditions of a uniquely fascinating, yet disturbingly violent and unjust era in world history, a time and a place almost entirely elided in my formal education. I expect Hayes would be pleased that the diary given to his cousin once removed, John Donaldson, deeply influenced John Donaldson's grandson, John Martin. If my condensation of Hayes' diary moves readers drawn to Hayes' adventure Africa toward an all too real colonial Africa, I hope Hayes would have been pleased about that as well.

1. Before Africa, 1878-1906

Hayes Perkins was born where Lampa Creek meets the Coquille River on the southern Oregon coast on February 10, 1878, the third of nine children and the only boy to survive to maturity. Timber and rich agricultural lands were Oregon's primary wealth, but gold was discovered there too. In the 1880s two men washed up $80,000 at Whiskey Run by shoveling sand over rough boards. Large native populations still lived in these Northwestern forests, but smallpox, tuberculosis, forced displacement, and liquor had already devastated their communities.

Neither William nor Malinda Perkins, Hayes' parents, had more than grade school educations but both had taught school and stayed informed, even purchasing "encyclopedias of general knowledge" from traveling sellers. Africa first captured Hayes' imagination reading in his parents' encyclopedias. But Hayes had more than books. The Perkins' isolated cabin on the Coquille River welcomed travelers in from the rain to stay a night and share what news they had of the broader world. One of the most exotic and thrilling stories, told in installments as his super-human deeds unfolded, recounted the African adventures of Henry Morton Stanley in the darkest heart of Africa "opening up the Congo Free State and later in the rescue of Emin Pasha." Hayes hung on every word. As a ten-year-old boy Hayes feared only that, "all the elephants and cannibals would be killed off before I was old enough to assist in the game."

Young Hayes lived in Oregon during a wild, unsettled moment. 1880s Oregon had no time for childhood beyond the chores of feeding a homesteading family. Hayes attended the yearly four-month school sessions; however, his marks for deportment published in the Coquille newspaper reveal the quality of his scholarship: 56 out of a possible 100.

When Hayes was twelve, his father, originally from Tennessee, "determined to return to his native South." Hayes hated to leave Oregon but thrilled at the long journey east. He saw his first railway, rode a steamship, visited a real city, and marveled at the barren country of Arizona and New Mexico so different from the "unbroken forest" he had known all his life. William Perkins took his family east and south seeking a "more godly" place to raise his family. Hayes remarked, "Of this I knew nothing, but the spirit of adventure that actuated me in every waking moment encouraged me to go."

The Perkins family settled in Hico, Texas, in 1890, where, as elsewhere in the former Confederacy, deep resentments remained from the Civil War. A boy newly arrived from a "Northern state" had to fight frequent scraps with the local ruffians loyal to the gray. Hayes recalled it as not so bad until two or three boys ganged up on him at once.

After the crops were gathered in August around Hico, "camp meetings" provided the only entertainment in this deeply religious countryside. One could choose from several tents, Methodist or Presbyterian who "sprinkled their converts," or Baptist and Christians, "who immersed the novitiates." Hayes' father, William Perkins, was a sprinkler, "a Methodist of the strictest sort." Even as the boys of Hico continued fighting the battle of North and South by day, one after another came to kneel at the rail of an evening, until Hayes alone remained without salvation. Late in life, when reconstructing the diary of these years, Hayes recalled that the floggings his father administered him for stubborn refusal to convert troubled him less than the vivid preaching of the "terrors of Hell Fire" promised to sinners like him. Despite intense pressure from the entire community and his own worries about damnation, Hayes "turned from the whole proceeding with something like disgust."

By the time Hayes turned thirteen, the battle with his father over religion had escalated to such frequent beatings, the boy took to living on the streets. On warm Texas nights he could sleep in boxcars and barns. In the winter, as temperatures dipped below zero, he buried himself to the neck in a neighbor's bin of slightly fermenting cottonseed for warmth. In a letter Hayes wrote to a young nephew in 1952, Hayes said the cruelty of those days decided his life-long bachelorhood: "I am wholly thankful ... that there is no child coming up to blame me for bringing him into this world."

Despite all the hardship, Hayes kept up with school until age fourteen, even as he sought his first paid employment. He earned, though did not receive, his first paycheck: $18 picking cotton for a month. Before Hayes could collect his salary, his father William intervened with the farmer: "Dad's dictum was that I was his property and what I had was his."

Unable to eat at home, unable to earn his own fare, in desperation Hayes began running with Bill Evans, another waif on the streets of Hico. Bill's .22 rifle provided birds and squirrels; sometimes they caught a fish from the creek. Eventually the two began stealing – apples from the grocer, butter, cheese, bread, a nest of eggs at a farm, chickens, even cartridges for the .22 – with only this apology: "At least we were free from church, and we stuck to school as much as was possible."

On New Year's Eve 1892, with freezing rain howling across the Texas plains, Hayes snuck home to wolf sandwiches his mother and sisters slipped into an inadequate hiding place behind the woodstove. Without warning, the door banged and a blast of cold air blew Hayes' father William, fresh from tending the horses, into the kitchen. Spying his fourteen-year-old son behind the stove, William bawled, "Aha my young man! I have you now." And set to with a shot-loaded mule whip. Raw and bleeding, Hayes escaped into the night wearing a thin cotton shirt only because his father turned the whip on Hayes' mother Matilda when she tried to intercede.

Hayes shivered around town all night before rescue materialized in the gray dawn: a "bright, well dressed mulatto" woman looking for a boy to clean up after the New Year's dance party at Hico's leading hotel. Hayes' diligent work on the first day of 1893 led to a live-in job, paid $8 a month, working twelve to fifteen hours a day, at every sort of job around the hotel. When this first hotel job soured after ten months, Hayes caught on with a very kindly woman at another hotel. Sadly, the softhearted woman believed William Perkins when the apparently bereft father came begging for the return of his only son for proper education.

On the fourth day "home" (Hayes used quotes to indicate the irony) William informed Matilda that Hayes was "due a beating." Hayes stared his father down, bid his mother and sisters farewell and, biting back tears of rage, left the family never to return. Thus, at age fifteen, Hayes began his life on the road. He would live at no permanent residence until age sixty, constantly traveling as a self-described "adventurer," working when broke, wandering when able. A young friend on the streets of Hico set him on what Hayes often called "the long path" with this advice: "If I was you, I would pay my way as far as I could and then trust God for the rest."

At the Hico bus station, Hayes asked for a ticket to San Francisco but his $15 would take him only as far as Sacramento. On his first days walking the streets of the not-so-prosperous capital of California, some of the most down-and-out residents of the city recognized a boy adrift and responded with kindness. A shaky gambler handed Hayes a dollar, a gesture the boy would never forget. The prostitutes helped the lone boy too. Small town rural Texas and Oregon had failed to introduce Hayes to "fallen women." They appeared to Hayes "the most beautiful girls I had ever seen, sitting at their casement windows, beckoning to passers-by."

To Hayes, a boy obviously alone in the world, these women always offered a coin, some food, or even a place to sleep. From these "waifs in the world," the gamblers and prostitutes, Hayes learned that those with the least are often the most generous with what little they have.

For the next few years Hayes lived by all manner of work, wandering about the western United States: trapping for a couple of years around Coquille, Oregon; threshing wheat in the Palouse region of Washington; mining in the Arizona desert; cutting and milling redwood in California. He walked a good bit from one situation to another but also became adept at hopping freight trains.

These teenage experiences among men with rough hands and rougher morals began to teach Hayes a hard philosophy: "The prizes of this life were to those who took them." Along with the philosophy came a stern code of retribution. Any who wronged him "were special objects to wreak vengeance upon." Eventually Hayes determined that a smart man in an unjust world, wronged or not, must take all he can by whatever means possible.

Drifting about western North America through his late teens, Hayes never stopped dreaming of Africa. At age twenty, he knew that if he ever hoped to make any kind of African adventure a reality he would have to find his way onto an ocean-going ship. By 1898 steam-powered ocean liners had not entirely replaced wind-powered sailing ships. Hayes couldn't afford paid passage on the former, but he knew the latter must need able seamen. He decided the only way to become an able seaman was to start as an unable seaman. At Portland, Oregon, with no previous experience at sea, Hayes signed onto the three-mast barque *Austrasia* sailing around the Horn of South America for Liverpool. He had confidence (ill-formed, as it turned out) that a seasoned sailor, as he would be on arrival, could easily reach Africa from England. Experienced sailors on the *Austrasia* earned $25 a month. Completely green hands like Hayes got $20. All were assessed (aka swindled out of) two month's pay before the voyage against purchase of their gear:

Two cheap cotton suits of underwear
Two suits of dungarees
A cheap suit of duck for oil skins
A 35 cent blanket
A 10 cent straw tick
Some tobacco (which Hayes didn't use)
A couple pairs of socks

With this meager outfit, Hayes sailed four months around the Horn, then, sick and starving in Liverpool, sailed directly back across the Atlantic to the East Coast of the United States. If anything, his brutish shipmates – Tom the Australian, Tom the Negro, Dublin, Fagan, Old Jack, Charley Bews, Liverpool – reinforced his hard outlook on life. Sailing up the English Channel toward London, Hayes expressed a decided worry about himself, writing in his diary that he wondered if he wasn't "going bad."

It took Hayes another eight years following that first trip around The Horn to reach Africa for the first time. What may have been the deciding events making Africa possible for him took place in the gold boomtown of Victor, Colorado, in 1899. Though he never did much prospecting himself, Hayes loved boomtowns. Seven years after the initial rushes at Victor and Cripple Creek, much of the early gold fever had cooled; a few big corporate mines dominated the towns by the time Hayes got there. He refused, on principle, to pay the union bribe necessary to get work at the big outfits and hadn't the time or the stake necessary for prospecting, so he took a job slinging hash at Charley the German's chophouse.

The twenty-one-year-old, still living "gone bad," spent nights after work in Victor hanging on the fringes of the "sporting crowd" watching gamblers and prostitutes relieve miners of hard-earned dollars at the casinos. For diversion some nights, in company with a couple of prostitutes trying to go straight, women he had met at Charley's, Hayes would stop around the Salvation Army tent and listen to the tambourine and a sermon. The examples of young Salvation Army men and women living clean lives of devotion to a higher good affected him far more than anything they said. After a couple weeks of regular attendance at the tent, Hayes decided to abandon his sure-fire scheme for "doubling up on the red or black" at the roulette table, and try something along a more straight-and-narrow path. When most of Victor burned to the ground two months later, Hayes, moral conviction still intact, helped a friend rescue all the chairs and the organ from the Salvation Army mission before setting out on the long trail again.

The new moral arc Hayes began at Victor had a few wobbles. Immediately after leaving Colorado, Hayes enlisted in the Revenue Cutter Service aboard the *USS McCulloch* out of San Francisco. Three months later, following most of the ship's crew who'd already fled the *McCulloch*'s inhuman working conditions, Hayes deserted.

Less morally wobbly, Hayes worked sawmills in Eureka, California, through most of the years 1900-01. In order to clear his conscience from the "gone bad" years, Hayes decided on a grand gesture: he would send reparation to every man he had ever swindled. For most of two years he worked, saved, and mailed out cash. From some of the men he received notes of thanks; others returned only derision at his naiveté. By the middle of 1901 he had paid his self-imposed debts sufficiently to return to wandering the world. The long, expensive penance cleared his conscience but also solidified a lifetime ethic of abstention from alcohol, gambling, shady business dealings, and women. At the end of his wandering life, in another letter to the enquiring nephew, Hayes recommended this austere ethic as mandatory for any would-be lifetime adventurer. The dissipations of the sporting life would kill a young man more certainly than all the elephants, lions, or cannibals in Africa.

Leaving Eureka, Hayes briefly took up steel work in San Francisco but violent union strikes in the city made another trip around Cape Horn seem safe by comparison. This time, he sailed on the *Crown of India.* Six months of poor food brought scurvy to most of the crew and would cost Hayes all his teeth. Loosened on the *Crown of India*, they pained him until age 50 when he finally had them all pulled.

In 1903, an uncle in Washington, DC, set Hayes up as boatman and camp roustabout on a United States Geological Survey (USGS) team to Alaska. Returning to the lower US after that summer in Alaska, Hayes hit what may have been the lowest point in his life following a trip to see his mother in Texas.

For a time William and Matilda Perkins shared two separate halves of a house in Hico. Quite exceptionally for the time, Matilda had left William, eventually securing a formal divorce. After tramping Alaska in the summer of 1903, Hayes blew into Hico to check on his mom and sisters. While there, word came that William had been killed in a coach accident in Walsenburg, Colorado. Broke and unable to find work to supplement his mother's earnings from taking in laundry, Hayes took off again. He signed on as a bullpusher, the lowest, least-paid sailor, doing exactly what the job title says – wrangling seasick cows – on the *Norseman* out from Galveston to Liverpool. Still broke in Liverpool, he signed back on to the *Norseman,* this time (and not for the last time in his life) as a "workaway," an unpaid sailor working for passage, just to get back to Galveston.

Still broke back in Texas, he reluctantly accepted a $25 loan from his sister Jenny and began walking west from San Antonio, Texas, stopping only when he arrived in Los Angeles, California! He left San Antonio on Jan 21, 1904, and arrived in Los Angeles on March 29, 1904, walking nearly 1,400 miles in two months. In one 24-hour period, a full moon lighting the desert that night, he walked 60 miles. Unless he saw a shortcut, he followed the railroad tracks. He could fill a quart jar he carried at water stations spaced along the track for the trains' steam engines. He worked a day or two for food at some of the stops. Twice, kindly porters threw edible scraps out a dining car window into the gravel at the feet of the lonely walker. He walked entirely voluntarily. Some years previously he had followed this same route end-to-end in four days by hopping freights, but, after the conversion at Victor, he considered hopping freights stealing from the rail company. So he abstained riding – even as hoboes jeered him from atop passing railcars. Threadbare, his shoes tied on with twine, swollen and sunburned, he knocked on a farmhouse door in Los Angeles. The young woman who opened the door cried out, "Oh mama, come look at this poor man!" The girl's father let Hayes hoe a half-acre of beans in return for a meal and a dollar.

After Hayes got back on his feet again, first breaking rocks at a gravel quarry, then back at the mills in Eureka, the USGS came calling again. Hayes spent the summer of 1905 working in the same capacity for the Alaskan survey as he had in 1903.

Though Hayes learned all his engineering and practical skills with only minimal instruction while on various jobs, he did have some formal schooling beyond the rudiments offered at Coquille, Oregon, and Hico, Texas. Returning to the lower forty-eight following his second USGS trip to Alaska, Hayes paid two-year's tuition and board at the Free Methodist Seminary in Fremont, Washington. He entered high school as a twenty-seven-year-old freshman alongside eight teenage girls and five teenage boys. He planned to finish high school in two years so he could apply to the University of Washington. The studies at Fremont went fine. He completed three year's work in the five months he lasted there, quickly excelling his instructors in geography, geology and "general knowledge of the world." But the Fremont seminary taught children. Hayes, an adult, could not abide the rigid social structure imposed by men little older than he, sheltered academics with scant knowledge of the world. Furthermore, the religious fervor of the Methodists amused him. He tried to maintain his composure when "the spiritual unction and ecstasy falls on the assembled throng [and] they lose self-control and run about the house, screaming at the top of their lungs." Hayes couldn't fully conceal his laughter behind a raised hand.

As during the old battle of wills with his father, Hayes refused Fremont's theatrically fervent altar calls. So the wily Methodists tried another strategy. Hayes couldn't help noticing the attractive young women seated to his left and right at every meal. An accident? He didn't think so. Free Methodists married and raised good citizens at home or married helpmates for missionary work. Either might be a praiseworthy ambition for others, but not for an adventurer yearning for Africa. At Fremont Hayes accepted neither conversion nor a wife. He left taking from Christianity pretty much only the bare bones he built on the Salvation Army examples at Victor: "to be good and kind, to help one's fellows who are unfortunate, to play the game as square as one wants it played toward himself." These simple precepts seemed to him "of more practical value than all this undue excitement and enthusiasm."

After leaving Fremont Seminary, broke, of course, Hayes returned to swinging a fourteen-pound sledgehammer making gravel. The quarry in Tacoma paid $2.75 for a nine-hour day, minus $1.00 for room and board. He stuck the job six full months, writing intermittently of premonitions concerning Africa. April 24, 1906: "For some reason or another I feel as if Africa was mine." August 12, 1906: "Time slips by quickly for me, for somehow I know that Africa is mine." He knew he sounded like a dreamer or a fanatic. Plenty of folks told him so. Colleagues at the quarry, Long Andy, Short Andy, Andy the Boob, Scotty, and Old Pete, laughed when Hayes, "so sure I am of my wish come true," started singing on the job.

Hayes quit the quarry on October 4, 1906, passed through San Francisco just after the great fire, said hello to the family for one day in Hico, and signed on to the steamer *Sangara* out of Galveston on October 27. Why would the *Sangara* come through Galveston when regularly routed down the West African coast? Hayes' premonitions seemed to be holding: "Why, unless to pick me up, I cannot say why she is here." The *Sangara* would return from Galveston to London with a load of cotton, where Hayes planned to sign on again, a sailor paid to visit every port of call on the West African coast. Hayes immediately began pumping the *Sangara's* coal trimmers, "Kroo boys from Sierra Leone and Liberia" for all the details they would share.

At London, Hayes opened his diary entry with a one-word sentence: "Discouraged." When he went to sign on again, the skipper of the *Sangara* informed Hayes its parent company, Elder-Dempster Lines, forbid his hiring more men. A kindly mate told Hayes it was all bunk, and then added, fare thee well.

Deflated but not defeated, Hayes shook himself off, screwed up his resolve and decided that, sometimes, a premonition can only be realized by paying for it: "Anyway, I have a few dollars yet, and am returning to Liverpool and will pay my way from there." On December 5, 1906, Hayes sailed out of Liverpool, second class, because "no European is permitted to go third, else I would," on a one-way ticket paid through to Lagos, Nigeria.

2. Logging up the Jamieson River, Nigeria, 1907

Hayes first glimpsed Africa on December 15, 1906, sighting a sandy stretch of barren coast somewhere near the mouth of the Senegal River. The *Mandingo* had sailed south in the deep Atlantic to approach the westernmost point of Africa below the arid Saharan shores. Now porpoises – "I never saw so many before" – leapt about the small steamer just starting a coastal delivery route to a succession of "factories," West African colonial trading stations, at Dakar, Konakry, Freetown, Monrovia, Half Jack, Grand Lahou, Grand Bassam, Axim, Sekondi, Salt Pond, Cape Coast Castle, Accra, "and at some place whose name I missed in the excitement."

Every anchor stop called tantalizingly to the young adventurer. As lazy rollers off the Atlantic beat long stretches of barren sand, palm trees obscured sleepy factories. A white-clad Frenchmen or Brit, always with a helmet, bossed "naked giants" who expertly wrestled cargo ashore across a heavy, pounding surf.

Africa at last!

As the sandy beaches gave way to more densely forested coastline, Hayes kept watch from the deck of the *Mandingo*, chatting up both "Old Coasters," Europeans returning to positions at these isolated factories, and "Kroo boys," African men recruited by the steamship lines to work as deckhands and coalers. From the jaded, perpetually drunken Old Coasters in pith helmets and whites, Hayes sifted for useful bits of information scattered within their self-inflating tales of JuJu, cannibalism, blackwater fever, malaria, chiggers, and Guinea Worm. Much more relevantly, from the native Kroo seamen Hayes learned the 300 or so words of pidgin English by which colonizers and colonized communicated across European and West African languages. Hayes had a facility for languages. He picked up working knowledge of several over his years in Africa.

Paying his last dollar to get to Africa had been reckless perhaps, but easy enough. Now he had to find a job to stay in Africa. One of the Old Coasters Hayes had chatted up on the *Mandingo* held a colonial office: chief forester for Nigeria. While pumping the Brit for information about employment prospects in Lagos, Hayes had spoken of his enthusiasm for African adventure and of his many years' experience cutting and finishing redwood at various mills in the Pacific Northwest of the United States.

Turned out a good recommendation from the head forester of Nigeria carried weight: Hayes had job offers from two companies on his first day in Africa. The offer extended by Miller, Bro. & Co. paid the best: £100 per year on a two-year contract cutting mahogany at an isolated Miller's station north of Sapele. Hayes accepted on the spot.

The next day, January 10, 1907, Hayes and a Miller's district commissioner boarded a small passenger launch headed toward Siluko, 250 miles east through "an endless maze of broad, winding channels." Hayes admired the skill of the African pilot navigating the river labyrinth. The district commissioner gave most of his attention to a native steward: "'Boy! Cocktail! Boy, Gin-and-bitters! Boy, Whiskey-and-soda!'"

At some point in the day, Hayes dove headfirst into a wide lagoon. Releasing frustration about all the booze? He had seen case after case of cheap liquor off-loaded from the launch to "seedy natives, a chief clad in a silk hat and a G-string." Or maybe Hayes dove in sheer exuberant delight at finally reaching the real Africa. Regaining the surface, the green American noticed a jaded, "phlegmatic district commissioner" tip his highball glass toward a floating crocodile that had raised its head as soon as Hayes hit the water. That night's diary entry read, "I'll have to watch my step after this."

Hayes spent the five days on the launch between Lagos and Siluko thrilling to the new sights and sounds of Africa: gorgeous butterflies, birds with vast toes specialized to walk on lily pads, ducks, egrets, raucous-voiced parrots flying in flocks and pairs over the forests. Everywhere he noted evidence of the JuJu.

Hayes used the word JuJu in at least three different ways: as a broad term for the pagan religion practiced by most native Africans; to refer to a single god from among the "gods, and gods, and gods everywhere in both animate and inanimate objects;" or, when describing statuary or tribute offered to those gods. At intervals along the riverbank out from Lagos, Hayes saw goats or fowl tied by the water's edge or sometimes a bolt of cloth, a bunch of bananas, "or any sort of material wealth the simple natives possess," offered to the god of the water.

Hayes left Siluko three days after his arrival there in the company of J.F. Herald, head forester for Miller & Co. Setting a casual two-day pace overland toward a station on the Osse River, the stern older man, a devout Catholic Englishman feared across the region "as a bogey man," tested Hayes' forest knowledge and abilities. About these topics Hayes quickly became Herald's instructor, recommending the tools and techniques of modern logging as practiced in the Pacific Northwest: jackscrews, crosscut saws, and wheeled trucks for dragging the logs to waterways. Hayes could show these African colonialists a thing or two about extracting resources.

With a sigh of relief, Hayes parted company with Herald and continued on "alone," traveling by canoe up the Osse River accompanied only by Nigerian men. The boatmen knew the way to the isolated bush station where Miller & Co. had scheduled training for Hayes by a young Scottish agent named McPherson.

Two days paddling up the Osse River in comparative solitude allowed Hayes to turn from his disgust with colonial alcohol excesses to his delight in the natural world. Light rains of the dry season in Southern Nigeria fell daily, pushed by Harmattan winds off the Sahara. Nights cooled to the point of cold. The river Osse flowed sluggishly, travelers' progress impeded by shallows and endless sandbars piled with enormous snags of detritus from a riotous evergreen forest looming on all sides. An occasional crocodile pushed off a sand bar, "small ones perhaps five or six feet in length." The boatmen spoke of hippos in these waters but the shapes Hayes saw floating submerged in the Osse were only sodden tree trunks too dense to float.

Hayes' newness to the continent and to the universal pidgin of his crew did nothing to prevent him taking charge. His African guides were "willing to dawdle," but Hayes pushed them to reach McPherson's station in two days - a pace McPherson immediately doubted.

If Hayes first impressed McPherson as a greenhorn braggart, McPherson's dilapidated appearance stunned Hayes. Miller & Co. had sent the young Scot alone into the bush to establish a logging camp - exactly the same assignment given Hayes. McPherson looked "very seedy from fever and poor living alone in the bush." Hayes was immediately certain that "unless he gets out of Africa soon he will stay here in the White Man's Grave."

After a few days sharing "a bush hut thrown together by natives" with McPherson, Hayes elaborated on McPherson's squalor: droves of ants of various species, jiggers that bore under the men's toes, and a choir of crickets "that make the night hideous with their shrill noises" lived inside with the two men.

Setting aside both his amateur naturalist bent and his inner entranced ten-year-old boy, Hayes eagerly turned to the business at hand: logging. The 29-year-old expert forester from the great Pacific Northwest woods of the US had come to McPherson's station to learn by observation the forestry methods of Miller & Co. After a few days watching he wrote a succinct summary: "None of these men have any idea of handling timber."

Consider, for instance, the matter of saws. Mahogany trees in the Niger Delta grow to enormous girth, often with spreading roots that form buttressing side supports partway up the trunk. In 1907, British regulations forbade cutting any tree smaller than twelve feet in circumference ten feet above the ground. This seemed a sensible conservation requirement to Hayes – completely subverted by Miller & Co.'s inability to sharpen a saw properly.

Efficient felling of these trees would have employed a two-handled crosscut saw. The difference between a crosscut saw and a ripsaw is only how the teeth are sharpened: crosscut sharpening for sawing across the grain as when felling; ripcut sharpening for sawing with the grain as when finishing. To the extent that Miller & Co. sharpened their saws at all, only rip sharpening seemed to be known.

One *can* fell a tree four feet in diameter with a ripsaw – over the course of many days with much wasted effort. Ignorant of proper sharpening, Miller & Co. preferred axes for felling. Once a tree had been certified as large enough to meet regulations and close enough to the river for subsequent transport, "men with clumsy axes are turned loose on its trunk, and in two or three days it will crash the way it leans."

Miller & Co's techniques were both incredibly dangerous and hugely wasteful. Just accounting for axes gnawing like beaver teeth around their trunks, two to three feet of valuable timber ended up on the forest floor from every tree cut - an equal amount from every log cut to length. But beyond the waste from cutting cross grain with axes, a massive tree falling willy-nilly could damage smaller stems nearby, or, worse, shatter into worthless shards on impact with the ground.

At McPherson's station Hayes located a couple of saws abandoned in a tumbledown shed, sharpened them for crosscut, and demonstrated a preliminary wedge-cut to control the direction his tree would fall. Before making the horizontal felling cut, Hayes showed McPherson's men where to pile branches on the forest floor. Knowing his tree would fall into the wedge-cut, the cushion from the branches would prevent the big trunk from shattering. And yes, knowing the direction the big tee would fall also gave the sawyers advance warning about which way to run.

The savings on every tree cut? Lives. And 20% on every trunk? At international mahogany prices, the latter efficiency meant real money. Hayes valued one particularly nice trunk at £2,000, the equivalent of about £240,000 today.

So what to do with a thirty-ton mahogany trunk lying flat somewhere out in the dense Nigerian forest? Hayes knew the American way: cut the trunk to lengths, hitch up horses or oxen, and drag timbers to the water's edge for floating to market. If McPherson could round up some draft animals, Hayes knew how to drive any team.

McPherson must have laughed. Across a broad swath of equatorial Africa the tsetse fly, responsible for sleeping sickness in humans, effectively prevented oxen, horses, and even the dogs of early European explorers surviving more than a few months.

Lack of draft animals explained why only logs relatively near water's edge – no more than two miles – could be marked for cutting. Once a tree had been felled, measured by a European, cut to length, and laboriously squared, a team of men dragged it out of the forest to the water's edge, requiring "at least a hundred men to drag a log of ordinary size to water … and when possible whips are used on the men."

Some days after leaving McPherson's tawdry station, Hayes began his diary entry on March 2, 1907, with a great sigh of satisfaction: "Alone at last." By "alone," he meant in Africa separate from all Europeans, while surrounded by "many, many, blacks." He went on euphorically: "The past few days have been among the most interesting of my life."

On his way overland from the McPherson's station toward the site of his own prospective outpost up the Jamieson River, Hayes had detoured to the fabled city of Benin.

Hayes had undoubtedly heard of Benin City before his visit. The "Benin Massacre" of a British expeditionary force in January 1897 and the subsequent sacking of Benin by a second, larger, force of British marines in February 1897 headlined British and US newspapers. Hayes could not have missed Sir Reginald Bacon's book *Benin: City of Blood* published that same year. Bacon had accompanied the second "Benin Punitive Expedition." Rumors, based on a false report, of a "city of blood" at Benin began as early as 1892. Suppression of the ritual sacrifices attributed to Benin, luridly described as "sub-human," provided Britain a more noble justification for military conquest of the city than mere commercial interest, justification Hayes seemed to believe.

In 1907, Hayes, at that time still in company with Herald, walked east from McPherson's station for more than thirty miles on a road "straight as if surveyed" through dense forest. Hayes, Herald, and their small crew entered Benin City near sunset through a wide rift British forces had cut in the outer fortifying wall just ten years previously. Hayes described the wall as ancient, circular, six miles in diameter, and thirty feet tall, enhanced beyond that height by a deep surrounding moat. Ever attuned to tools and feats of engineering, Hayes marveled at a fortification nearly twenty miles in circumference, thirty feet tall, that he assumed could only have been built using pointed sticks and carrying baskets by "the labor of countless slaves working under the lash."

Inside this tall outer fortification, two smaller and much older walls surrounded an inner city emphasizing the antiquity of Benin. Much of the area between the two outer walls had been left open for cultivation in times of siege. A few huts spilled beyond the second wall and from these issued "snarls and catcalls" from hidden locals growing more menacing as Hayes and company entered the more densely populated inner city.

Ten years after its initial sacking, British subjugation of Benin City remained tenuous. Having put down "another rising" at Benin City just before Hayes arrived, the British had installed two regiments of Hausa troops, Moslem Africans from Northern Nigeria under British Imperial command, "to keep order." To Hayes, the tense "order" imposed by the Hausa troops felt more like a lull in an ongoing revolt. He was "very glad to meet the few whites at the post," standing among grinning Hausa soldiers.

Leaving behind both the lurid past and the uneasy present of Benin City, Hayes continued overland south toward his own isolated station far up the Jamieson River. At Sapele, some thirty miles from Benin City, the Jamieson and Ethiope Rivers meet to form the Benin River. Boatmen paddled Hayes across the mile-wide Benin River to Miller & Co.'s "great trading station among many at this place."

At Sapele, Hayes departed by canoe to continue "alone" northeast forty miles up the Jamieson River to Sapoba. The village squatted on an island mid-river near the source of the Jamieson at tremendous springs issuing from the forest floor. Already one hundred feet deep at Sapoba, the Jamieson flowed on both sides of the island "so pellucid one may see a bit of broken dish at its bottom anywhere."

At the request of Sapoba's "king," Hayes took up residence at the royal palace. On Herald's advice, Hayes shortened the king's name from Apajah to Pajah "to save letters" in official correspondence. Apajah's principal advisor, Comay, immediately and unfavorably impressed Hayes as "a renegade mission convert who can read and write just a trifle, and much learning has gone to this backslider's head."

Not that the backslider wasn't capable. Comay had built the royal palace from whipsawn mahogany "worth a fortune if it was in Europe or America." The palace stood on twelve-foot mahogany stilts providing shelter for razor-backed hogs, starved dogs, goats, and fowl - plus the royal court in case of rain. Comay still affected vestiges of Christianity but not in ways that interfered with his leadership of the JuJu on Sapoba Island. His various elevated statures gave him "run of the womenfolk of the village."

To Hayes, both Apajah and Comay appeared "brutal, avaricious, lustful to the nth degree." Of course he disapproved, but their conduct was nothing he hadn't seen from men in power the world over: "They are two devils, though perhaps no worse than my own countrymen would be under the same circumstances."

The JuJu, "which is in full blast all the time," at Sapoba fascinated Hayes. From what he could piece together, it seemed their one universal god-of-all, benevolent creator of the universe, needed no attention. All the sacrifices went to appease "the thousand and one malign spirits that dwell in trees, in stones, in the water, in wild animals and insects even."

Following a daily ritual, JuJu headmen paddled canoes to shrines about Sapoba and the surrounding forest offering food and cloth to the larger and smaller spirits animating the world around them. A river spirit named Gulu required particular attention. Hayes himself had heard Gulu speaking from the depths of the river. In fact, he found it a "trifle uncanny," to hear, "'gulu, gulu, gulu…,'" bubbling up for perhaps five minutes on end. Trapped gases escaping the riverbed? Perhaps a scientist would say so, "but we who live at the village of Sapoba know better."

Of course, Hayes recorded his observations about village life and religion only while attending efficiently to company business. Within a week of his arrival, Hayes had scouted the nearby forest, marking the largest mahogany trees for cutting. Apajah wept, imploring that more should be tagged.

On one of his early scouting trips, Hayes ventured several miles downriver by canoe to salvage some cast-off tools at a bush station abandoned some years previously. Comay came along to keep an eye on Hayes and to oversee Apajah's enslaved paddlers. Mid-river, a small boy seated beside Hayes, possibly dawdling, cried out at a bite from Comay's whip. Quite on impulse, Hayes, an American completely new to Sapoba, snatched the hippo-hide lash from "the brutal semi-educated Negro" and cast it far out from the canoe to splash into the river. The king's first advisor, apparently composed, raised no immediate hand toward Hayes. It had been a rash and ultimately stupid act; with even a moment's reflection Hayes knew he would not suffer Comay's retribution directly. The next day, sight of the enslaved boy lying semi-conscious behind a hut, his face badly beaten, caused Hayes to regret his impulsive "interference" in the canoe.

On another river excursion the other direction, Hayes met a man named Richardson, an English agent bossing a similarly isolated logging station for a rival trading company, Cranstoun, a few miles from Sapoba. Hayes' boss Herald, familiar with the ruthless tactics of West African trading firms, knew Richardson's station and had warned Hayes "to lay off [Richardson] in every other way than to pass the time of day." Good advice but, much to Hayes' subsequent detriment, advice he did not heed.

Following a long paragraph describing a fearful march of driver ants through Sapoba, Hayes' third diary entry, written three weeks after his arrival, returned to the JuJu. Apajah had ordered a house built for Hayes on the riverbank opposite the island but work proceeded slowly. Hayes suspected Apajah had issued a "go-slow" work order to keep Hayes in residence at the royal palace where Apajah and Comay could keep an eye on him. From his involuntary ringside seat at the royal palace on stilts, Hayes had little choice but to watch the ebbs and flows of JuJu fervor acted out in the compound below his open window.

Every night, Apajah gathered his wives and children near to where Apajah sat on a high stool in front of a small sanctuary housing two small, especially revered, mud images. All the wives knelt, hands folded and placed to one side of their heads. All the children danced, joined by the king's courtiers, to the rhythm of a phalanx of drummers "who fairly raise the treetops with their clamor." At some point in a typical evening, the sacrifices began: "not human," but "dogs and goats and many fowls ... sawed across with a dull knife until their throats are cut." Screams of the dying animals only spurred the fervor of Apajah's kingdom, with the women, if anything, more enthusiastic than the men. Children broke from the dance to cavort with "bullroarers," a slat tied to a length of twine swung in a circle to roar like an airplane propeller.

As the revival down in the courtyard finally began to subside, before he retired Hayes bent to check the collection of fetishes placed beneath the head of his bed. Everything was in order: "gourds containing vile smelling grease, bundles of hair, crocodile's teeth, leopard's claws, and many other charms." One of Apajah's young wives who spoke a bit of pidgin had been assigned to hover close to Hayes with an implicit offer to share his loneliness. When Hayes rebuffed her advances, the fetishes had appeared to "influence the 'Ibo,' as White men are called." Tucking in his mosquito netting, Hayes concluded his diary entry: "It's a great life if I can stick it."

Hayes didn't update his journal through nearly the entire month of April 1907. In the silent weeks he must have been hard at work logging with gangs out in the forest. On April 20 he was preparing to depart Sapoba with a raft of more than one hundred logs bound down the Jamieson River for Sapele. He didn't state precisely how many men worked under his direction, but he did write that one particularly large log required 120 men pulling two days to reach the river. And, as on every job he'd ever worked anywhere in the world, management abused labor: "There is the same political hookup here that one finds in more enlightened communities." Apajah's sons all received the highest wages while some of the "real workers" swung axes and hauled logs without pay. King Apajah had the power to compel their work and, together with his advisor Comay, the knowledge to manage the British paymasters. Apajah's well-paid sons would accompany Hayes downriver to Sapele with the raft of logs.

Ordinarily Hayes could have handled a raft of a hundred logs downriver by himself without Apajah's sons, but less than two months after arriving at Sapoba Hayes was sick. Despite a strict health regimen including boiling all drinking water, limiting sun exposure, daily quinine, mosquito boots, and "always the protective mosquito net," the adventurer suspected he had malaria. Hayes planned to rest and recuperate for a few weeks in comparative comfort at the Miller & Co. trading post after delivering the logs.

Malaria aside, the real reason Hayes left Sapoba on April 20, 1907, probably had more to do with the events of the preceding week. An enraged Apajah had just booted Hayes out of the royal palace and ordered him escorted off the island by force. Sitting in his nearly completed riverside house, Hayes could hear the king, his sons, Comay, and the entire village raging through the night of the 19th with a "fervor that makes them dangerous."

Apajah had a jewel: "a gem of purest water, a beautiful object of real value resembling a sapphire … set in complicated bead work." When Hayes had offered to buy the stone, Apajah asked Hayes if the American would next offer to buy the king's own head? That exchange seemed to settle the matter for Hayes – if only the rival agent, Richardson, the scoundrel, hadn't come calling. If only Hayes hadn't told Richardson about the magnificent jewel.

Richardson complained to Hayes: "'He'd never sell the bloody thing; the only way's to swipe it.'" Then, acting independently of Hayes, Richardson went ahead and swiped it himself.

In the first moments following discovery of the theft, Apajah and a few of his wives turned Hayes' room upside down. As if Hayes was the aggrieved party, he complained, "and two shirts have disappeared in the hunt." Meanwhile outside, Richardson, to create a distraction or, more probably, to further disrupt his competitor's station, strolled out to the shed in the center of the compound and smashed Apajah's two mud idols. Others of Apajah's wives trying to stop the desecration fell back under fire as Richardson pelted them with chunks of the statuary.

Somehow Richardson must have made it to his canoe and away downriver but not before "Richardson dashed me a fine pair of shoes." Hayes didn't say how Richardson got away or what happened to Apajah's jewel, only that Hayes himself was now "marooned here" on Sapoba Island, a virtual prisoner of the royal palace.

Hayes lived the next eight days in "a fevered dream," partly from the malaria, partly from the incessant religious furor engulfing him. All logging ceased as every man, woman, and child at Sapoba joined in the JuJu extravagance. What slight freedom of movement Hayes exercised was always in company of Apajah's two big sons. Even while thus escorted, nearly naked spearmen in fearsome headdress lunged to "barely graze my shoulder." What could he do? How could he defend himself? "I never move; it would be useless." No spearman seriously followed up an initial display toward Hayes – or he would be dead – but the threats continued as yelling men and women of the village tore through walls, "rushing from one end of the island to another."

Apajah's big sons compelled Hayes' attendance at "ceremonials" in the compound below the royal palace, denying Hayes rest, or sleep, or peace for eight days and eight nights. The broken statuary could only be repaired by blood sacrifice. Numbers of dogs, goats, and razorbacks "beyond computation" bled out onto the altar before the "resurrected gods." The terrified cries of these animals "slowly massacred" by Apajah and his attendant priests punctuated the constant throbbing of fifty drums, countless bullroarers, and frantic yelling of men and women. Hayes had his suspicions, but, "If there be human sacrifice, I have not seen it."

On the eighth day, Hayes could stand no more. Feverish with malaria, he "appealed to Pajah to cease the row and let my aching head rest just a bit." In gleeful response, Apajah positioned his royal self directly beneath Hayes' window and called the entire village around him to redoubled clangor. At patience's end with despair, or fever, or perhaps arrogant disregard, Hayes leaned out and dumped a large kerosene tin full of water from the window, drenching the king and his retinue below.

With typical brevity when recounting a "spicy bit of danger," Hayes wrote only that, "[t]his insult to his majesty was too much to be borne." However, Apajah did not immediately spear Hayes through the chest, nor order him flogged. Instead, the king punished his White intruder exactly as Hayes wanted: tossed him into a canoe together with all his belongings and had him paddled to the not-quite completed mahogany house across the river. Alone and safe from the continuing hubbub on the island, Hayes faithfully recounted the previous eight thrilling days into his diary.

The furor at Sapoba continued through the night of the 19th and into the morning of the 20th even as Hayes and Apajah's sons launched their raft of one hundred logs down the Jamieson River toward Sapele. Once on the river, all became immediately calm.

Several days rest and familiar food at Miller & Co.'s Sapele station broke Hayes' malarial fever. With pride, he reported that the company's timber receiving agents had been surprised to see his one hundred logs cut, measured and checked, ready to be loaded onto a deep-water ship. An honest man does a job properly even when working for incompetents.

The river trip back to Sapoba merited no comment and Apajah's village apparently had enough time to settle during his absence downriver. There was "still a deal of trouble" but Hayes and an increasingly competent workforce carried on cutting trees. Quiet evenings allowed him time to reflect in his diary on the European presence in Africa.

First of all, Hayes wrote, a White man in Africa had to be careful of the women. Whenever Hayes went swimming in the Jamieson, the entire village turned out to see the spectacle of White skin exposed - especially the women, "who are desirous of mixing the blood if I will." Hayes' iron adherence to his own code of purity held up, even if he could not help noting that, "these young girls are often beautiful and attractive as any European maid." However, all around him Hayes could see that few White men in Africa shared his chaste discipline. Almost every European man took a temporary African "wife," though individual behavior varied by nationality: the Brits had enough "race pride" to conceal the relationships, the Germans less, and the French none at all. Hidden or flaunted, Hayes opined that these relationships seldom resulted in children, "for Europeans do not breed well in tropic lands."

African women were not the only danger Hayes perceived to European men in Nigeria. Only a month after Richardson had smashed the JuJu gods, sending all Sapoba onto a dangerous rampage, Hayes sat quietly in his mahogany house across the river calmly detailing rumors of powerful people like him being eaten nearby. Hayes wrote that the British military victories over the Edo and Jekri had driven human sacrifice underground but not eradicated the practice entirely. Quite near Sapoba, British forces had just broken up a JuJu house where gods were being fed on human flesh, the hands and jaws of sacrificial fetishes moving, "probably drawn strings in the hands of the priests doing it." Those sacrificed were undoubtedly African, but rumor had it that a White doctor had recently suffered a horrible death, taken from village to village, "a bit more carved from him at each place until he died." Hayes explained ritual cannibalism in the context of power: "The JuJu worshipers believe if they eat a bit of any white man, any superior person, the powers of that individual will enter them from that time on."

By the middle of June, the JuJu fervor had "died a natural death" at Sapoba. Maybe the rituals to recover the broken idols had been completed. Even with the big furor quieted, small difficulties remained, the casual violence prevalent at an isolated colonial logging station. Hayes got "crowned with a club" one night breaking up a gang fight. Usually he got on well with the native workmen, but not always on paydays. Apajah paid wages in square-face gin (cheap spirits, originally sold in square bottles) so vile the only two White men Hayes ever knew to drink it "died in a delirium shortly after." Hayes

40

wrote an ineffectual letter to R. Lenthall, head of the Niger Company at Burutu, complaining about the alcohol payments to native workers. He thought seriously about going higher, directly to British colonial authorities, but he knew to have any effect he'd have to reach as high as Sir George Goldie, British Administrator for all of Nigeria – an unlikely stretch for a backcountry logger.

Starting on July 2, 1907, six months after first arriving in Nigeria, Hayes' diary took on a despondent tone. He had decided to leave Africa. Partly the malaria drove him out; his recovery at Sapele had been only temporary. But his despondency ran much deeper than physical illness. He wrote with a broken spirit, that he, the idealistic young adventurer come to Africa to "assist in the game," had discovered that "the game" in Africa in 1907 was the exchange of liquor for land, resources, commodities, and power.

Alcohol, always alcohol. Hayes had seen the ravages booze inflicted on native Alaskan communities when working with the USGS, but in Alaska renegade White traders imported liquor illegally. In Africa, a British company exchanging cheap, soul-destroying, community-wrecking gin for mahogany extravagantly valued at a shilling a board foot back in Europe was considered good business. The last straw seems to have been Hayes' realization that most of the mahogany he cut shipped directly to the United States in return for rum imported directly from Jamaica. His conscience would not allow him to participate in this immoral exchange that devastated one community while enriching another.

Sick with malaria, Hayes had no more strength to fight a colonial system of theft and corruption. Lenthall had replied to Hayes' letter, hinting vaguely at a place in the Hausa territories to the north, a Moslem region where Hayes might fare better in regard to the liquor trade. But Richardson and McPherson, those corrupt little men, seemed to dash that last hope for Hayes in Nigeria. Their petty existence convinced

Hayes that, at least in Nigeria, "No one is honest, business means nothing more than robbery without going to jail."

Hayes left his Sapoba station and paddled "alone" downriver by canoe toward the end of July 1907. At Miller's headquarters in Sapele, he met with a few company officers sympathetic to his complaints – as long as all conversations remained behind closed doors. Bowie, a beach clerk for Miller & Co., the only other man brave enough to voice a protest publicly, found himself packed off alongside Hayes on the freighter *Zaria* sailing west along the African trading coast, headed for Liverpool.

At the mouth of the Niger River, departing Nigeria, Hayes wrote: "It seems the light will go out of my eyes." His boyhood dreams of wildest Africa had smashed hard against the reality of booze and whips, inflated kings and little colonial cogs in Nigeria. And he hadn't even lasted a year! Would he ever return? Would he ever want to return?

On August 8, 1907, the *Zaria* lay off the beach at Saltpond, Ghana. In a delirium of fever, Hayes, agonizing about his failure in Africa, slipped into a sentimental reverie and wrote tenderly, perhaps for the only time in his entire journal, about the intimate lives of women and children: "How vivid it is all to me now. I can see the villages now clearer than when I have been in them during the past seven months. The women, who do most of the work, tending their tiny babies never absent from any woman as long as she is youthful enough to bear. The babies painted a vivid red with the sap of the root of a certain tree. The mothers, chewing manioc, then forcing into the child's mouth the result. Larger children already weaned, all with immense stomachs from this forcible feeding…"

Hayes continued in a darker vein: "… Men guzzling gin, drunken, bleary eyed, often fighting. The younger women also drunken, selling their favors for the much-prized fiery liquor they all love. Children hanging onto the fringe of the crowd in an effort to get at least a swig. This is Africa and one wonders whether it has profited by the occupation of the European. The latter has stopped the slave trade and human sacrifice, but he has saddled this debauchery on them, and it is worse."

3. In the Meantime: Alaska, Australia, New Guinea, San Diego, etc., 1907-1913

After leaving Nigeria in August 1907, Hayes did not return to Africa until January 1914. The following compressed account of his wanderings in the six intervening years indicates at least something of the incredible scope and peril of his travels. Slipping the bounds of North America and Europe into the wildly foreign African continent seems to have emboldened him to seize the world.

Immediately upon arriving in England, still sick with malaria and heartbroken with the sense that he'd failed in Nigeria, Hayes sailed from Liverpool on *The Empress of Britain* with a crush of British immigrants seeking new lives in Canada. In the brisk air of the North Sea he regained enough vitality for at least one practical joke while at sea. *The Empress of Britain* had only a single saloon where all passengers dined after crashing, in a mob, through a narrow entry hall as soon as a harried porter cracked the door. One evening, early out from Liverpool, Hayes and five jaunty fellows linked arms across the hallway leading to the saloon, playfully delaying the hungry Brits' charge toward supper. Afterward, Hayes did not believe his ribs had been broken but feared they might have been had he tried that stunt when the otherwise congenial immigrants weren't weak from seasickness. Despite his pranks, Hayes wrote with great empathy for these unwashed, untutored immigrants forced by poverty and aspiration to gamble their lives into worlds for which they were entirely unprepared. "One is intrigued by the hopefulness of all these people."

From Quebec, Hayes rode an austere iron bench across the continent to Vancouver. The Canadian rail line would have rented him a thin seat-mattress, but 50¢ was too steep for Hayes and for most of the immigrants from *The Empress of Britain* now jostling him on the train. Race riots wracked Vancouver the week Hayes and the immigrants arrived. Burned-out buildings and shattered glass attested to the European workingmen's refusal to countenance Japanese and Chinese workers accepting lower wages that would reduce the standard for all. Instead of attacking unscrupulous employers exploiting racial animosities to divide workingmen, White workers lashed out with violence and death for their "Asiatic" competitors. Hayes would not seek work here.

If one geographic locale could be called "home" for Hayes Perkins during his wandering years, the North and Central California coasts came closest. A nightmarish ride south from Vancouver in the hold, fouled with the seasickness of previous passengers, of "an old time wooden vessel," the *Pueblo*, finally landed Hayes "home" in San Francisco. The soft California sunshine cured him of the malaria, the Canadian cold, and the seasickness, but Hayes would not seek work in San Francisco either. He marveled at how San Francisco had rebuilt in the short year since he'd passed through a city destroyed by the great earthquake and subsequent fire of 1906. Much restoration work remained to be done, but San Francisco was a union town. Any work Hayes might find there meant paying a bribe to the union bosses, so Hayes moved on south to find something independent.

Of Southern California, Hayes wrote: "There is plenty to do here if a man is not particular what he does." Hayes was never particular about what work he did; in the last three months of 1907 he found, and quit, several jobs. He drove a mule team four abreast leveling farm ground in the Imperial Valley near the Mexico border but quit when the farmer paired two wild broncos between two mules requiring double work, plowing while breaking horses. He drove another team at a brickyard in Los Angeles, hauling clay behind four mules now hitched two-and-two but quit along with the entire Mexican crew when the boss cut wages with no notification. He loaded and unloaded at a dock job for the Salt Lake Railway with a dozen men in San Pedro but quit because the boss was a brute.

Returning north to the rain and mud of a camp called Little River in the California redwood forests 30 miles north of Eureka, Hayes joined a roustabout gang setting up a Canadian timber mill. Pay at the various California jobs averaged around $50 per month, reduced to $45 when Hayes refused to work Sundays, and most provided meals and housing so he was able to save most of his salary.

By March 1908 labor discontent had the mill site at Little River in turmoil. Workers voluntarily contributed $1.50 per month to a hospital they had established for themselves to treat the many injured at this dangerous work. Now the "thrifty" company had built its own hospital and would require all workers to pay into company medical care instead. To a man, the workers threatened strike. Hayes said he'd honor the strike, but mainly as a way to get out of there. He believed the company hospital was a raw deal, but also, he had had enough of the Northern California rain. And more to the point of his departure, in six months work he'd saved a stake sufficient for another big venture.

By late May 1908 Hayes had made his way north up the Pacific coast of the United States to find work on the docks at Skagway, Alaska, shifting mountains of prospectors' baggage onto the rail line connecting Skagway to White Horse in the Yukon Territory, Canada. He knew the big gold rush of the late 1890s was essentially finished; still, wouldn't it be interesting to take a ride up the Yukon River to catch the tail end of the legendary boom? When news arrived in Skagway that the river ice had broken on the other side of White Horse Pass, Hayes quit the docks and boarded the narrow gauge train himself.

At Dawson on the Yukon River in the Alaskan interior, site of "perhaps the last great rush North America will ever see," Hayes found exactly what he had expected. From his time in Victor, Colorado, he knew the appearance of a boomtown past its prime. The population of Dawson, formerly peaked at 35,000, had dwindled to around 3,000 in the warm months, 1,000 in winter. Almost no independent mines or new exploitations remained. The Guggenheim Company had cornered all the claims and now worked great areas with massive dredges instead of the pick and shovel of an independent miner. Men still drawn by the romance of Alaska, fueled in no small part, Hayes noted, by the embroidery of Jack London and Robert Service, found "plenty of heavy work, poor food, [and] mosquitoes." No fortunes remained to be found for any man with a name other than Guggenheim. In addition to those working the big outfits, many idle men swindled by the company clogged the streets and saloons of Dawson. Company flyers posted around Seattle offered four-month contracts with return passage guaranteed upon completion. Many men paid the $75 passage north for the promise of work, only to be fired after three and a half month's hard labor. Hayes sidestepped that losing game.

Continuing west from Dawson along the Yukon, Hayes changed to a ferry small enough to navigate east up the Tanana River on the way to the more recently discovered goldfields at Fairbanks. Upwards of 3,000 independent prospectors at Fairbanks rattled rocker boxes out in the creeks. At least another 3,000 ran wheeled carts from the deep diggings following a three to four foot gravel "pay streak" beneath overburden as much as 160 feet deep. The independent fortune hunters on the creeks must not have been even moderately successful; barrow men working for the big companies fought to get those jobs, running ten hours a day stooped behind heavy carts in a low tunnel for $2.25 plus board.

Aboveground, another 2,000 unemployed would-be miners idled among "the pimps, gamblers, prostitutes, musicians about the dance halls, prize fighters, politicians and other shady characters who hang on the fringe of crime in every gold camp that has ever been or ever will be to the world's end." An entire unemployed labor force waited, eager to seize the handles of the wheelbarrow, and the salary, from any man unable to keep pace in the tunnels. Worse, this early in the season, the big companies placed "flattering advertisements" in the Seattle papers to draw a steady flood of ever more men north to try their chances at quick fortune in the brief Fairbanks summer.

Passage south out of Alaska back to Seattle cost more than the $75 men were paid to come north. Fifty-six day's work running the tunnels would earn a man the necessary $125 to get out before the snow started to fly. As usual for Hayes, after paying passage and expenses north, he didn't have $125. Nor had he any desire to run the tunnels. Among all the unemployed men at Fairbanks increasingly desperate for work as the short summer lengthened, Hayes miraculously turned up work on July 5, handling cargo on a small river steamer, the *Relief*.

The cargo riverboat *Relief* paid $75 a month, easily enough for Hayes to save passage south had he stuck with the job. He lasted only two days, not even time enough to finish straightening out the "mare's nest" of ship's gear. When the *Relief* had arrived back at Fort Gibbon, the first river stop west of Fairbanks, Hayes had unloaded all the "ordinary cargo," then locked eyes with the captain. Hayes had clearly told the man Hayes would not handle liquor. The skipper shrugged and nodded toward the knot of men on the dock seeking work. Hayes understood the threat but, true to his resolve, lifted his slight rucksack and walked off the boat. An unruffled skipper glanced past Hayes' retreating back and pointed to one of the half-dozen men surging forward to replace the lunatic stepping ashore.

The next day, as Hayes lounged on the riverbank conversing with a well-educated but soft-handed Bulgarian named Feodor, four late arrivals at Fort Gibbon pulled ashore in a small, open boat they'd rowed down the Yukon River from White Horse. In a sweat to get to the diggings unencumbered, one of the fellows called out an offer to Hayes: five bucks for the boat, twenty pounds of flour, eleven pounds of bacon, and two pounds of prunes, plus cooking gear – take it or leave it, Mister. Hayes could barely restrain himself; he thought he and Feodor might scrape together five dollars between them.

The morning of July 7, 1908, greeted Hayes and Feodor under full sail behind a blanket tied to a tree branch braced in the bottom of a leaky boat, chinked with bits of moss, bound north and west toward the Bering Sea. Twelve days later, the pair pulled ashore at St. Michael having sailed and rowed their little *Maryann of White Horse* 900 miles down Alaska's Yukon River. Just before reaching Norton Sound on the Bering Sea, helplessly lost in the spreading maze of the Yukon River delta, the two sailors survived only with the help of an indigenous guide picked up along the way. "We demanded a salmon in payment for his passage, while he wanted a free trip and grub besides for showing us the way."

The Inuit man paid a fine King salmon and guided the *Maryann of White Horse* safely to a semi-permanent settlement of tents and igloos at the mouth of a river channel on Pastol Bay just past Kotlik. Waving farewell to their guide on the last day of their journey, Hayes and Feodor rowed, sailed, and baled thirteen-hours, forty-miles across open ocean in a raging squall. Barely alive, Feodor stepped ashore and wandered off to town without a word. No more alive than Feodor, Hayes sold the boat for two dollars, and then followed into town where he would lay down all the money he had for passage on the *Ohio* bound south for Seattle. The rigors of prospecting on the wild Yukon River so punished men, Hayes and Feodor weren't the passengers most badly broken sailing out from St

Michael on the *Ohio*. Assessing the crowd of unsuccessful prospectors on board, crewmembers judged Hayes and Feodor weak but sane enough they would not need watching.

Hayes put himself back together over the next year working mills, hayfields, and farms in Oregon and Washington, including a brief stint in October 1909 on the farm of my great-grandparents, Joe and Minnie Donaldson, at Riverton, Oregon. Hayes and Minnie were first cousins. The Donaldson farm offered Hayes a seductively secure life, but no, "One never runs out of work on a farm." Incredible that Hayes would pretend to blanch at hard work. The same work day after day under the same twenty-two cows must have been his true aversion. John Donaldson, my grandfather, to whom Hayes gave his diaries in 1964 just before Hayes died, would have been a ten-year-old working son of the Riverton farm in 1909.

Fit again by the beginning of 1910, Hayes signed on as a deckhand on the *Foxley* bound for Australia out of North Bend, Oregon. The *Foxley* needed a new man because most of the crew had deserted her thuggish captain. Ashore at Sydney with, by Hayes' standards, little mishap with said captain, Hayes chanced across a magazine advertisement announcing the prospectus for a new company exploiting "millions of feet of timber," "thousands of acres of sago," and "hundreds of acres of coconuts," in Papua New Guinea. As he was down to his last £20, he strolled round to their offices and accepted a job opening up plantation land for those soon to follow.

Steaming north toward New Guinea, Hayes just missed Jack London at a plantation known as Pendufferyn on Guadalcanal. Probably just as well; Hayes' comments regarding London's work shed some light on Hayes' own self-appointed role as a traveling truth-teller: "Jack London, noted author, has been here recently, and the whites who run the plantation laugh at his adventures. These he set down as real, but they were entirely vicarious. In truth he sat on the veranda of the wide bungalow and penned these thrilling episodes in safety, drinking numerous highballs the while. But the non-traveling public eats up this sort of adventure, and give the lie to men who say little and see much."

Undoubtedly Hayes included himself among those who say little and see much. Not to single out London, a few pages later Hayes dressed down Louis Bekke and Beatrice Grimshaw for romanticizing "the trader, the beachcomber, the miner until it gives no comprehensive picture of island life as it is."

Perhaps there is no irony in noting that, late in life, Hayes himself wrote a novel, *The Rearguard*, featuring a noble White elephant hunter and an equally elevated Moslem Tuareg man arguing theology in the deserts of North Africa. Hayes seemed to be trying to write more factually, drawing from his lived experiences, than the novelists he criticizes. Unfortunately, Hayes' lived experiences with women were so fragmentary and stilted he wrote all the relationships to his heroine, "Zeitoun, pearl of the desert," in cartoonishly elevated terms. None of his writings, including *The Rearguard*, the five volumes of his diary, nor his three non-fiction synopses of his time in Africa, Alaska, and at the Hearst mansion, have ever been published.

By October 1910, five months on New Guinea had convinced Hayes that the development he had carefully scouted and partially cleared while living almost entirely off the land was an investment fraud. He quit and returned to Sydney where he was called before the investment council to lay bare his view of the swindle. Disturbed, the council did a little internal housecleaning, then offered Hayes another job scouting timber on Muyua, largest of the Woodlark Islands in the Solomon Sea east of New Guinea. Somewhat surprisingly given the ethics of the company, Hayes accepted their offer and spent another few months traipsing about Muyua hoping to meet cannibals. He found the residents he met pleasant and generous to a lone traveler.

Back in Australia in March 1911 with his savings from the previous year's work in New Guinea weighing heavily in his pocket, Hayes thought about what to do next: "I don't care to return to the states, for there hard work and little recompense await. In Africa adventure, perhaps riches, surely hardship, a fifty-fifty chance of death."

Two weeks later he paid passage on the Norddeutscher Lloyd liner *Seydlitz* bound west from Sydney for Aden at the mouth of the Red Sea. The *Seydlitz* crossed the Indian Ocean carrying Hayes and a throng of wealthy Australians traveling to London for the coronation of George V. At Aden, Hayes intended to transfer to a ship bound for Mombasa, Kenya, then walk west from Mombasa overland into the African interior.

Hayes arrived successfully in Mombasa aboard the German liner *Windhuk* out of Aden, but on this ship, chatting up fellow passengers backfired on him. The two missionaries with whom he'd discussed his adventure plans denounced him to an immigration officer at Mombasa as "a penniless wanderer who will corrupt the natives." The insult stung deeply especially since officials required Hayes to put down a £10 deposit, insurance to carry him out of the country in the event he should go broke in East Africa. He stayed only eight days sightseeing around Mombasa before retracing his three-month journey back to Aden and across the Indian Ocean to Australia.

While still in Mombasa, Hayes chanced across a type he'd meet again later in his travels:, this one named Dixon, an elephant hunter, "a true man of the wilderness, [who] has little regard for his life." Without identifying precisely the haunt, Hayes wrote that he watched Dixon silence a room full of "four flush bad men." The gamblers had been bragging about their steely nerve when Dixon tossed £600 onto the table with a challenge to cut a single card with any man willing to match the amount. No takers. Hayes almost signed on with Dixon's plan to return to the center of the continent hunting elephants. At the last minute, though, Hayes decided that newly imposed joint British/Belgian hunting restrictions made Dixon's enterprise too "hot" to risk traveling with him.

Back in Australia in July 1911 after 3,300 rough miles re-crossing the Indian Ocean from Aden by way of Colombo, Ceylon (Sri Lanka) to Fremantle, Hayes continued on to Sydney, idling a month there as "parlor poodle" among a chic social set: "Well-dressed men who know no hardship, beautiful women whose eyes are langourous [sic] and alluring, whose every action is bent on getting a suitable mate." Hayes described himself as "a rank amateur among these people" and plotted his escape before he too went soft; besides, he was nearly broke again.

When a proposed coconut and rubber plantation scheme in the New Hebrides he'd been discussing with some Sydneysiders fell through, Hayes decided on a return to New Guinea. He knew the island well enough and had some financial connections he thought he could trust from the previous investment group. He partnered with two men, Hammond and Greer, who agreed to foot the bill if Hayes did the heavy work on the ground to establish a plantation on the Regurani [Wegulani] River at the eastern tip of New Guinea.

Hayes lived comfortably with the Papuans, a lone White man in the region, for the last three months of 1911. The village donated him a newly built house where he ate entirely native foods, mostly sago, taro, crabs, and fish. When his private pantry ran low, he ate, but did not like eating, from the communal stew pot into which went "snakes, goanas (huge lizards seven or eight feet in length at times), alligator flesh or eggs, and human flesh for all I know." He absolutely refused to eat pork if he knew it came from a pig suckled by a woman of the village.

Support from the women and the young men of the village during fireside council meetings allowed Hayes to successfully negotiate a land purchase with the elders. He believed the Papuans welcomed a good neighbor bringing jobs for their young men: "Even the elders realize it is good to encourage the European occupation of the country, for even bad white men are better than bad natives."

Hayes left the plantation site in January 1912 when it became clear Greer and Hammond weren't upholding the money end of the partnership. Back in Sydney, a smooth-talking Hammond, treading on their friendship, induced Hayes to accept £25 and 200 shares of stock in the company to compensate his many months' work in the bush.

The cash and stock settlement would have satisfied Hayes had it been more equitable. Both Greer and Hammond "set themselves down for 900 shares and other emoluments as well." Hayes cynically excused Greer: "He is a so-called business man, and we all know such are on the borderline of robbery." But Hayes thought Hammond, one of the most noted Christian ministers in all Australia, would have acted more ethically.

Nearly broke again, Hayes walked 100 miles south from Sydney to Jervis Bay where he had heard a new Australian naval station would soon be built. While waiting for construction to commence in early summer, he camped out alone in the bush for two months in 1912 eating kangaroo and sago.

After six months working at Jervis Bay breaking road stones with a two-pound hammer and mixing cement by hand for want of the simplest machinery, Hayes had saved enough for return passage "home" to California following a westerly route that would take him completely around the globe for the first time. This first circumnavigation of the globe goes entirely unremarked in Hayes' diary.

Returned to Sydney from Jervis Bay with a little cash, Hayes booked passage on the *G.M.S. Zeiten* all the way to Southampton, England. January and early February of 1913 passed pleasantly for Hayes, his diary recording idle ship's gossip at various stops on the Australian continent, across the Indian Ocean, up the Red Sea, through the Suez Canal, across a placid Mediterranean, out the Strait of Gibraltar, and up the North Atlantic to Southampton.

Hayes celebrated his 35th birthday, February 10, 1913, his first night in Southampton, discussing Harvey Logan, Butch Cassidy and Harry Longabaugh, better known as The Sundance Kid, with a Yank late of Buenos Aires, Argentina, where the Wild West outlaws had recently relocated.

The steamship *Majestic* carried Hayes from England across the Atlantic, the ship close packed with Jews and Poles and a few "splendid blonde Scandinavians … who will make real Americans." At Fire Island, New York, US doctors and immigration officials boarded the *Majestic* poking and prodding every new arrival absent the slightest common decency. Hayes went ashore at the Tomkinsville pier but everyone else aboard the *Majestic* was sent on to Ellis Island, "where doubtless they will be put through the mill by other inquisitors there."

A train south to Florida and then a steamer from Tampa brought Hayes to Houston for a ten-day visit with his mother and two of his sisters, Jennie and Pearl. Seeing his family members for the first time in ten years, Hayes wrote only that his mother looked older and that his sisters, "have had a hard, uphill fight for an education," and, having achieved educations, "I fear it has slightly gone to their heads." The next paragraph in his diary describes the bright industrial prospects for the port of Houston, a discussion bearing considerably more warmth than the one regarding his family.

Arriving "home" in San Francisco, Hayes worked a typical succession of jobs on the West Coast of the United States between April and August of 1913: more farming with cousin Minnie and Joe in Riverton; sorting green lumber at a mill in North Bend; running a planer at Hammond's mill in Eureka (a large company run so much like a penitentiary that Hayes, never a fan of labor unions, wrote approvingly of IWW organizing there) and, finally, back to the Imperial Valley driving a mule team leveling farm ground.

En route to the job at El Centro in the Imperial Valley, Hayes stopped for a few days to see the sights and a few old friends around Los Angeles. One of his Christian acquaintances in the city asked him to speak about West Africa, the Solomon Islands, and New Guinea at the mission hall. Later, in the press of bodies in the hall after his talk, Hayes shook hands with an Englishman, George Studd, whose more famous brother, CT Studd, sat at that moment on a riverbank in the Belgian Congo waiting for God to send a handyman to erect the Heart of Africa Mission.

George Studd, something of an evangelist himself, pressed Hayes to apply. Hayes hesitated to get his hopes up for Africa again after the disappointments in Nigeria and Kenya: "It sounds good, but it is futile to try." So he dashed off a cursory outline of his adventures around the world telling George Studd, "…they must read between the lines if they wanted more." Then Hayes forgot all about the Heart of Africa Mission and left Los Angeles toward that mule team in the Imperial Valley.

A Fresno scraper is a dump-bucket pulled by mules yoked four abreast; Hayes bossed a Fresno scraper around the Imperial Valley for two months. He quit the job partly because the Indian and Mexican drivers abused the mules with whips and goads, and partly in protest over reduced wages offered a crew of unskilled Italian men brought in to replace the Mexicans and Indians.

A letter caught up with an unemployed Hayes near the Mexico/US border. Fred Sidler, his friend on the other end of the Salvation Army pew back in Victor, Colorado, years previously, encouraged Hayes to come up to San Diego. Fred could get Hayes ridiculously easy work driving a Fresno scraper, two abreast, with a sideman dumping! Fred already had work at the job: blasting tree trunks on the future site of Balboa Park. Hayes came north and the two took up "housekeeping" in a small apartment with a kitchenette.

For the first time in more than ten years beating about the world, "good food and congenial surroundings" nearly convinced Hayes to abandon wandering: "This is the place I have been looking for all my life." Soft winds and gentle sunshine seduced the adventurer. Could he put down roots in this most beautiful of all places? Maybe: "I'm almost forgetting about Africa even."

Not a week after penning a long paean to the beauty of San Diego, on the night of October 19, 1913, Hayes woke to "a haunting, sub-conscious warning of evil to come that thrills me like an electric shock." A letter arrived from London the next morning. Would Mr. Henry H. Perkins travel forthwith to England to interview for a position at the Heart of Africa Mission at Niangara, Belgian Congo? How easily a call to Africa broke the spell of San Diego.

4. Up the Nile, Across the Continental Divide, to the Heart of Africa Mission, Niangara, Belgian Congo, 1913-14

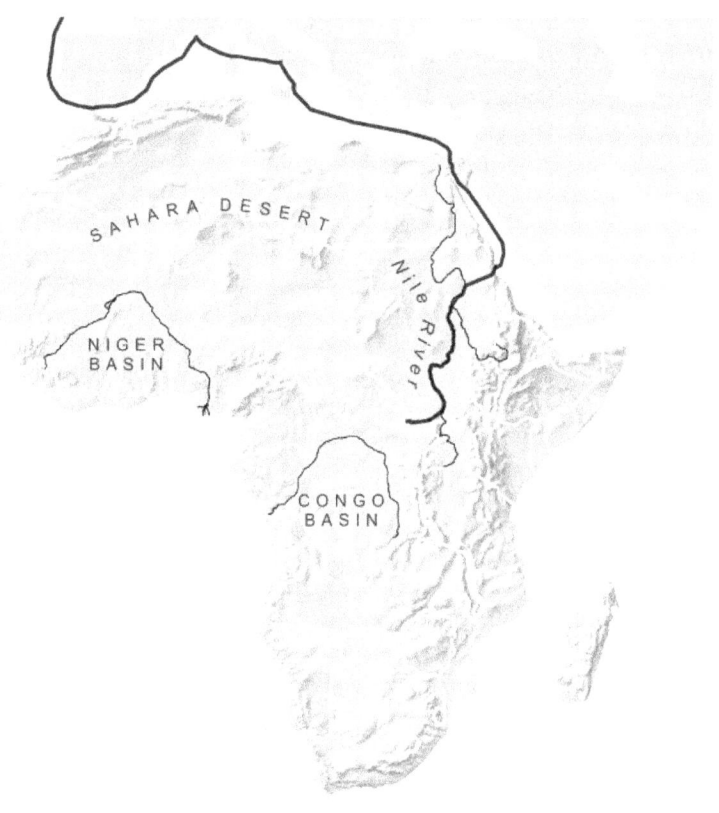

Five days after receiving a summons to the Heart of Africa Mission Society in London, Hayes boarded a boat to Los Angeles where George Studd gave him letters for the Studd family in England. An unheated train puffed Hayes across the North American continent to Montreal. The

Cunard Line's steamer *Ausonia* tossed him across stormy North Atlantic seas to arrive in London on November 12, 1913.

Hayes took an inexpensive room in Edgeware Road, "a slightly dingy part of town." He wasn't flat broke but he couldn't afford Piccadilly or Regent Street, or even Mayfair, any of the nicest accommodations. The night before his first interview, he pressed the better of his two suits, hoping to make a favorable impression.

Hayes first spoke with Martin Sutton, "the greatest seed merchant in the world" and principal benefactor to the Heart of Africa Mission. Hayes liked the straight-talking industrialist. Apparently the liking was mutual: immediately following their meeting, Sutton had Hayes transferred to the Wilton Hotel, "not far from the Houses of Parliament and from Buckingham Palace." Even with Sutton picking up the tab, Hayes thought the better hotel not worth the money.

The next day Hayes interviewed with CT Studd's wife, Priscilla, at the Studd home near the Crystal Palace in Hyde Park. Afterward he wrote with shock and a little irony, "These people are all aristocrats, and evidently think I am." They had given Hayes a hyphen. Everyone seemed to be addressing him as "Mr. Hayes-Perkins."

Over the course of a month in London, Hayes learned more detail about "THE Studds." Edward Studd had established the family fortune planting indigo in India. Converted to Christianity by the American evangelist Dwight Moody, Edward exhorted his three sons, George, Kynaston, and CT, then at Eton, toward Moody's "muscular Christianity." Moody's Christians were "men's men," square of jaw and strong of arm, eschewing effeminate intellectualism in favor of the moral purities exemplified by athleticism and team sports.

Adopting Moody's teachings, the three boys went on to Cambridge where, as successive captains of the cricket team, they became known as The Studd Brothers. CT, the most accomplished of the boys, played on the losing Cambridge side that started the "ashes" test matches with Australia.

Just after finishing at Cambridge, CT internalized Pentecostal Christianity much more profoundly than he had at Eton or Cambridge. Still in his early twenties, CT decided that the fleeting fame of cricket, or any other accomplishments of this world, paled by comparison to the work of saving souls. Renouncing both his cricket career and a very large inheritance in favor of radical dependence on God's providence, in 1885 CT joined a group of six other students, "the Cambridge Seven," in making widely publicized volunteer commitments to the China Inland Mission. At age 52, after nine years missionary work in China, six years as a pastor in India, and against doctor's advice, CT answered what he understood to be another call from God: to bring the word of Christ to the darkest corner of Africa.

Not exactly Hayes' take on Christianity but he knew how to speak discretely to powerful people; the interviews went well. All the important people at the Heart of Africa Mission Society were assured the American would serve CT Studd well and faithfully. Granted the job, scheduled to leave forthwith, Hayes might have been expected to be overjoyed. Instead he wrote into his diary a sequence of disturbing premonitions of "a haunting sense of evil to come, that all is not well in Africa."

One last errand before leaving London: on his way to the docks at Tilbury, Hayes stopped off to speak with a dinner guest he had met at the home of Salvation Grace Faith Sutton ne Studd, 26 year old wife of Martin Sutton, eldest daughter of CT Studd. Fearing a special Miss Edith Donnithorne had formed an unfortunate attachment to an improper image of him, Hayes wanted to let her down as gently as possible: "Poor girl, she doesn't realize I am an adventurer, and I am really rough and uncouth."

At Tilbury, the rough and uncouth adventurer boarded "a typical British India liner," the *Golconda*, traveling second class with eight other passengers bound for Port Sudan on the Red Sea.

Exiting the Suez Canal, the *Golconda* took a short jaunt down a remarkably pellucid Red Sea along the eastern coast of Egypt to Port Sudan. If Hayes' diaries recorded any foreshadowing of the World War that would break out six months hence, it was with references to German hotel staff at Port Sudan. As in London, young, officious German men staffed all the finest hotels, "a key position to give them the opportunity for information they relay to their home government." Hayes didn't know a specific purpose for the information, only that "Germany aspires to be next top dog for world power."

By entering Africa at Port Sudan, Hayes cut off 1400 river miles south up the Nile from Cairo to Khartoum in exchange for a 500-mile train ride west across the barren desert from Port Sudan to Khartoum. Hayes regretted missing the wonders of the lower Nile but he was in something of a hurry to get across the continent and into Northern Congo. The desert towns along the rail line held nearly as much fascination for the adventurer as the Egyptian Nile.

At Atbara on the confluence of the Atbara River with the Nile River, Hayes commented on "a medley of Dongalawis, Arabs, Nubians, and pilgrims from the western Soudan" on hajj, the Moslem pilgrimage to Mecca. He wrote with some compassion for these mendicants who he believed may have been traveling toward the holy city for as long as five years. Especially were the women following behind their men to be pitied: "for some authorities say she has no soul." This close to the Red Sea with Mecca just across the water, the faces of the men shone radiantly. Not so for the woman: "Never have I seen utter hopelessness implanted on a human face as in the face of these women."

At Meroë, identified by Hayes as the capitol of Ethiopia far in the past, Hayes marveled at "pyramids, ruined temples and even cliff dwellings," but puzzled how this arid waste where neither "jackal nor gazelle can now live" ever supported such an expansive population.

As the sun cast long rays low in the evening sky, Hayes' "wondering eye" saw out the train window desert mirages so clear he could count ripples on the surface of chimerical water. For Hayes, every bit of the exotic desert panorama unreeling just outside the car window anticipated romantic adventure at "Khartoum!"

The adventures of "Chinese Gordon" disobeying orders from London to abandon Khartoum in 1885 to the rebels lead by the Mahdi, a Sudanese religious and political leader, had ended in a massacre when the city's defenses failed. The unfolding story of the Mahdist rebellion had dominated the world's newspapers in the early 1880s when Hayes was an impressionable boy. Thus, Hayes was surprised to depart the train at a modern Khartoum at the confluence of the Blue Nile and the White Nile: "There are many fine government buildings, a magnificent cathedral, mosques, shops, bazaars, the railway shops at Khartoum north…." Gunboats patrolling the rivers "just in case" seemed the only evidence recalling any violence from the Mahdist rebellion.

Before leaving Khartoum, Hayes wrote a description of the confluence of the two Niles, a first-hand comparison of rivers few in the world then or now could make: "There is an air of enchantment and mystery about it all. The Niles have none of the lilt and swing of the Yukon nor the sparkling blue of the St. Lawrence. They are patient plodding rivers, uniting their forces here for a common purpose, that to conquer the desert." Departing Khartoum, Hayes would float the White Nile as far south as navigation permitted, then undertake some patient plodding of his own.

The month and a half following Hayes' departure from Khartoum may have been the happiest of his life. Between January 8 and February 21, 1914, Hayes traveled 1200 miles by steamship up the White Nile to Rejaf, walked 400 miles across the continental divide into the Belgian Congo, and poled 50 miles down the Welle River with a crew of native boatmen to arrive at the Heart of Africa Mission at Niangara, Congo. He wrote extensive journal entries nearly every day as if trying to hold onto each moment forever.

On the sixth night of his trip up the White Nile, Hayes wrote, "I wish this river was longer than it is." At Rejaf, "a fair sized hamlet" and center of trade for a vast area of the country, he wrote: "Eighteen days from Khartoum, every one of them filled with vivid interest. I have lived more in these past eighteen days than in a year in a sawmill at Eureka or in Oregon." Just enough adventure, just enough danger, a riverboat steamer up a river just exotic enough to realize the romance Hayes sought all his life.

As much as Hayes loved the sights and sounds of the river, he was equally excited to begin travel overland by "hamrah, or bullock transport" out of Sudan into the Congo River drainage: "Now for the bush in its fullness. I am glad to see it, eager to learn what lies beyond."

Red tape at Rejaf, "the Sudan regulations are irksome to a traveler," dampened Hayes' enthusiasm only slightly. Castle-Smith, the "bimbashi or major" commanding the post, would not allow redistribution of Hayes' many large crates, supplies for the Heart of Africa Mission, into loads appropriate for porters. The bambishi fussed officiously over Hayes' papers, threatening two-week's sleeping sickness quarantine. Hayes' porters were all either old men or boys; none could manage a 67-pound load! Castle-Smith would not budge. Hayes slipped the heaviest boxes onto a hamrah; old men and boys shouldered those they could manage, any expedient to get out of Rejaf.

As the caravan was about to depart Rejaf, the officious Castle-Smith handed Hayes a sheaf of documents. Because Hayes was the "lone European" traveling into the Congo, Castle-Smith entrusted Hayes with the papers necessary for crossing the international border. Included with the official papers Hayes discovered a small volume. The Heart of Africa

Mission, anticipating his arrival at Rejaf, had sent him a slim vocabulary of Bangala, a trade language common to many of the local tribes. Alfred Buxton, CT Studd's young missionary assistant, had compiled this godsend. None of the drivers, soldiers, or porters in the caravan spoke any English. With Hayes' facility for languages, Bangala would soon be their common tongue.

On January 27, 1914, Castle-Smith's papers in order, the hamrah finally crept out of Rejaf, two oxen drawing each wagon. A driver flanked by an askari, an African soldier in service to some colonial authority, walked beside each team. Porters carried the manageable loads on their heads.

Among the documents given him by Castle-Smith, Hayes read the name "Mr. Grogan's servant." Hayes didn't know who Mr. Grogan might be but his servant could only be the "comely Bari girl, she bound for some Englishman upcountry as a temporary wife." Hayes began to practice his Bangala, of an evening, with this young woman, Mr. Grogan's servant Maliboro.

In the daytime, Hayes saw elephant spoor everywhere along the path. The natives had been burning the dry-season grasses to catch the large and small animals fleeing the flames. By one small pool in a dry khor, the ox carts rumbled past a large steam truck abandoned by the Belgians when they relinquished this territory. When King Leopold II of Belgium ceded private ownership of the Congo Free State to the Belgian government in 1908, this area, in the east, had come under British control: "Leopold did what he could to exploit this country of its easily negotiable riches before turning it over to the British, which had to be done at his death." Porters were scarce in the days of the Belgian atrocities so Leopold imported the trucks that soon failed "and were left to rust in the bush."

After a four-hour night march on January 30, 1914, the caravan reached Loka and the first "considerable watercourse" since leaving the Nile. This close to the Congo basin tsetse flies had become prevalent. Walking the oxen at night and tethering them away from shade during the day postponed the animal's inevitable deaths from sleeping sickness.

Two days later, the hamrah drivers spent half the night coaxing oxen across the Yei River flowing swiftly out of "timbered hills to the south." When safely across at the town of Yei, a "Colonel Bey (Colonel Dove, of the Anglo-Egyptian Army)" greeted Hayes cordially. What a relief to meet, at this out of the way place, the kind of commonsense British army officer upon which an empire could stand: "This man is a gentleman by instinct as well as by training, and makes up for a lot of boors like those out shooting on the way up the Nile." At Yei, Hayes first mentioned that he also carried a firearm, not an elephant gun, a shotgun for hunting dinner. Bey removed the wire bonds (installed by Castle-Smith?) from Hayes' shotgun, recommending guinea fowl on this side of the continental divide. Yes, he told Hayes, by all means, redistribute loads for the porters sensibly.

While at Yei, Hayes toured a medical camp crowded with more than 450 victims of sleeping sickness. The two British doctors overseeing the camp assured Hayes they had hope for some of the cases: the recently infected lived normal lives, marrying and raising children. Among the more advanced cases, though, some "imagine they are hyenas or other wild animals and simulate these beasts in their actions." The worst cases "lie prostrate on the ground, sprawled as a man falling before a gun." Doctors told Hayes these men and women might linger three or four years but all had begun "their last long sleep."

When Mr. Grogan arrived at Yei from his home in the nearby bush to greet his "wife," Maliboro, Hayes learned Mr. Grogan was Quentin Grogan, an elephant hunter of "world-wide reputation." Quentin Grogan had guided Theodore Roosevelt's big game safari of 1909-10 that recorded killing 17 lions, 3 leopards, 7 cheetahs, 9 hyenas, 11 elephants, 10 buffalos, 11 black rhinos, 9 white rhinos and various smaller game over the course of 11 months.

Unlike others of Quentin Grogan's biographers, Hayes didn't explicitly label Grogan a poacher. At an overnight stop at the elephant hunter's home, Hayes described Grogan's job as "a sinecure obtained through influence to permit him to hunt in the supposedly closed Mongalla district." Hayes gave a rough estimate of Grogan's lucrative sinecure: By regulation, Grogan could kill two elephants in the district yearly. To this could be added another two from the Belgian Congo and two more from Uganda. Grogan had just "taken" his elephants from the local district. The tusks weighed 111 pounds left and right on the first and 125 left, 134 right on the second, for a total of 481 pounds. Hayes put the value of ivory at between $5 and $6 per pound. Accordingly, Grogan profited roughly $2,500 for the ivory from these two elephants, $7,500 if the other four he shot legally averaged similar weight. Adjusted for inflation, Grogan's six dead elephants yielded roughly $200,000 in contemporary dollars.

As much as Hayes thrilled to the sights and sounds along both the Upper Nile and the bullock track through the highlands, he wrote with some relief to finally exit the Sudan. Neither British Sudan nor Belgian Congo maintained an official post at the border where Hayes crossed. Thirty-eight miles west of Yei, the official Sudanese post, and twelve miles east of Aba, the official Congolese post, at another small village "(also called Libogo)," Hayes sighed into his diary: "I now bid farewell to the hamrah and regulation-ridden Sudan, and leave it gladly hoping never to see it again."

One last intolerable Egyptian sub-officer had accompanied Hayes the final few miles to the border at Libogo. The man's excessive religiosity bothered Hayes, writing that the man "aired his religion by praying in the open square when we stopped." Nevertheless, some good came of the man; he spoke enough English to help Hayes sort through the "wild, excited crowd of seventy porters" pushing and shoving at Libogo hoping to carry Hayes' loads forward into the Congo.

Hayes does not detail how many men he hired or what they carried but it must have been many and a lot. Upon arrival at Niangara Hayes unpacked a coal stove! Martin Sutton had considered the stove essential gear: "I have had to lug this heavy iron stove thousands of miles at great cost when there are no coal beds within thousands of miles on either hand. … I demurred at bringing it but was ignored."

Standing at the continental divide looking west into the Congo, Hayes "could not but observe the greener vegetation on the Congo side when compared with that sloping distinctly to the Nile." Across 130 miles climbing the Sudanese slope up from the Nile, the party had crossed only two running streams. Not a half-mile down the Congo side out of Libogo, he and the porters walked beside "a sparkling clear rivulet." Great evergreen trees, evidencing a much rainier region, graced the official port of entry at Aba, twelve miles further on.

Hayes and the porters walked fifty miles west from Aba to Faradje in three days, "good time in Africa with heavy loads." Mostly they walked through high open forests except where streams supported "galleries resembling the lush jungle of the equatorial regions" reminiscent of Nigeria. This near the end of the dry season, local residents had burned most of the grass and low vegetation for hunting. In some of the swampier areas that would not burn "walls of grass ten to fifteen feet tall" lined the track.

To avoid the full heat of the afternoon sun, each day's march began in the full dark of night, as early as 2:00 a.m. Elephant tracks, broken branches, and "great heaps of dung" littered the way. The few native residents they encountered begged Hayes to kill the elephants so destructive to their gardens. Neither properly armed nor inclined to shoot the playful, elegant beasts, Hayes declined.

When Hayes began to hear lions roaring off in the forest, none of the porters seemed the least bit concerned, "mimicking the roars and laughing" into the jungle. Their example allowed Hayes to remain calm when, on the third morning out of Aba, he encountered his first lion face-to-face. Hayes had fallen far behind his carriers. Alone, as he glanced to one side, a lioness parted the tall grass "and sat on her haunches beside the road, looking like nothing more than a Great Dane dog." Hayes calmly returned her stare for some minutes before she bounded off into the forest.

Hayes celebrated his 36th birthday at a hut in a Greek compound surrounded by African women "as handsome according to European standards as any people in the world." The Greek men had purchased their wives, now sitting around Hayes, manicuring, braiding each other's hair, and arranging bright new calicos. The Belgian officers all had wives too but not purchased; theirs had been "drafted" when needed.

In a reflective mood, Hayes ticked off a list of the locations of his previous few birthdays: "The last one was in Southampton... The ones preceding had been in Sydney, the Woodlark Islands, in New Guinea, Ellice Islands, North Bend, Oregon; at Little River, California; in Nigeria, at Seattle, and so on."

One of the Greek men, Makris, produced a bit of "tough, dry, stringy" meat, waterbuck, a type of antelope, for a small birthday celebration, a welcome gesture of kindness. Hayes savored the meat "as if it were a sirloin steak." He declined the "strong intoxicants" Makris offered to go with the waterbuck and listened with some surprise to hear his host use the word "musungu" to mean both White man and strong drink. Hayes wrote ironically: "I wonder if there be any connection between the two?"

Despite the safari walking by moonlight, on the night of February 13 tsetse flies twice bit Hayes. Flies not even as large as the American horsefly but "the bite is as painful as a red hot needle." Hayes reassured himself in his diary that night, writing that few flies carried sleeping sickness so "it is improbable any untoward happening will take place." At the sleeping sickness camp back in Yei, the doctors had told Hayes tsetse flies must bite an infected animal to transmit the disease. In fact, "It is supposed they become infected from biting crocodiles." In the days going forward, as Hayes hoped, nothing beyond the immediate sting came of the two bites.

Just outside Faradje, a beggar waved as Hayes passed. The man's "fingers and thumbs had been severed at the palms of his hands." Hayes had seen another man similarly disfigured back in the village. That man told Hayes that Faradje's chief had mutilated both his hands as punishment for adultery. This beggar by the roadside seemed to be blaming "Bula Matadi."

Henry Morton Stanley had originally been given the name Bula Matadi (or Bula Matari), a phrase meaning "he who breaks rocks" in Kikongo, by Congolese men working on the rail line between Matadi and Stanley Pool. Later users expanded the term to mean "the Belgians." If Hayes understood the man's Bangala correctly, Belgian soldiers had cut off his fingers and cauterized the bleeding with a quick plunge in boiling palm oil.

In all likelihood, Hayes would have been on the lookout for amputated hands and feet in the Congo. He certainly would have known something of the dark history of Leopold's Congo Free State.

Between 1885 and 1908, under Leopold's personal ownership, the Congo Free State became an increasingly severe forced labor state. Leopold's Anglo-Belgian India Rubber (ABIR) Company taxed Congolese villages with rubber quotas. His Force Publique enforced those quotas by village destruction, mass murder, enslavement, and hostage taking.

With his interest in all things Africa, Hayes could not possibly have been ignorant of the international outcry denouncing atrocities in the Congo. Though Joseph Conrad's

1899 *Heart of Darkness* received little popular attention at the time of its publication, pamphlets written by journalist and pacifist E.D. Morel airing true conditions in the Congo Free State were widely read from 1903 on. As the term "Blood Diamonds" would galvanize worldwide condemnation in the 1990s, so too for Morel's term "Red Rubber" in the first decade of the twentieth century.

In 1905 Mark Twain published a 68-page booklet called "King Leopold's Soliloquy" lampooning Leopold's counter-propaganda campaign. Twain's pamphlet included ghastly photographs of Congolese children, their arms ending in stumps, hands severed to enforce rubber quotas. Hayes had certainly read about "the excesses" of the Belgians, although he may not have believed Twain's estimate of ten to twenty million Congolese killed by Leopold. The fact of Leopold's genocide cannot be questioned. Its scope is difficult to establish with any precision but modern scholars argue figures within Twain's range.

Seeing men with mutilated hands just after he had crossed into the Belgian Congo in 1914 darkened Hayes' mood generally. Immediately after encountering the fingerless beggar on the road, Hayes mentioned yet again "an insistent warning of evil to come that will not be denied." Hayes had come to quite dread arrival at the Heart of Africa Mission but, "[i]t is too late to draw back now, and I would not if there was an opportunity for it." Shaking off a sense of "foreboding, of certain disaster," Hayes roused his porters back onto the trail.

Upon arrival at the village of Dungu, where the Dungu River meets the Kibali River to form the Welle River, Hayes wrote that his safari had walked 150 miles in nine days "actual marching." At Dungu, Hayes no longer needed porters; the men could transfer their loads (one happily dropping a cast iron stove) into one enormous canoe as soon as Hayes found a French translator to make the arrangements.

From the cabin of a "genial Greek" in Dungu, Hayes gathered what information he could about his future employer, CT Studd. Nothing he heard allayed his forebodings. A couple of English missionaries building a house on a hill at Dungu had worked briefly with CT Studd. The missionaries told Hayes that Studd had initially started in collaboration with Charles Hurlburt, an American who headed the Africa Inland Mission, but Studd and Hurlburt had quarreled: "They suggest I will find Mr. Studd difficult to get along with. This adds to my fears of strife, but it is too late now to remedy matters."

Hayes waited two days beside his loads on the Welle riverbank before the Chef De Poste at Dungu found him a large canoe and a crew of Bakango boatmen. Hayes spent two glorious days traveling "alone" in company with his boatmen toward Niangara on the Welle River, the "lacustrine reaches of still, deep water overhung by greenest trees," calming his forebodings. The loafing, singing boatmen postured at effort only when passing a couple of young women working on the riverbank. Hayes ridiculed the boatmen as idlers until the "Rapides D'Ananasi" challenged their magnificent skill, guiding the massive canoe using only slender poles.

However, before tackling the rapids, The Bakango men put Hayes and all his goods off the canoe. Only after portaging Hayes and his cargo beyond the cataracts would they take the wild, joyous ride themselves. No fuss would ensue should one of them perish on the river but "they would be held responsible if a white man was lost."

From a vantage point below the rapids, Hayes watched as the African men, stripped naked, crouched in the canoe center stream in still water above the rapids. Then with "every man yelling his best," they "drove the canoe into the white water." Their exquisite display lasted no more than a few seconds: "All knew their work, for with poles they warded off every rock thrust up through the surge of foam, kept their craft headed into the main channel and finally out into the boiling maelstrom and on into quiet water beyond." Some triumphant shouting and five minutes' hard paddling followed, but soon the men were back to "lethargic songs, slapping of flies and chit-chat of the day." Hayes always admired skilled men performing dangerous work without braggadocio.

The day before arriving at the Heart of Africa Mission could not have been better. Hayes killed a spur-winged goose for dinner for the crew. His grinning boatmen chided Hayes good-naturedly about his choice of armaments. A shotgun? Why not a rifle to shoot a hippo for a real feast? Those "monsters" of the river had been harassing their canoe all day. Once the canoe stalled for a full hour while a "giant head remained close by."

While his boatmen prepared the goose for roasting on shore that night, driver ants "swarmed in on us, driving us to the river again." Monkeys laughed from riverbank treetops at men slapping ants on moonlit water. In company with these able men in this beautiful place, Hayes wrote: "Africa always offers entertainment." For the past six weeks he had steamed, walked, and canoed through the Africa of his boyhood dreams in close company with the vivid memories of his lifelong heroes.

The next day he would meet CT Studd and Alfred Buxton.

5. Heart of Africa Mission, Niangara, Belgian Congo, 1914

In London, Hayes had signed a two-year contract with the Heart of Africa Mission at Niangara in the Northeast Belgian Congo. From talks with Martin Sutton, Hayes understood that the mission buildings Hayes would build for CT Studd and Alfred Buxton would be the first of a chain, stretching south and west into unevangelized regions of the African interior. Hayes carried letters to Studd from London stipulating payment to him of £20 for travel expenses. As a gesture of good will, Hayes donated that £20 and every cent he had to the mission's "community chest." His donation cannot have been large; as a foreigner entering the Congo, Hayes had been compelled to post an £88 bond.

Alfred Buxton, CT Studd's twenty-two-year-old acolyte and future son-in-law (betrothed to Studd's third daughter Edith), met Hayes with a canoe at Makassi Rapids seven miles up the Welle River from Niangara on February 20, 1914. From the first impression Hayes recorded of the young man, Hayes' reader assumes Buxton was not paddling his own canoe: "Buxton is a tall, callow youth, apparently out of place in the bush. It is easy to see he knows his position of family and breeding is superior to most folks, and this will not sit well with me." In his diary entries for the ten months Hayes lasted at the Heart of Africa Mission, the only vaguely positive remark he directed toward Buxton's character appears a few weeks after their initial meeting: "He is not naturally a bad boy, but has been spoiled by his people's petting." On another occasion, Hayes spoke well of Buxton's work; the vocabulary of Bangala Buxton compiled speeded Hayes' progress learning the language that Buxton already spoke quite well.

No diary entry Hayes made in those ten months records one positive remark about the missionary CT Studd or his work. Every mention of Studd goes downhill from the first: "Studd, so-called pioneer and founder of this mission is decidedly a self-centered man." The former cricketer was not quite as tall as Hayes: "He is about five feet eight inches in height, of sallow complexion, has a thin beard and the dreamy eyes of a fanatic."

The impulsive donation Hayes made to the mission fund upon arrival at Niangara demonstrates Hayes' initial determination to meet the two-year commitment he'd made to the Heart of Africa, but even on this first meeting with the two evangelists he could see the position would be uncongenial: "Both [Studd] and Buxton are aware of a special dispensation from the Almighty to evangelize the world, beginning with the Dark Continent, and do not propose to let anything stand in their way of doing it." On his first night at the mission Hayes retired from the two missionaries, "too downhearted to say anything about the surroundings, other than that the country is very beautiful."

The morning after meeting Studd in Africa dawned a little brighter for Hayes. The first paragraph of his diary entry for that day describes the beauty of the mission site: "The situation here is a splendid one." Three hectares of open ground fronted "the enchanting blue river, here some 200 metres in width and flowing strongly between high banks." Mature oil palms planted by previous native residents rose high above jungle scrub where Hayes could see a lime tree laden with fruit growing beside pineapples gone to riot. Hayes planned to direct rapid reclamation of all extant fruit trees. Surveying the mission site more fully, he saw, best of all, a spring well back from the river that provided "an ample supply of pure water, half the battle here in the tropics." He could see Studd and Buxton, his "two associates," had directed some small attempts at pushing back the encroaching jungle: blackened marks indicated they'd nearly destroyed their own tents burning dry leaves and grasses.

Their small ineptitude with the fire returned Hayes' pen to the subject of Buxton and Studd: "They are snobs of the worst sort among the British aristocracy, and regard me as a servant." The kindness he'd recognized under the exterior phlegm of men like Martin Sutton back in London had given Hayes hope relations might be more egalitarian between the "three of us alone in the bush." How different Hayes' vision of shared work: "I came here to act as a friend and companion to these men, and have given two years of my life freely to help them establish an oasis of culture and uplift among these barbaric people." Compare Hayes' expectation with the vision of his aristocratic companions: "On overhearing Buxton ask whether I should not be relegated to a table by myself it hurts."

In his next diary entry three days later, February 25, 1914, Hayes took himself in hand: "What's the use grouching? Do the best you can, boy." While not fully resigned to a servant's role, he reminded himself he'd signed a two-year contract to obey Studd. If aristocratic disdain was the worst Studd and Buxton had to offer, Hayes admonished himself to buck up and find a way forward.

Looking about beyond the two missionaries, Hayes identified the "barbaric people" of the region a either Azandes, living north of the Welle River, or Mangbettus, living to the south, with "a considerable feeling of hostility between the two peoples." Studd and Buxton had sited the mission on the south, Mangbettu, side of the river but recruited Azande men from the north bank for fieldwork on the mission grounds, because, as Hayes noted, "Mangbettus feel it a disgrace to work, their women doing all labor in the fields."

Despite deep reservations about his mission companions, Hayes threw himself into the work his first week at the mission "so have not leisure to worry about my troubles." He built tables, chairs, and stools from some whipsawn lumber discarded by the Belgians who had previously occupied this site, and organized a crew of a half dozen Azande workers to clear and burn brush to prepare ground for planting a kitchen garden.

On a rest day a week after his arrival, Hayes accompanied Studd and Buxton into town to lunch with Comte De Grunne, commander of the Belgian post at Niangara. Studd negotiated the purchase of two elephant hunting licenses, one for Buxton, one for Studd, "out of my money [donated to the community fund]," saying "nothing about [a license] for me."

As Studd pocketed his two missionary elephant hunting licenses, he brought conversation to the main reason for their visit: the missionaries needed a house. De Grunne had used Bangba workmen for similar tasks previously and would arrange with Bukinda, chief of the tribe to the south and west, to supply 75 men to erect a house 36'x 72' on the mission site. The Bangba men spoke Bangala so Hayes expressed confidence he could oversee their work while keeping "my own men" busy clearing and planting.

Hayes next wrote in his diary a week later, March 8, 1914. While overseeing two work crews and building furniture, evidently Hayes had also been quarreling with young Alfred: "Buxton criticizes all I do with all the wisdom gained in 22 years of pink tea fights, under the supervision of nurses and governesses and at school." To bring Hayes to heel, Studd placed Hayes on two meals a day: breakfast at seven in the morning, supper at eight at night, "my working at hard labor in between." Bananas and whatever else he could scrounge from the jungle simply wouldn't fuel Hayes sufficiently for the heavy work building a mission and restoring its grounds. Already, he weakened toward sickness.

While the Bangba men worked to erect the house Studd had dubbed "Buckingham Palace," the three Europeans at the mission lived in a mess tent discarded by Adolph Friedrich Albrecht Heinrich, Duke of Mecklenburg. The German nobleman had led a three-part expedition in 1910-11 exploring the river system of the region around Niangara. Hayes recommends the Duke's two volume account of his travels as "one of the most informative and interesting tales of African journeying I have ever seen." The discarded tent "big as a house" had ample room for all three men: the "two apostles" inside and Hayes outside "under a fly and in a sump where water drains inward from every side." When Hayes protested bedding down in a water-filled depression, Studd cited "some 'Professor Drummond'" advising missionaries not to pitch tents on elevated ground in Africa for fear of infection by "native disease from former occupation."

Hayes acquiesced to Studd's meal restrictions and sleeping order and, predictably, by the middle of March he could barely rise from his bed with the pain of lumbago. Hayes wrote that he felt like a human guinea pig Studd used to test this Professor Drummond's theories.

After three weeks at Niangara, Hayes' critique of Studd and his acolyte Buxton escalated beyond chafing at their boorish aristocratic snobbery. He now had them diagnosed as vainglorious hypocrites: "This mission is strictly a family affair, destined to enhance the reputation of the name of Studd." He went on to charge that Studd's family members ruled the board back in London and Studd's daughters married for influence. Lacking sons of his own, Studd was "grooming Buxton to act as crown prince when he himself passes off the scene."

Thoroughly disgusted with these two representatives of English aristocracy and hoping to walk out the stiffness in his joints, Hayes hiked south the Bangba village to meet Bukinda, "small chief" to the men building Studd's Buckingham Palace. Hayes says he photographed Bukinda surrounded by fourteen wives in a village "scrupulously clean and neat." (These images are now apparently lost.) The mud walls of every Bangba house had been coated with "decomposed feldspar or gypsum" then painted to murals depicting "men and animals, especially leopards and horses." Hayes observed that the colors available, red, white, and black, "stand up well" in a difficult climate.

Hayes' general assessment of Mangbettu men closely resembled what he'd written concerning aristocratic Englishmen a few months earlier; he always held men he considered effeminate and/or lazy in lowest regard. He did, though, admire their handcrafting skills, praising Mangbettu men as, "the most ingenious of all Africans I have seen thus far." Hayes watched one man examine a folding chair from every angle, then set it down after ten minutes. A week later the man returned offering to sell Hayes an improved model "fully planed and sandpapered and iron hinged for five francs, a fortune to him." The Mangbettus smelted iron for the hinges, their work in iron and copper "equal to any in more civilized countries." Commenting further on Mangbettu cleverness, Hayes described the musical instruments the men played as "marvelous," stringed instruments resembling banjos and fiddles on which they played "real music."

Wherever she went, a Mangbettu woman carried with her a delicately carved low stool for sitting while resting. Behind each Mangbettu man of the least prominence, a small boy toted a deck chair designed on a European model with woven mats that Hayes thought improved on canvas in this climate. Mangbettu men did not carry their own chairs; that would be work. Hayes couldn't understand how such capable crafters could "scorn work." He much favored Azande men who "are willing to work at anything to advance themselves."

Returning to the mission from his visit to Chief Bukinda and the Bangba village, Hayes found Studd down with dysentery: "Naturally a fellow feels sympathetic with one so ill, but [Studd's] absence is appreciated always."

Hayes' sympathy extended exactly that far. He went on to blame Studd's dysentery on the missionary's own stubbornness, calling him, "as arbitrary a man as I have ever seen." Studd ate what he wanted, when he wanted, and made

Hayes and Buxton follow his example. Where did Studd think Hayes' lumbago came from? A man of any common sense would easily surmise that eating poorly and sleeping in a "sump hole" in Africa could not be contributory to good health. But, unfortunately for Hayes, "there is no viewpoint but [Studd's] own."

With Studd bedridden, De Grunne, the Belgian commander at Niagara, took Buxton out shooting. After wounding several animals, the pair returned to the mission to find Studd roused from his sickbed long enough to lunch with the two hunters and the mission's American manservant, Hayes Perkins. Studd knew the importance of official connections to the Belgian rulers at whose pleasure English missionaries served.

After recounting a thrilling tale of the morning's hunt with young Alfred, De Grunne leaned toward Hayes with a polite invitation to the next day's shooting. An apoplectic CT Studd "half raised himself from across the table, glaring like a maniac, for me to say no." De Grunne could not have missed the stilted deference Hayes showed his aristocratic missionary boss when declining: "In [De Grunne's] eyes I read full sympathy."

March 29, 1914, six weeks after arriving at Niangara, Hayes recorded having a fever of 102°. Despite the lumbago and fever, "I have kept going." Buxton was, "decent, for once, now that I am ill." Studd, too, left off the usual hectoring, but not out of decency, rather because his own sickness lingered. An ailing CT Studd, British head missionary, savior to the barbaric heathen, had to reserve what strength he had for swindling Bukinda and the Bangba house builders.

Bukinda had failed to negotiate prior payment for construction of the mission house "trusting to the white man's idea of fairness and justice to pay him what it was worth." Studd's idea of fairness came to 150 Belgian francs, which Hayes converted to $30 American. When the Bangba chief protested that an average of 75 men had worked more than a month building the house, supplying their own food and shelter, Studd sweetened his offer to 160 francs. The missionary had "cannily asked De Grunne," head of Belgian military forces at Niangara, to be present, with a few askaris, "to aid in settling with Bukinda." What recourse had the Bangba leader faced with an armed mandate?

Hayes knew many of the Bangba men would receive nothing for their labor and that their reproach would fall mainly on Hayes, their immediate supervisor. In fact, Hayes felt complicit in the swindle. How could he expect the Bangba men to appreciate that these so-called men of God exploited their White workman as well? Hayes ended the day's diary entry concerning Studd's payment for "Buckingham Palace" with wry cynicism: "So this is missionary uplift with a vengeance."

As early as April 5, 1914, less than two months after arriving at Studd's Heart of Africa Mission, Hayes considered walking out. Never mind he was broke. Never mind leaving alone without arms and porters would mean certain death. If he could have left he would have, but the rains had begun. Hayes noted, "the dry season north of the equator begins about December 1st, and lasts until somewhere near the first of March." By April 5, rains fell "with increasing violence," blocking overland travel. As the river rose, native boatmen increasingly feared crocodiles stalking in the murky waters. Hayes could not leave, probably not until the following December.

At the newly completed "Buckingham Palace," Studd and Buxton quartered in the dry end of the house. They allowed Hayes inside but only at the end, lashed by daily rains pushed by "vast thunderings and strong winds." To prevent rains driven horizontally melting the mud wall of the end where he slept, Hayes wove a grass screen to catch the brunt of the storms.

Outside the palace, in the dry mornings Hayes worked with a crew to establish gardens for the mission. The "warlike" Azandes scrapped continuously with the Mangbettus, or with each other when necessary, but worked well when not fighting. De Grunne had to jail two of the more exuberant Azande men, but with those remaining Hayes managed to plant "bananas, plantains, pineapples, and such fruit trees as can be obtained." In the ten years since the Belgians had arrived in Niangara, they'd planted nothing but mangos and a few custard apples. Hayes chided Belgians at the post for neglecting soils so fertile lime trees sprung up overnight wherever seeds dropped.

"Strangely," both Studd and Buxton recognized that Hayes knew his work. After retiring to bed at night on his windward side of Buckingham Palace, he could hear the two quietly praising him. How much more easily the work would have proceeded had the mission head and his acolyte expressed this confidence in their foreman to the Azande workmen. But no, only Studd wielded authority at the Heart of Africa: "He calls the men together and harangues them, saying he is master, and that if he says build a house, I must build it, and if he says not, that goes too." How could Hayes possibly maintain discipline among workmen told not to listen to him but to appeal only and directly to Studd? When sent for timber or bundles of grass on Hayes' order, the men lounged in the bush insulting him when called to task. As neither Studd nor Buxton "have the least idea of handling men or cultivating a plantation," anything planted took root despite their "interference." For a second time Hayes wrote about leaving but, "[n]o one could make it in the rains."

Two weeks later, April 19, 1914, Hayes favorably assessed the work he'd accomplished on the mission gardens with a chuckle at the machinations of the two English missionaries. Hayes' plan for the site had begun to unfold so beautifully Studd and Buxton "sometimes forget and offer praise."

Despite the issues with authority undercut by Studd, Hayes felt he had the workmen – except for "a couple of malcontents" – well "in hand." Apparently the two missionaries agreed. One night lying awake in Buckingham Palace, Hayes overheard Studd plotting with Buxton a way to keep Hayes on as foreman, "too valuable a man to lose." Surely a missionary wife could tame this recalcitrant commoner. Studd would send to Europe for a handpicked "helpmate" to domesticate the American.

Hayes repressed a laugh upon hearing their whispered conversation because a) he was planning to leave the Heart of Africa at the soonest possible dry moment anyone could leave Niangara, and b) one needn't look to England for a helpmate. Mangbettu and Azande mothers, fathers, and brothers urged any reluctant European to "wed" one of the local women, who all "want to marry a white man, even for a brief time." Hayes wrote appreciatively about his prospects among the beautiful women at Niangara: "cupid's bow form of lip … Grecian noses … lithe and lissome …" Overcoming his admitted temptation toward the local women, Hayes remained only an admiring observer.

Adding to Hayes' ongoing problems with malcontent workmen, temptations, and undercut authority, every year the Mangbettu men harvested murru, a kind of millet, from which the women brewed "vast quantities of a sort of beer." The month-long "orgy" of singing and dancing following fermentation of this weak intoxicant reminded Hayes for all the world of the slums of London's East End: "As in European countries the people spend too much of their time and income for intoxicants, so are debauched."

Surely, at a minimum, any sense of Christian decency ought to exclude drunkenness? Why then did Hayes' flippant derogation of drink and drunkenness receive sneers from CT and young Alfred? Hayes thought he might know. Like Studd, Buxton came from a wealthy English family. Though Alfred's father, Barclay Fowell Buxton, established an early Christian mission in Japan, Hayes seemed to recall the Buxton family fortune rooted in the manufacture of alcoholic spirits.

Even so, distant English investments would not explain Mombidi, Mangbettu chieftain of the district, confronting Hayes with loud demands for liquor. According to Mombidi, Studd had been "sweetening the chiefs with booze" in order to obtain concessions for missions in other territories. Mombidi expected to receive the same from Hayes, Studd's underling.

Could Mombidi's allegations be true? While not entirely incredulous, Hayes would wait for more immediate evidence than the word of an African man asking for whiskey.

Hayes apparently passed on an opportunity to leave Niangara and the Heart of Africa Mission on May 10, 1914. He wrote that James Evans, an American engineer with the Forminiere, a joint Belgian and American concessionaire establishing gold and diamond mines in southern Congo, passed through with a substantial caravan en route home by way of Cairo. Evans told Hayes he could easily get on with the Forminiere at the rich diamond mines in the Kasai. Hayes wrote, "I can't see how." By which Hayes must have meant that he still felt bound to the two-year commitment he'd made to the mission. He certainly would not have doubted his technical skill for gold or diamond mining work.

Soon the gardens Hayes and his Azande men had planted would be supplying much of the mission's food. Seedlings sprang from the fertile ground growing an inch or two overnight. By the middle of May, three months after Hayes arrived at Niangara, he and his gardeners had planted 1,100 bananas and plantains, 1,000 pineapples, and more than 200 fruit trees: mango, avocado, lime, lemon, oranges, and custard apples. Sweet potatoes grew in profusion on vast termite hills, "one thirty feet in height." A generous garden of European vegetables, including maize fifteen feet tall with three ears per stalk, from a store of seeds presented Hayes by the late Martin J. Sutton back in London, flourished nearby. Belgians visiting the mission from the post at Niangara loudly voiced their admiration for Hayes' accomplishments in so short a time.

By 1914 much of the easy profit King Leopold had realized on rubber and ivory from the Congo had been exhausted. To sustain profit from the colony, its new owners, the Belgian State, imposed a head tax on the Congolese: five shillings, or the equivalent of one month's pay per person per year. On paying the head tax, native men received a medal stamped with the current year as receipt. Two of Hayes men took the day off garden work to pay their taxes and returned from the post at Niangara with medals stamped 1909. Hayes immediately reported the "ruse" perpetrated by the "canny Bula Matadi" to Studd.

To Hayes, a tax paid to the Belgian government by the Congolese in return for "protection against an aggressor [Arab raiders enslaving Congolese] and the plague [various readily curable diseases]" seemed reasonable. Hayes had no objection to the tax in principle, only to its corrupt implementation. He went to Studd because a protest lodged with Belgian authorities from the head of the mission would carry more weight than the word of a simple workman. Instead of rallying to the cause, Studd "forbade me to speak of it again." Flabbergasted, Hayes pressed the point of justice forcefully enough that Buxton inserted himself into the resulting quarrel, admonishing Hayes: "'Father says it and that's an end.'"

The mission board in London heard nothing about Studd's complicity in the tax medal fraud; indeed, they heard nothing critical about any activities on the ground at the Heart of Africa Mission. Studd forbade Hayes writing any letters to London and monitored all outgoing mail. The board did, however, correspond with Studd, inquiring about progress with evangelizing the natives.

In response, Studd instituted formal evening services at the mission. At the end of each day's work in the gardens, Buxton lined up the Azande men to deliver a two-hour evangelical harangue. Buxton gave the sermons because Studd spoke Bangala insufficiently to preach himself. The Mangbettu men, however, refused to attend. They were still piqued about the scant payment for building Buckingham Palace and, since they would not work, did not fear dismissal like the Azandes.

If King Leopold saw the Congolese people as only bodies for the extraction of wealth, CT Studd saw the Congolese people as only souls to be saved. Doubtless Buxton's sermons, under Studd's direction, dwelt heavily on the terrors of hell, the goodness of God, renunciation of sin, and salvation through Jesus Christ. In early June, the disciples decided two-hour evening "services" (Hayes' quote) weren't enough. So they instituted morning theological lectures as well: "These last until ten A.M., the men's eyes wondering in utter bewilderment, it all going over their heads."

According to Hayes, every European arriving in Africa received from the natives a nickname based on "some physical characteristics or whim of temperament." Initially the Africans at Niangara called CT Studd "the old man" until Studd insisted they use "Bwana." Hayes noted that "Bwana" means master in Swahili, a word unknown to these Bangala speakers. Hayes answered to "Yellow Tooth," a reference to a gold crown showing in his smile, or sometimes flatteringly the men called him "Bocaboka, meaning a man who can do any sort of work." The Africans referred to Alfred Buxton as "the White Child," a name Hayes heard as an insult, and approved.

Much to Hayes' relief – "[n]ever have I been cursed by such uncongenial companionship as these two men afford me" – Studd and Buxton left Hayes alone at the mission on June 16, 1914, departing fifteen days behind schedule to scout south into previously uncontacted mission fields. At their departure, Hayes wrote a long paragraph critiquing the two as posturing "unscrupulous adventurers posing as altruistic and self-sacrificing men" whose only interest in "heathen uplift" is the fame thereby afforded in London. He charged Studd with playing up his cricket fame – and its renunciation even more – with the British aristocracy to whom he "poses as an unselfish martyr when his whole thought is to drink the wine of fame equal to that of Livingstone." (A reference to David

85

Livingstone, beloved Scottish medical missionary legendary for his exploits in south central Africa in the mid-nineteenth century.)

Studd and Buxton took the best Azande workers south with them but Hayes got along fine with those remaining. All the men worked harder now they were free from Buxton's morning and evening oratories. Just before departing, Studd pleaded with Hayes to keep on with the important work of sermonizing. The American reluctantly consented to say what he knew, if asked(!), but that he would "never endeavor to cram a plan of salvation town their necks." None of the Azande men asked, so Hayes suspended sermons.

Following the departure of the two "pseudo apostles," the Mangbettu made friendly approaches toward Hayes. They told Hayes they could see Studd and Buxton treated him no better than an African. As a token of their newfound esteem, wouldn't Hayes like to take a daughter or perhaps a wife of one of the Mangbettu men for his own? Hayes wrote privately of his loneliness, calling any "normal man" immune to the temptations of these girls a liar. Nevertheless, he declined "the well-rounded arms and towering breasts of these Mangbettu houris." The male emissaries didn't press the point when Hayes demurred, but the women became so insistent that he claimed he had to dose several with Croton oil, a powerful laxative, to quell their amorous advances, a remedy that seemed to work: "They don't bother me again."

Four days after declining marriage, on June 21, 1914, Hayes' relations with the Mangbettu had soured considerably. Their constant begging for corn and other vegetables from the mission's now flourishing garden wore thin, especially so because the Mangbettu men held themselves above the work of growing food. Worse, Mombidi, principal chief of the Mangbettu, had a new interpretation for the ill treatment Hayes received at the hands of Studd and Buxton.

In Hayes' presence, Mombidi explained to his subjects that the real missionaries' ill regard for Hayes must indicate

Hayes held lower rank than either Studd or Buxton – perhaps on the level of the Greek traders excluded even from the rest houses of the Belgians. According to Mombidi's reckoning, he, principal Mangbettu chief of the entire district, ranked equal to Studd or Buxton. Hayes, of inferior rank, must bring Mombidi gifts in their absence. Whiskey would be preferable, but foodstuffs from the garden would suffice. Hayes burst out laughing and sent the chief on his way with a congenial slap on the back.

An hour later, "six husky henchmen" arrived demanding loads of ripe corn. When Hayes and the Azande workmen chased off his henchmen, Mombidi loosed a fighting bull "reputed to have killed two men" – a gift to Mombidi from the Belgians – into the mission garden. From the safety of a tall anthill, Hayes ordered the Azande men to run the bull back into the forest. They complied, chasing an increasingly bloodied bull into the forest – then on into the center of Mombidi's village. In the meantime, Hayes took the "rather cheeky" herdsman "in hand." Trouble would doubtless follow thrashing both the man and the animal, but "I am ready for anything now."

A week later, Hayes wrote that trouble with Mombidi still simmered. Mombidi's bloodied bull crashing around Mombidi's own village entailed considerable loss of face. To regain stature, the chief increased his attempts at "bluffing me into making matabishes (gifts, tribute)." Mombidi wanted whiskey. Could it really be possible that "these two charlatans have been sweetening this old cannibal with booze to get a concession?" The thought seemed too "unchristian" for Hayes to accept. On the other hand, Mombidi swore he enjoyed English whiskey, and his subjects, to a man, swore it came directly from the missionaries. Hayes respected the word of his workmen and, despite his disbelief in African veracity, had to grant that "[w]hen all Negroes agree on one thing, it is usually so."

The comparative idyll of dealing only with Mangbettu squabbles ended for Hayes on August 1, 1914, with the return of Studd and Buxton. The pair had traveled south to Wamba "on the edge of the great Ituri Forest," successfully securing further concessions for additional missions. Reinstalled at Buckingham Palace, Studd scribbled while Buxton pounded the typewriter composing letters to London. The adventuring missionaries took turns reading aloud to each other, particularly pleased with a section recounting how the Lord preserved them from hungry leopards and myriad other dangers. Hayes observed: "Even a leopard has some scruples as to what he eats, so they need not blame this lack of attention on the Deity."

Listening to self-congratulatory aggrandizement was annoying, but re-integrating the Azande carriers Studd and Buxton had ruined on the trip south back into his work gang was dangerous. Their "cheek" immediately spread to the Azande gardeners Hayes had cultivated so assiduously while free of the corrosive influence of the two missionaries. All the workmen began openly demanding whiskey from Hayes. Those who had traveled south claimed that "these two men who pose as missionaries" had distributed strong drink freely on the scouting trip.

Deaf to the havoc occasioned by their return, the two English missionaries were delighted at the beautiful order Hayes had established at the mission during their absence – "they could not be otherwise." Once again Hayes heard furtive whispers in the night from the English end of Buckingham Palace: surely they could find an Englishwoman missionary wife to bind this capable man at Niangara. The morning after the whispers, Studd broached the subject directly with Hayes, asking for "a free hand to act as agent on my behalf." When Hayes refused, Studd broke out in special prayers "that my 'beloved' may be led to join me here."

Describing the two missionaries as "rotten hypocrites," Hayes summed up his prospects for departure: 65 francs in pocket, 2,000 miles to the nearest ocean, and the river "booming along with muddy flow that is boiling like a pot." Poverty and danger prevented leaving, at least until the coming of the dry season no sooner than December.

A telegram arrived at the Heart of Africa on August 19, 1914, that jerked the attention of every European at Niangara away from local squabbles toward the looming disaster at home. For several days African drums had chattered of a great war sweeping Europe. Garbled news spread from village to village, announcing Britain at war with Belgium! Fantastic gossip brought by drum could be uneasily ignored – until the telegram arriving on the 19th delivered the correct and terrifying story: After Austria declared war on Serbia, all the pacts previously supporting a fragile European peace cascaded to world war in a blink. Russia honored a joint-defense pact with Serbia, declaring war on Austria. Germany attacked France by way of Belgium. And the British came in on the side of Russia, Serbia, and France. "Studd's hands shook like a leaf" as he opened the telegram.

Hayes wrote that he would have joined the British Navy given his British and French ancestry if not so far away. However, he thanked goodness all Englishmen were not like the two in Niangara, else "I would be yelling my head off for Germany."

Telegrams arrived in flurries over the next several weeks, telling always of Allied victories and the hope for a quick end to the fighting. Hayes thought otherwise. He described Germany as "the bully of Europe," wishing her "a good drubbing," but acknowledged that she was stronger than generally believed, "and this will be a terrible war." Hayes' travels about the world had given him a pretty good sense of worldwide geo-political realities; his assessment proved disastrously prescient.

The initial shock of the outbreak of European war could only suppress local squabbles temporarily. Once again, "Studd got nasty over the tax program." When Buxton intervened to settle the ensuing conflict between Hayes and Studd, Buxton proclaimed a theological principle Hayes truly abhorred: "[T]o do the lesser evil to gain the greater good." The missionaries employed a simple calculus: the lesser evil of complicity with tax fraud, committed to accomplish the greater good of saving African souls. Hayes accounted Buxton's principle as purest sophistry, exposing rather than hiding the shame of two men who "fairly grovel at the feet of these men [Belgian authorities] whose sole aim in life is to exploit the peoples of the Congo."

On Sept. 1, 1914, Hayes wrote, "The bottom has fallen out of everything, and the apostles are beginning to realize it." In lieu of work, the men sat at the feet of Buxton, "a very minor prophet," until 10:00 every morning, smiling as the young aristocrat struggled to translate the progenitors of Christ to Bangala. One favored acolyte of Buxton smuggled a young girl into the proceedings, much to the discomfort of the preacher. Hayes couldn't bear to think of the length of his full commitment here: "To think of fifteen months more of this is appalling." Rains had swollen the river again. Hayes still had no way out.

All the news from Europe announced Allied victories. The map, though, showed Hayes another story: Belgium almost completely occupied and Germany advancing farther into France. With the war news came word that the helpmate Studd had requisitioned from London to come marry Hayes in Africa had been delayed. The war blocked passage to a missionary party just ready to leave England. Hayes secretly gave thanks. About this time, he began work on a house of his own separate from the would-be apostles.

By September 25, 1914, nearly all the Belgian officers stationed at Niangara had been redeployed to African fronts of the Great War. Some went west to the fighting in German Kamerun (Cameroon), others east to German East Africa (Tanzania). Those remaining at Niangara had to contend with the real fear of an Azande uprising: "Renzi, Mopoie, and

Bukoyo, to say nothing of Akengai, all have several thousands of warriors behind them, all they lack is arms to drive the Belgians out of the northern Congo."

The departing Belgian officers took most of the askaris from the post at Niangara with them to the various inter-colonial fights. At enlistment, each askari had been provided a wife by some Belgian quartermaster. Wives could not travel with the army. Accordingly, hundreds of abandoned young women now roamed the countryside about Niangara. Jenssen-Tusch, an itinerant Danish missionary from across the Welle, attempted to aid the women, but the daily allotment of 10 centimes he offered left many seeking "their living in the only way they know."

By now, Hayes understood Bangala well. He spoke to one of the young women about alternatives to prostitution and translated her frank, heartbreaking reply: "Musungu, we were taken from our homes against our wills and given to this soldier. He has gone away, and we have no garden, no home, no place where we may find a living. The men who belonged to us have been taken away. If we return (which we may not, it is very far) we will but be made slaves what else can we do?"

For once Hayes had no solution to a problem at hand. He estimated more than 800 women had been left behind at the Niangara post by Belgian askaris departed to fight German askaris. He lamented bitterly: "Little do the Belgians care, for there are always more women when these are gone, more where they are going, so why worry?"

The following morning, as Hayes worked on the roof of the second house, Studd called up a command barring Hayes from denouncing polygamy among the workmen. Hayes had never given polygamy any thought. Setting another nail, he decided it must have been a proactive injunction: Studd planned to depart soon for Léopoldville (Kinshasa) seeking more concessions for mission fields from the Belgian government. Stirring up trouble condemning African social norms couldn't possibly help the application process. This could only be another instance of the "Lesser evil/greater good" theology Hayes so loathed.

The list of substantive indictments against CT Studd on Hayes' ledger now stood at four: bilking the men who built Buckingham Palace; complicity with the Belgian tax medal fraud; the increasingly believable allegation of supplying African men with intoxicants; and now refusal to denounce polygamy.

On October 6, 1914, Studd and Buxton once again departed Niangara in a great canoe piloted by Bakango boatmen toward Bambili, 160 miles downriver. Studd had canceled the trip to Léopoldville in favor of the direct work of evangelism. Hayes rejoiced at their departure: "Of course I am glad to see the last of them, would be glad it was the final parting." As the canoe disappeared around the river bend, Hayes waved with one hand and pulled a coin from his pocket with the other. One toss would decide if he should seize this moment to go his separate way. He had those 66 pounds to his name and was still 2,000 miles from the nearest coast. The coin fell "no," so he honored fortune and stayed.

On October 25, 1914, with the end of the rainy season nearing, Hayes took a decisive step that ensured his departure from the Heart of Africa Mission. In violation of Studd's direct prohibition on correspondence, Hayes wrote the London Committee a detailed account of "the activities of my two colleagues here." Presumably Hayes outlined his four substantive accusations, but the self-promotion, the "constant furthering of the House of Studd" seemed to bother him most.

With both Studd and Buxton "barn-storming" to the south, Hayes had free run of the supplies of the mission. In all his work Hayes suffered a chronic shortage of tools. He had frequently asked Studd to allow him to investigate several cases marked "tools" among the stores. Studd had always directed him elsewhere. But with the missionaries gone, Hayes had all the keys. He searched through the cases "not through inquisitiveness, but to find perhaps a hammer or saw to aid in my work." No hammer, no saw, instead Hayes found French cognac in the first and old Scotch whiskey in the second – a total of seven boxes of intoxicants in all. Two boxes stood empty, their "tools" already put to use. Mombidi and the Azande workmen had been telling the truth.

When the missionaries had departed, Studd had once again instructed Hayes to "keep up the sermons they [Studd and Buxton] so delighted in and of which the men were filled with disgust." Instead Bokaboca, following his recent discoveries in the "tool" boxes, lined up his workmen to announce forced attendance at sermons would be discontinued. When their "shouts of glee" subsided, Hayes did offer to explain what he knew of the bible as best he understood it.

At this late date, "strangely, these men took me up on it. I pleaded lack of familiarity with their language at first, but that would no longer stand up as an excuse." So, for several evenings, all his Azande workmen squatted about a fire, "on their haunches in African fashion," listening as Hayes translated "the Lord's prayer, the Sermon on the Mount and such simple things as Jesus taught his disciples in those days of long ago."

Hayes wrote that he didn't consider himself good enough to be a missionary. Nevertheless, the workmen "sat rapt, their eyes shining, attentive to every word" as he gave them his best interpretation of the gospels. He reasoned that if Christianity had any worth for these Azande men it lay in the precepts laid down by Jesus, spoken in the straightforward manner "Christ himself taught his disciples."

On a morning following several of the evening fireside chats, Hayes stood blowing a police whistle calling his workmen to assemble. Usually all responded promptly but today no one came. Hearing loud cries from the men's common house, Hayes scrambled over to break up what he assumed must be another fight. Just outside the door he paused, curious that he hadn't heard the expected crashes and bellows of rage. After listening for a few moments, he tiptoed away, then waited more than half an hour for the Azande men to assemble.

The workmen expected condemnation for their tardiness but Hayes sent them on their way without a word of censure: "What I had heard was one of the most enthusiastic prayer meetings it has ever been my lot to hear. Especially were they praying for their natural enemies, the Mangbettus." Hayes translated their prayers: "Oh Nzambe (God), we want to thank you for taking the bitterness toward the Mangbettus out of our hearts. Even old Mombidi, worst of all. We want to thank you for giving us victory over our enemies in battle, but we want them to love us as we love them, then we will fight no more."

Oddly, Hayes wrote that he felt "ashamed" that the Azande men seemed to have understood what he said "and to have the spirit of it in their hearts." Perhaps he made an awkward word choice about what he felt when trying to express modesty.

With the missionaries still absent, Hayes received a telegram from a WJW Roome, "a noted architect, traveler, and enthusiast in the establishing of foreign missions," advising that Roome's party had arrived in Rejaf. News to Hayes. Roome and six missionary reinforcements, one of them Hayes' prospective Christian bride, had traveled, during wartime to join Studd and Buxton's work at the Heart of Africa. Hayes determined he would hand Roome, a member of the London board of the Heart of Africa Mission, his letter of resignation. But first, at least until Buxton arrived back at the mission, "I must stay for a time to ready all for these lambs being led to the slaughter for they are as helpless as babes and know nothing of the great bush."

On November 20, 1914, just when Hayes moaned his fortunes had reached lowest ebb – recently threatened with jail by the Belgians for some hijinks concerning the Mangbettu, anemia making him prone to sickness, and facing a 2,000-mile hike alone, and broke, out to the east African coast – he got a financial boost. The 88 francs bond he'd posted at Aba when first entering the Congo arrived fully refunded. Hayes now counted his purse: 155.80 francs. Enough, he calculated, just possibly, to carry him to the gold fields of the Ituri where he knew he could find work. First, though, he must discharge his duty to settle Roome and the imminent arrivals. Duty, but also perhaps curiosity; surely Hayes wondered about a woman traveling all the way from London intended as his "helpmate." Didn't she deserve at least a glance? He'd wait a little longer.

Before Roome and the mission recruits arrived, Hayes received another visitor: Renzi, paramount Azande chief of the entire region, accompanied by a large entourage of wives. Initially Renzi seemed to want nothing more than an educated ear for reminiscences about old military adventures. According to the old chief, in 1897, just as Arab forces had nearly defeated a Belgian force in the Lado Enclave (on the south side of the Nile in what is now South Sudan), Renzi threw his troops in on the Belgian side "ending Arab rule on the upper Nile."

Hayes listened patiently until Renzi eventually came around to the point of his history lesson. The Azande chief said he could raise 12,000 warriors on a moment's notice. He'd been dickering with the British officers in Sudan, offering now to sweep the Belgians from the northern Congo. Hayes knew the reason for the proposed revolt but wanted to hear it directly from Renzi: "Tax medal, tax medal, another and another! They never finish, every day they demand another, are crying for another tax medal."

As Renzi struggled to recompose himself in the shade outside Hayes' house, one of his "numerous wives" doused her husband with cheap perfume and another began trimming the chief's beard. The old man could barely walk, with a dry ulcer from knee to ankle on one leg. Hayes offered to treat the wound and, while kneeling at Renzi's feet, tried to explain the

European alliances of WWI. Britain was unlikely to encourage an Azande attack on Belgium while the two were allied against Germany. Renzi worked to understand but had heard only vaguely of "Alemania."

Toward the end of November, Hayes became so dispirited – he used the word "aweary" – he began to write of dying in Africa. With his sickness and his disillusionment at the mission, life seemed barely worth living. He finished one despondent passage trying to rally himself: "I do hope to die game."

Standing on the porch of his new house one evening shortly after describing his weariness unto death, Hayes looked along the pointed finger of his new friend Mombidi toward a welcome sight: Orion, shining brightly, low on the horizon, announced the beginning of the dry season. Within just a few days the level of the Welle fell 15 feet and grass fires blazed everywhere. Maybe, just maybe, Hayes' 155.80 francs would get him out of here – or at least away, toward a dignified death.

But Hayes got one last astonishing temptation before leaving: he stood flabbergasted when a cadre of young Azande men knocked on his door to urge the American to lead the African warriors against the Belgian post at Niangara! Ten prospective wives waited on offer outside as Hayes tried to explain to the Azande men that Great Britain would intercede on behalf of Belgium. Yes, the men countered, but Renzi himself backed their offer: Hayes would be appointed Prime Minister to their paramount chief. One man pointed to the ten wives of such an important man. Hayes confessed some temptation with regard to the women, especially one named Numba … but no! No to any military appointment, and, he regained himself, no to any wives.

Not long after the young men and the ten wives on offer left Hayes' new house, thirty-five boxes arrived at Niangara, in advance of Roome and the five missionary re-enforcements. Those boxes marked with the name Bowers, who had died en route at Rejaf, particularly disturbed Hayes. When Alfred Buxton breezed back into the mission accompanied by one of the new missionaries, "one of his dupes named Coles," Hayes could not muster even the pretense of congeniality as Buxton dripped "sugar itself, trying to patch things up."

By December 21, 1914, Roome's entire party had arrived. Hayes recorded his initial impressions of each: Of the dead man, Bowers, Hayes wrote at least Bowers had been spared the choice of "becoming disillusioned and disgusted even as I am" or succumbing to "the general hero worship of Studd." Coles, "an inexperienced boy" took to his bed after asking, and then hearing bluntly, why Hayes would soon depart. Miss Chapman, a maiden of 38, seemed "unspoiled and kindly," never having experienced evil. "She would learn much here." Miss Flangham, "a spoiled kiddy of 28," appeared to be the helpmate designated for Hayes. He tried to be nice to her; she hadn't set the snare. But even congeniality toward Miss Flangham required superhuman effort. Being accustomed to servants, Miss Flangham expected the same in Africa. The only "real man" in the group, Richardson, had resigned as chief engineer on a destroyer in the British Navy just before the war broke out, saying, "God gave him no commission to kill his brother." Mrs. Richardson accompanied Mr. Richardson. As for Roome? He had a "cunning reliance on the powers that be," rather than any sense of what might be right. Certainly not a man to whom Hayes could confide information to send back to London.

With the new recruits fully installed, Buxton came to Hayes' house near midnight one night in late December 1914. Setting aside the "the past month's bullying," Buxton calmly offered Hayes a severance package: forty pounds to carry Hayes to the coast. Hayes interpreted the offer as "hush money" and refused. Richardson, "the bluff Scot," agreed the money could only have been a bribe and congratulated Hayes for sticking to principle, "though God knows I need this money and it is really mine."

At 2:00 a.m. on December 24, 1914, Hayes departed the Heart of Africa Mission accompanied by three Azande porters and a cook, Bundajuo. None carried a firearm. The African men were fit but "I am tired, broken, run down." Only the Richardsons rose to see Hayes depart. Mrs. Richardson cried out, "He'll never make it. He'll die in the bush." Mr. Richardson held her back, offering scant reassurance. "If God wants him to get through, he will be safe enough."

Hayes agreed with Mr. Richardson, but if Mrs. Richardson should prove right? Well, Hayes preferred her outcome to another day in the company of CT Studd and Alfred Buxton.

6. Down the Nile, 1914-1915

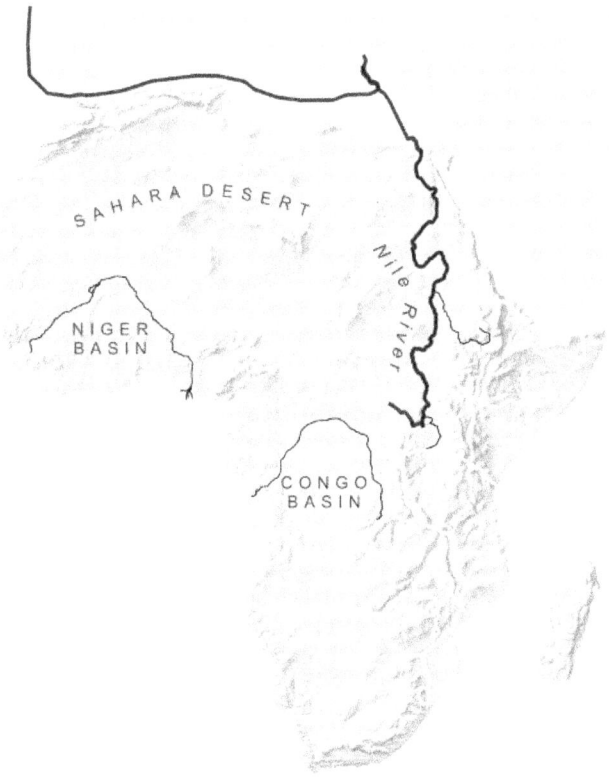

When Hayes departed the Heart of Africa Mission so precipitously on Christmas Eve 1914, he had only the vaguest of plans. He would travel east from Niangara toward the Indian Ocean with his tiny safari. Deserts blocked travel north and Hayes feared entering the Congo River basin with its forests and swamps to the south and west. Walking east would take him toward the fighting of WWI – British East Africa

(Kenya) squaring off with German East Africa (Tanzania) – but, if he couldn't make it all the way to the coast, he could turn north and travel up the Nile to Alexandria.

That first night out from the Mission, Hayes and his small troop walked twelve miles to a rest house at Jubberi's village "on the way to where I know not." Hayes collapsed, sick and exhausted, into the rest house, bidding his porters collect wood for cook fires. Shortly before sundown that Christmas evening a "gang of cheeky ex-askaris and their women" sauntered up to the rest house, took the woodpile and chased Hayes' porters into the forest. Doubtless the drums had publicized every particular of this feeble safari. Lying inside, tended by Bundajuo, Hayes heard raucous jeering: he was no musungu, only a Greek with no arms and no status to use a rest house. Hayes knew if he didn't defend his men they'd desert him, forcing an ignoble return twelve miles back to Studd and Buxton.

From his sick bed, Hayes sent out the fearless Bundajuo, hoping to quell the hideous row developing outside by parlay. Predictably, the "guffaws of laughter and utmost derision" sounded only louder. With all attention on Bundajuo, Hayes dashed from the rest house to seize a long brand protruding from the fire. Some of the men and women fled before Hayes' wild, flaming swings into the only door to the rest house where Hayes had just exited. Hayes gave chase, thrashing about with the smoking brand in the confined space. His assailants immediately elbowed back toward the exit where Bundajuo and the three revitalized porters "formed a reception committee at the door" to deliver a few last licks.

Hayes' little safari mounted their loads and departed Jubberi's village long before first light the next morning. A strenuous, fevered march brought the party to a second rest house at a fork in the road: east to Dungu returning to the path by which Hayes had originally come to Niangara, or south to Kilo and Moto, goldmining towns in the Great Lakes region. Hayes had no strength to decide; he told Bundajuo to send a drum message to Dungu should Hayes die in the night. The three porters, unsupervised, had an impromptu party: "With the local harlots they enjoyed a session, worship at the shrine of Venus, with a compliment to Bacchus thrown in." Hayes surprised them, waking still alive the next morning.

Only anger buttressed by a "quinine and aspirin diet" sustained Hayes' stumble through a long, wobbly morning. No matter how sick, he must walk out of this dangerous region, and "strangely I grew better as we kept on." That afternoon the fever broke in a beautiful park-like region on the path leading south to Kilo and Moto. True to form, even in the extremity of sickness, Hayes had chosen the path he'd not traveled before.

Monkeys chattered in the trees above the many small streams crossed as they stepped past well-swept courtyards grown to cheery hibiscus in what seemed like one continuous village. Women ran after the slight safari, offering eggs and fowl and delicious fruits, accepting whatever the travelers gave in return, "for it is seldom a white man comes this way."

In this beautiful region, a runner from the Heart of Africa Mission caught up to Hayes' safari bearing gifts: references from Studd and Roome to church dignitaries in East Africa, a draft for twenty pounds, and two apologies. Both Buxton and Studd wrote letters expressing contrition about their conduct toward their American handyman. Reading no sincerity in any of it, Hayes sent everything back to Niangara with the runner: "I don't care to hear from this crowd again. It is better to perish in the bush than to compromise with them."

The party stayed the night of the 29th at Nafraka's village, the last Mangbettu household before entering into Azande territory ruled by chief Bukoyo. By firelight, Nafraka delivered hair-raising warnings concerning the strength and cruelty of Bukoyo. The Azande had 8,000 fighting men. Sometimes Bukoyo sold his own people, along with captured Mangbettus, to the great Belgian goldmines at Kilo and Moto. "This causes much fear among my men, all Mangbettus, but Bundajuo who fears nothing."

Two "genial post officers" at the tiny Belgian outpost at Gombari filled Hayes in on news of the European war: a German fleet had been destroyed at the Falkland Islands. At least the British controlled the seas. A genial offer of fresh porters and abundant food at Gombari allowed Hayes to purchase a feast for his tired crew before sending them back to Niangara. Bundajuo, cook and companion, stayed on with Hayes.

Fresh carriers double marched the next day through beautiful open forest with granite pinnacles rising above a plain decorating the way to Alimassi's village. With Hayes' fever broken and stomach "returned to normal functioning," Africa became disarmingly beautiful again: "If the country was enchanting, Alimassi's village crowns it all in its sublime magnificence and infinite charm."

Two day's march out from Alimassi's village, Hayes noted a change in the geology. The rough granite outcroppings were giving way to sedimentary rock. From his previous mining experience, Hayes knew that gold collects at these lines of geological transition. Soon he began to see sluice boxes and prospectors running wheelbarrows filled with gravel. Hayes mentioned two prospectors he met at Moto by name: James Giliot and Charley Groves, memorable because they imposed charity on him.

Initially the two Australian miners greeted the small safari and its scruffy leader emerging from the forest "with some reserve." They begin to thaw when it became evident Hayes knew much about gold mining; melted entirely upon learning the Hayes had traveled in the Australian outback; and fairly bubbled with welcome after discovering a shared disdain for CT Studd and Alfred Buxton. Giliot and Groves told Hayes that shortly after CT and Alfred had pedaled into Moto on the west side of Lake Albert two years previously, the two independent gold miners had "learned to despise them completely." Their regard for Hayes was just the reverse. Giliot and Graves recognized a man down on his luck. Unasked, the pair pressed 200 francs on Hayes. "It is humiliating to receive charity, but what can one do?" That Hayes would accept charity at all indicates the extent of his privation on his way out from the Heart of Africa Mission.

Along with the geology, the predominant language changed below Moto. Bangala gave way to Swahili. An itinerant Syrian trader who walked a while with Hayes took a few moments "when he was not buying women from the avaricious natives" to translate a few Swahili words. Hayes made more linguistic progress after meeting an African resident of the region who spoke both Bangala and Swahili. With some pride, Hayes wrote in his journal "'Leta angu chumbi, mimi nunna'" with its translation: "'Bring me salt, I will buy it.'"

On the evening of January 7, 1915, from a squalid bush hut masquerading as a rest house, Hayes wrote a careful description of the Ituri forest from the inside. In this lush and exotic forest, every acre supported eight or ten trees, three feet in diameter at the base, 75 to 100 feet to the first branch, buttressed by wide-spreading fan-shaped roots "and their naked white boles appear ghostly in the dim light where sunlight never enters." Smaller trees competing with the ghosts shot up until, vanquished, they died, crashing to tangle the jungle floor. Giant creepers festooned every forest layer blossoming to loud crimson, lavender, or white flowers in sunlight at the upper forest reaches. Seemingly anodyne fig vines catching root in the crotch of a forest giant quietly sent taproots down the outer bark and, reaching ground, leapt upward with undeniable vigor until only a hollow shaft indicated where the host had been, replaced by a giant fig standing as large as any tree in the forest.

Hayes saw few animals, but those he did sight were unfamiliar and enchanting: the fabulous okapi, near relative to the giraffe; the bangana or bongo, a ferocious bush buck; the tiny dik-dik; leopards preying on small antelopes; the red river hog; a giant forest pig; river rats with flat, hairless tails; and buffaloes with no natural enemies in the absence of White men with guns. Elephants roamed at will: "for these great beasts can accommodate themselves to forest or plain, mountain or morass as the case may be."

Despite its exotic novelty, Hayes found the forest a gloomy place: "The somber shades cause one's spirits to droop, and the constant squish of the porters' feet gives one an eerie feeling as we slip and slide on the clay of the earthen floor." In this ghostly forest Hayes' safari happily caught up to a column of askaris carrying ammunition to Lake Kivu. Safer to be traveling in an armed column of 40 when the bull elephant refused to surrender the narrow track. As every man scattered into the trees to avoid the trumpeting charge. Hayes lay in the mud close enough to hear "the strange internal rumblings constantly going on inside these animals."

A "bedraggled" White man stepping from the forest into the mining compound at Kilo faced considerable danger. A mockery of the name "Congo Free State," the compound surrounding the rich gold mines bristled with guns. Hayes walked carefully, directly to the office of Monsieur Braive, chief engineer of the mines, to enquire about a job. No. Applicants must enquire at the main offices in Bruxelles. Monsieur Braive had no place for a ruffian from the forest, "for there are any number of adventurous men here and elsewhere about these golden hills whom he fears and counts me one of them." The monsieur could offer fresh porters for an immediate departure but no more.

As Hayes stepped off the porch of M. Braive's engineering office, he heard a call from a tall, impeccably dressed Englishman: "He resembled an American cowboy but was faultlessly neat in attire, his clothes fitting his giant frame as if a tailor had measured him for his suit. His eyes were steel blue, his tongue like a sword." This would turn out to be Frank Bowen, elephant hunter, a man worthy of a novel.

Inquiring neither if Hayes spoke English, nor his nationality, Bowen launched a blue tirade directed at all Belgians.

Amused, Hayes asked, "'How do you know I am not a Belgian?'"

"'Know them! O God!'" Bowen threw up his hands and began the entire rant over from the beginning.

Presently "another frail, sandy complexioned man" walked up behind Bowen: "This last entry had a reddish beard, well clipped and pointed, but his eyes were the antithesis of his companion's." This would turn out to be Ernest Bishop, "a trader and hunter whose home is Africa, anywhere between Sahara and Good Hope."

Bishop shared Bowen's low regard for Braive's countrymen. Still not asking Hayes' nationality, Bishop joined Bowen's flamboyant denunciation of all things Belgian, standing, all the while, on the step of the Belgian mining engineer's office. Later they told Hayes they'd recognized him as a Yank the moment they saw him.

Finished berating Belgians, Bowen and Bishop sauntered across the street to introduce Hayes to Joe Rogers, a retired prizefighter who ran the trading post at Kilo. Hayes must have favorably impressed Bishop while chatting in the shade of Rogers' store; the smaller trader asked Hayes to accompany him across Lake Albert into Uganda, saving Hayes a long walk south around the lake. Hayes immediately discharged his porters, sold any superfluous baggage, and paid off Bundajuo.

Under the de facto protection of Bowen and Bishop, Hayes enjoyed some leisure to assess the mining operations at Kilo otherwise closed to outsiders. The Belgians developed the Kilo mines with "men working perforce in a condition little removed from slavery." When Hayes passed through, hundreds of men worked the gold sands: "I see men staggering under loads of pure gold, askaris with fixed bayonets behind them, coming in from the creeks." Belgian military/industrial forces impressed these miners from every village within hundreds of miles. Chiefs had to supply strictly enforced quotas of workers who were paid 10 francs a month, plus food, on three-year contracts. Women who accompanied impressed men were put to work in the vast plantations of bananas and manioc. Other women came as prostitutes or temporary wives to the Europeans. "The women are the brightest blaze of color about this camp."

On January 17, 1915, Hayes and the two British elephant hunters left Kilo, headed toward Bowen's thousand-hectare ranch seventeen miles outside Kilo. Bishop had, as yet, made little impression on Hayes, only that the small trader had nerve enough to sluice some gold on the sly at Kilo and had bought a large box of fishhooks from the retired prizefighter's shop – on the off chance they'd sell around Lake Albert.

Bowen, on the other hand, both fascinated and repelled Hayes. He wrote on three separate occasions of "the diabolical glare of [Bowen's] eyes." Hayes learned something of the big man's background while riding on a creaking ox-cart plodding toward his isolated ranch. Bowen, "perhaps the greatest living elephant hunter," first arrived in Africa as an enlisted soldier in the British army fighting the Boers (Dutch settlers) for colonial control of South Africa. Taken prisoner, Bowen's élan so impressed "the rugged Boers," they adopted him as one of their own at war's end. Hating civilization, Bowen drifted north until settling on this huge concession in central Africa.

In Bowen, Hayes saw the resolve he believed necessary to "pioneering" wild lands: "There is something terrible about this man. His grim eyes bespeak the iron will behind them, and woe unto any native who brooks his wrath." As for any Belgian who sought to constrain Bowen's will: "He despises them as weaklings, tells them so to their faces and dares them to offer a return." Something about the sheer strength of character that allowed a man like Bowen to make and enforce his own law in the world, no matter the consequence, attracted Hayes despite all its repugnance.

At Bowen's expansive ranch Hayes met an African leader every bit as imposing as Bowen himself, the powerful native leader Julu. Hayes described Julu as "one of the most striking men I have met in Africa, white or black." The Belgians all feared Julu as a man: "He is one of the biggest men I have ever seen. At least six feet four inches in height, perhaps more, upright as an American Indian and well-muscled over a giant frame." They feared Julu even more as a leader of free African warriors: "It is said he has slain 10,000 people in the last two years." So, to control their fears, if not the man, the Belgians hired Julu. The African king walked Bowen's ranch on a contract to rid the region of White elephant poachers.

When Hayes met Julu, the tall African wore an immaculate white duck uniform, French helmet, and white shoes, "for the Belgians left nothing out in dealing with this savage king." Julu ceremonially saluted, then extended his hand to Hayes for a solemn handshake. Julu, or perhaps Bowen or Bishop later, told Hayes that when Julu captured one English elephant hunter named Bennett hunting illegally on Congo territory, Julu stripped Bennett of all his goods, down to, and including, his trousers. Before abandoning the poacher naked in the sun, Julu returned Bennett's pith helmet and a bathtub, "saying he had heard no Englishman could do without the latter."

The few days Hayes spent listening to yarns at Bowen's ranch renewed his "strength and courage for the open road." The rich milk, fresh vegetables, and beef steaks helped as well. Hayes would have stayed longer but the smaller elephant hunter, Bishop, hustled them back onto the trail. Bishop carried a sack from his prospecting at Kilo containing seven pounds of gold. Hayes saw a single nugget weighing fully one pound. The sack made Bishop antsy to get off Bowen's ranch, out of Belgian territory and into British Uganda to unload his gold at a non-Belgian market. Bowen said he'd come along part way, driving his six-ox cart to pick up some freight near Lake Albert for the mines at Kilo.

Two days out from Bowen's ranch, despite being paid off at Kilo, Bundajuo caught up to the slow-moving oxcart. Hayes happily greeted his cook a half-day's walk from their first view of Lake Albert. When Hayes tried to explain to Bundajuo the extent of the great lake they would soon see, Bundajuo laughed, "like all Africans who have never seen the sea," thinking his boss must be joking.

All morning the six oxen trudged toward a low mountain range. The first glimpse of Lake Albert from the summit evoked Hayes' characteristic elation at natural wonders. A "vast sheet of blue water" stretched far below with the western shore of Uganda barely visible in the haze. To the south "a narrow ribbon of silver" wound across a wide plain set between two rock walls rising sheer to the viewer's level. Where the ribbon, the Semliki River, met Lake Albert, a long tongue of papyrus reached miles into the blue water. Looking to the north, Hayes saw only blue water stretching to the horizon. Bundajuo stood silently for a long time gazing at the panorama, "his mouth agape." Eventually Bundajuo managed two words, "'Nyeri assiri!' (the earth has finished)." Hayes doubted anything he wrote could improve on Bundajuo's description.

The low hills they'd climbed now sloped steeply down a mountainside into the Albertine Rift before them. The safari wound down a rugged path to the small village of Bogoro, still 4000 feet above the lake, about a half-mile from what had been Kavili, the gathering point where Stanley dickered with Emin Pasha about evacuating Equatoria. When chief Kavili died, the local residents changed the name of the place to Bogoro, the living chief.

Ernest Dymond, a lone Belgian trader at Bogoro, received goods from the village of Kusendji on the lakeside for transfer on to the mines at Kilo. Dymond had bad news: the sporadic boat from Butiabwa, north, on the Ugandan side of the lake, had come through just one day previously. Worse, finding little cargo at Kusendji, the slow steamer would skip its next scheduled stop, not returning for six weeks. Hayes wrote that he'd made a mistake. He should have continued south, walking around the lower shore of the lake; he hadn't money for idling six weeks at Bogoro.

Bowen loaded his oxcart with Dymond's trade goods and rumbled back up the slope toward his ranch. Bishop stayed on at Bogoro, fidgety not because he was broke, like Hayes, but rather because he was rich – seven pounds of illicit gold in his pocket – and still on the Belgian side of the lake.

At the end of four long weeks, Hayes and Bishop got away from Bogoro, scrabbling six miles down a hillside of "decomposed granite wash," then twelve miles across a dry flat, previously lake bottom, to arrive at Kusendji, "a vile little hamlet by the lakeside." They had heard the *Samuel Baker*, an antiquated steam-driven paddle wheeler, flagship of the Albert Marine, was due at Kusendji on February 17, 1915. Hayes does not mention parting from Bundajuo, who remained at either Bogoro or Kusendji.

At supper aboard the *Samuel Baker* that night, an impudent Bishop generously offered butter he'd carried from Bowen's ranch to the assembled passengers – including a Belgian officer charged with intercepting gold smugglers. Hayes alone declined. He'd seen Bishop pour the butter, liquid in the heat of Bogoro, into a tin half-filled with gold nuggets: "Bishop loves to dare." The polite customs officer knifed only shallowly into the re-solidified butter. Some coffee for the Belgian officer? Ja, bedankt. The remainder of Bishop's nuggets washing around the bottom of the pot made no telltale rattle.

After checking in at British offices on the Ugandan side of the lake, Hayes retired with Bishop to a camp the trader maintained eleven miles south of Butiabwa at a hot springs and salt manufactory outside the village of Kibero. Local women diverted hot salty water over level ground, let it dry for a few days, then scraped the salt-impregnated soil into earthen pots. Water poured into the pots dripped out tiny holes, purifying the salt. "Vast heaps of earth remain where they have tossed it after being worked for the precious salt."

On February 20, 1915, Bishop jumped on a bicycle, planning to pedal 200 miles south toward Kampala on the north shore of Lake Victoria: "He has the gold with him and will dispose of it there."

Immediately upon being left alone at Kibero, Hayes diagnosed himself with spirillum fever, a bacterial infection vectored by tics. He thought maybe he'd picked it up sleeping in a grass hut. It flared intermittently over the next few weeks while he waited for Bishop, expecting they would travel together east toward the fighting in East Africa. On bad days Hayes lay "bedfast and aching from head to foot."

Hayes felt considerable relief when Bishop pedaled back into camp two weeks later. Hayes was a little bored and maybe now Bishop's African "wife" would leave off suggesting Hayes join her in Bishop's large, comfortable tent. The gold merchant had fared reasonably well in Kampala. No one paid much attention to him at first: another wanderer in from the bush on a bicycle. But when Bishop started trying to sell a few of his nuggets, something of a crowd gathered. Eventually, the lieutenant governor of Uganda came wading through a swarm of Indian traders to deliver Bishop an invitation to dine, in the absence of the Governor, with the lieutenant governor and his lady at the Governor's mansion. Bishop was in no danger, the opposite: "All of them want to get in on the ground floor, thinking Bishop has discovered a gold deposit in Uganda."

Through the end of March and all of April 1915, between intermittent attacks of spirillum fever that both now suffered, Hayes and Bishop traipsed around Uganda east of Lake Albert looking for a route to British East Africa.

On April 25, 1915, finding no other way out of Uganda, Hayes wrote, "We are considering going down the Nile to Egypt and entering the war against Turkey."

Accordingly, Hayes and Bishop reboarded the *Samuel Baker* exiting Lake Albert onto the White Nile to steam 165 miles downriver to Nimule in Anglo-Egyptian Sudan. Cataracts stopped river traffic at this once prosperous post now gone to weeds.

At Nimule, defying the enormity of Africa, Hayes once again met someone he knew (and disliked), an Egyptian named Mukhsin who had been at Port Sudan when Hayes arrived there a year earlier. Now Hayes learned that Mukhsin had bribed the mamur of Nimule concerning the porters. Mukhsin hoped to travel with the Europeans in a larger, safer safari. Hayes objected: "Like so many of his countrymen, he is a sodomite." Mukhsin petted Hasan, a young African boy forcibly converted to Islam, "like a sixteen-year old boy and girl just hearkening to their first sex call might." Hayes had encountered older, more powerful men preying sexually on younger boys many years previously, in the Yukon. While not entirely shocked by Mukhsin and Hasan, his previous experiences did nothing to soften his revulsion for Mukhsin.

The Englishman and the American surely would have abandoned Mukhsin at Nimule except for Mukhsin's cook, Suleiman, a man who loved nothing more than tending a roast sheep all night. As Hayes and Bishop reclined on carpets before a raised dais, "Arab style," Mukhsin tossed great hunks of mutton onto their plates. For this gustatory delight, the high-minded travelers could disregard Mukhsin's displays of affection and the "frowning, sullen countenance" of small Hasan, who knew these reclining men would do nothing to help him.

Two days' march brought the safari to Rejaf. Hayes, familiar with the ever-officious Castle-Smith still in command at Rejaf, immediately tried to have Mukhsin arrested, charging "subversive political activities." Out on the trail, Mukhsin had loudly proclaimed support for the German war effort. Castle-Smith laughed at Hayes' accusations: "'We know what we have, that's why these chaps are here. We know them, so we bring them here where they can do no harm and yet be of some use."

At Rejaf, Hayes and Bishop boarded the *Amara*, a steamer pushing passenger barges downriver from Rejaf to Mongalla. They traveled third class - Hayes said nothing about why Bishop, with all that gold, would travel third, only that Castle-Smith came aboard to "stick us for as much in the way of fees as he could." Shaking the officious bambishi, the travelers staked out a corner of a barge in common cause with two Greek traders, also bound for Cairo, surrounded by "British, Syrians, Greeks, Egyptians, Arabs, Baris, Azandes, and last the inky black Sudanese."

On the river outside Mongalla, Meredith, Engineer on the *Amara* and a heavy drinker, urged his pilot - at first politely, then increasingly ornately - toward a smooth course. In what seemed to Hayes the most recent skirmishes in a long-standing feud, the pilot intentionally drove Meredith's barge, also carrying Hayes and Bishop, "headlong into the bank at every bend in the river." So Meredith calmly cast free from the *Amara* to drift with the current. The crowded barge bumped along from bank to bank overnight until the *Amara* caught up in the morning at the southern edge of the Sudd.

Hayes had passed through the Sudd traveling up the Nile on his way toward the Heart of Africa mission. He described it as "a vast swamp said to encompass some 35,000 square miles" where the White Nile spreads into an enormous shallow bowl choked with dense vegetation "450 miles long where the Nile flows through it." The impassable water flora obstructing any natural channel through the Sudd explains why the source of the Nile remained a geographic mystery until the middle of the nineteenth century. Nero's expedition learned as early as 61 CE that a solid mat of vegetation at the Sudd prevents sailing all the way up the Nile to its source. Navigating through the Sudd was only possible when Hayes came through because a specially equipped vegetation cutting steamer maintained a tenuous passage.

Before entering the narrow channel cut through the Sudd, Meredith, now sober, took the wheel of the *Amara* and blasted his steam whistle just to smile at an awkward stampede of thirty swinging trunks and sixty flapping ears gamboling across the last plain before entering the dark corridor.

Hayes could see nothing inside the Sudd beyond the two straight, ten-foot-tall corridors of papyrus bounding a channel, maintained 250 feet wide by the British Sudd cutter. A massive crocodile refused to relinquish the channel until Meredith rammed the *Amara* "full tilt" into jaws snapping on steel. How to be stuck in this place? One of Hayes' barge mates told a story: Gessi Pasha, Romolo Gessi, an Italian mercenary in the employ of Gordon of Khartoum, had once been imprisoned for five months, caught fast by vegetation in the Sudd on return from exploring the upper Nile. More than half the passengers and crew on Gessi's steamer died when the food gave out: "The Arabs were first to turn to cannibalism." Rescue arrived just as Gessi would have been next on the menu. Health broken, Gessi died soon after returning to Egypt.

Exiting the tunnel through the Sudd, the *Amara* hopscotched from one small village to the next, taking on wood for fuel. Hayes thought the Dinka and Shillook silhouetted silently with spears on the riverbank could have been the same one-legged men described by the party Nero sent exploring for the source of the Nile. Hayes found the statuesque watchers exquisitely handsome – except for the cow dung hairpieces.

Disembarking the *Amara* at Khartoum, Hayes and Bishop scraped together a few piasters for a room in the Victoria Hotel, "not a bad caravanserai run by a Greek." Between a "wet huboob," a sandstorm during which rain fell as mud, and recurrent spirillum fever, the pair used the Victoria as a base for photographic excursions. They couldn't develop the film because of the heat but caught some nice "wild game" shots by clever framing at the Khartoum Zoo.

Bishop became so antsy waiting for a steamer at Khartoum he hatched a plan to purchase some sort of boat and run the Nile to Cairo – just the two of them. Fourteen hundred miles down the Nile in a rowboat didn't frighten Hayes but he counseled Bishop against the idea during wartime. The British maintained a significant military force at Khartoum since Kitchener retook it from forces of the Mahdi, but all the seasoned British troops had been transferred out for redeployment against the Turks and Germans on European fronts. The new men, "territorials - they are called," sent as replacements, suffered horribly from forced desert training. Eight had died outright. Jumpy, inexperienced solders frightened Hayes.

However, when the temperature hit 113° in Khartoum, Hayes seriously reconsidered Bishop's plan with that small boat. Hold on – what about all the money from Bishop's gold? Bishop had the money all right, just not in the right form. At Khartoum the elephant hunter/prospector/trader finally unloaded a great stack of Congo francs "at par." Flush with money they could actually spend, the pair paid rail fare from Khartoum to Cairo and left the next day.

At midnight on June 7, 1915, on the train stopped at Abu Hamed, Hayes and Bishop munched on fine sweet dates purchased through a window from a young vendor. All day the train had followed the path of the Nile through desert sands blown through open windows by "bitter Khamsin" winds. The vast stretches of time associated with the ruins at Meroë provoked from Hayes a long, pensive passage on mortality: "The temple of the sun, the rock hewn city on the cliffs, the miles of rubble telling of a people once alive and flourishing makes one marvel why men contend with one another for the possession of the earth when all know they will someday be one with these." Perhaps Hayes was thinking more about the carnage rending Europe in 1915 than ancient Meroë.

A 200-mile stretch of track diverged from the Nile to shortcut a bend in the river. The train rejoined the Nile at Wadi Halfa, "a town that has seen better days, like Bishop and me." Officious "Gyppos" gave their luggage "an extra good frisking." Hayes scoffed at their zeal, after all, "[t]here is little to smuggle in from the Sudan."

Rail service from Khartoum to Cairo had a gap of some 230-rivermiles between Wadi Halfa and Shillal (Aswan). The Aswan High Dam, completed in 1970, currently backs the Nile up at Aswan to form Lakes Nasser and Nubia, flooding those 230-rivermiles. However, when Hayes came through the area in 1915, only the Aswan Low Dam had been built. The Low Dam, completed in 1902, was height-limited to prevent flooding the ancient Egyptian temple at Philae near Aswan.

At dusk the *Sultan Hussein* pushed passenger barges, one carrying Hayes, Bishop, and a couple of Syrians "with rather pretty wives" slowly past "the great temple of Abu Simbel, where Rameses [sic] the Great made sure of being remembered for a long time." Hayes thought the statues contrasted well with the emerald green of the river but, characteristically, his thoughts turned to the working hands Ramesses impressed to their building: "[Ramesses] counted not the sweat of slaves who carved these gigantic monuments to his vanity, desiring only to be remembered as a great king."

As the 70-foot statues of Ramesses II faded into the dusk astern, Hayes sat on deck looking for other wonders of ancient Egypt. He wrote that he missed much in the dark but eagerly returned to his lookout at first light. That day, Hayes counted sixteen separate ancient temple sites, some encroached by waters risen behind the Low Dam.

Hayes wished the *Sultan Hussein* had dawdled longer down this magnificent stretch of river: "Everywhere it is enclosed by indescribably weird cliffs, and at every sharp turn we are afforded a new vista different from the rest." But even a slow steamer pushing two barges eventually reaches its destination, in this case the railhead at Shillal.

When the train finally came, the now threadbare Hayes and Bishop boarded third class surrounded by their baggage, and sat cross-legged on wooden planks with fellahin, Egyptian peasants who "were courteous, something the educated class of Egyptians never are." The view from the window of the train following the Nile equaled that from the steamer: Temples at Edfu and Kom Ombo then a stop at Luxor where "ruins extend 23 miles on either bank of the Nile."

The train followed the course of the Nile between Aswan and Cairo through a river valley from one to four miles wide. Everywhere Hayes could see industrious cultivation extending north and south along the verdant river: cotton, vegetables, fruit trees, "every square inch of soil where water can be made to flow being made to produce." All worked by "countless people," the fellahin, working under "the corvee, or forced labor system whereby all men may be called to labor without recompense as long as the wealthy pashas may see fit on the irrigation canals or any other public work."

The train pushed quickly past Minieh, Aby Girgeh, Assiout, Beni Souef, "and a lot of other places" before pulling into the great Egyptian station: "Cairo! Another of these dream cities of my boyhood that seemed half-mystical and non-existent as life on another planet." An energetic and voluble Russian "who seemed to speak all tongues and know everything sized us up and escorted us to the Grand Royal Hotel on the Bab El Bahri, a street out of the Arabian nights." Ten piastres a day for a double room with vast beds, mosquito nets, and a bath. Heaven to be clean again.

Cleaner, but still considerably travel-worn, Hayes reported: "Our clothes are worn and our sun helmets proclaim us from the desert." Their tanned faces and frayed clothing brought sidelong glances from the Europeans at the Grand Royal. Even Egyptians on the street turned for a second look at these battered men of the desert, contrasting so extremely with the "smartly dressed Australians who are established here until needed at the Dardanelles."

The two scruffy wanderers pushed their way through the thronging "vanity fair" on the Cairo streets looking for Australian military headquarters, where they planned to present their papers hoping to join the fighting of WWI. Both tried to enlist; both were denied. Hayes because he was a Yank and Bishop because, at 45, he was too old. The officers suggested the two might enquire in England or Australia about enlisting; a shame they'd just missed a pair of hospital ships recently departed Port Said bound for Australia "carrying 1,500 invalided soldiers who were so far gone with syphilis and other social diseases they were no further use to the army."

On the morning of June 11, 1915, Hayes and Bishop, seeking a respite of beauty and calm away from the "hell" of the city, fled Cairo for a tour of the pyramids. On the nine-mile trolley ride to Gizeh, "[t]he green palms in the gardens at Ezkebieh and Kasr El Nil, the famed Blue Mosque, and the creamy white of the houses of the city make a picture long to be remembered." Hayes admired the pyramids at Gizeh for their size and antiquity but complained that most of the syenite outer covering had been "stripped and built into mosques at Cairo by the ruthless Arabs." He and Bishop searched at some length but never located the Sphinx. Hayes used as many words in his diary describing his annoyance with the "pulling, hauling, guides" as he did his wonder at the pyramids. He congratulated himself and Bishop for setting a record never broken "from the days of the pharaohs down to the present day": neither had paid a bakshish, or bribe, to their porter. Perhaps that explains why they were unable to find the Sphinx.

On June 13, 1915, half a day's train ride from Cairo up the verdant Nile delta through several small agricultural town brought Hayes and Bishop to Alexandria, jump-off site for Anzac troops shipping out immediately to war in the Dardanelles.

Six months after leaving Niangara, Hayes had 30 shillings in his pocket, enough, he figured, to last him two weeks at the sailor's home in Alexandria. The spirillum fever still lodged in his left arm, swollen and painful, but not severely enough to stop him scouring the docks for a place on a ship.

A drab day tramping the docks landed Hayes nothing but conversation with skippers of ships with full crews. Bishop, who had gone the other direction, had better luck; he landed a berth on the *Southland*, a Red Star liner converted to troop transport between Alexandria and Turkey. Bishop told Hayes to hop it: the *Southland* lacked one man. A dash down the dock and a blunt Nova Scotia skipper looked over Hayes' papers before delivering the magic words: "'Yas, yuh go on this ship.'"

After a night anchored in harbor at Alexandria, the *Southland* set sail carrying 2,000 Australian soldiers, "as many as this ship can carry and a few more," for delivery to the meat-grinder at the Dardanelles. Luckily seas were calm, the weather "almost tropical." Anzacs sat all about the decks, many bare to the waist, picking lice from their shirts. Hayes vaguely liked them: "To be fair, I suppose they are as courageous as men of other races."

On the night of June 17, 1915, the *Southland* steamed into harbor at the island of Lemnos off the Gallipoli Peninsula past double booms guarding against German submarines, then continued slowly past "long lines of battleships, cruisers, torpedo boats, destroyers, submarines, mine sweepers, transports and hospital ships" of the Allied navy. The Australian fighting men aboard the *Southland* quickly transferred to swift boats for landing on the beaches. "Every face was blanched, some were vomiting from sheer funk."

A few new crewmen joined the *Southland* at Lemnos, "waifs" escaped from three ships torpedoed and sunk by German submarines, the *Goliath* (570 men killed), *Triumph* (49 men killed) and *Majestic* (78 men killed). Their spirits unbroken, the survivors spoke matter-of-factly of sighting their attackers from ships at anchor. They had been helpless to flee and had no defenses against submarines that need only "keep under water where no guns could be brought to bear on her and torpedo her victims at leisure." All through this telling, Hayes heard the rumble of guns from the peninsula some three hours distant. Rumor came of a huge battle with 7,000 Allied and 8,000 Turks killed.

Rumors of the great battle turned out to be an exaggeration but the actual fighting on a typical day on the Gallipoli Peninsula delivered horror enough. Two medical evacuation ships pulled alongside the *Southland* close enough Hayes could hear the screams of those still living – just a few here and there, in long lines of dead men, lying silent and still. "All young and in the full flush of life, yet it is all over."

Hayes assumed the *Southland* would take all those wounded onboard and sail right back to Alexandria. However, on June 24, 1915, Hayes realized his second long adventure in Africa had come to an end. He didn't know the *Southland's* destination but clearly it was somewhere other than Alexandria. The ship carried no wounded and had begun to zigzag across the Aegean in company of at least one transport ship and a couple of minesweepers.

Just as when he had left Nigeria in 1907, at age 29, Hayes departed Alexandria in 1915, at age 37, essentially broke – 30 shillings in his pocket – and sick – this time with spirillum fever instead of malaria. Leaving Nigeria, he had written of an intensely personal heartache, the failure of his own strength and courage. This time leaving Africa, he hadn't failed; his institutions had failed him. At their "pseudo mission," CT Studd and Alfred Buxton debased themselves, their Christian ideals, and the very "savages" whose uplift they intended. Worse, an entire civilized world – capable of building pyramids and Alexandrian civilization, of morality, and light, and compassion – chose instead worldwide, mechanized murder.

7. In the Meantime: Sailing the World, 1915-1918

The *Southland*, a White Star–Dominion liner converted for troop transport in 1915, steamed away from the fighting at Gallipoli past the Mediterranean islands of Cerigo (Cythera) and Crete. These names roused in Hayes "memories of books I had read telling of brave deeds by ancient mariners who had lived and fought in these seas." Now, fifty brave Anzac soldiers sat on the forecastle scanning the waters for submarines: five pounds to the first man to call one out. Should a man sight a torpedo already launched, speeding on a straight white line toward the ship, concentrated rifle fire would, in theory, explode it before impact. By strict order, every soldier not on the forecastle remained below deck: a transport ship apparently empty presented a less appealing target.

Off Gibraltar, word came over the wireless that a Leyland liner had been "subbed" with the loss of 21 men. Hourly ship's evacuation drills and constant checking of "the boat falls [ropes and blocks for lowering] to see everything clear" calmed Hayes' anxiety somewhat. Nevertheless, he suspected that, in an emergency, "the boats will be stormed" by panicked troops. Accordingly, he took to sleeping in some horseboxes on deck alongside two light planks, "and if the old ship gets it these go overboard and me after them." The planks would float him so "there will be a chance of being picked up at least."

On July 9, 1915, the *Southland* docked safely at Hornsby at the north end of Liverpool. An Irish shipmate, Old Mick, begged Hayes to raise a pint, a toast to safety at the end of a long fearsome road: "'At laste wayther!' he insisted." Hayes joined in a solemn toast, with water, to safety and friendship among sailors.

At Liverpool Hayes lost his traveling companion. The Royal Navy paid both "Good old Bishop!" and Hayes one pound for services rendered the *Southland* in wartime. (Evidently, they had shipped as workaways just to get back to England.) With one pound added to his thirty shillings reserve, Hayes retired to the sailor's home in Canning Place, a little desperate to find the next ship. Bishop, considerably more flush than Hayes, could afford to visit his old mother in Norfolk. Hayes guessed Bishop would return to South Africa, then drift back north into the interior of the continent. Throughout his life Hayes had many colleagues but few companions. Bishop's departure elicited an emotion Hayes never mentioned at any other time: "I am lonely, for he was the best pal I have ever known."

Britain did not introduce military conscription for the Great War until January of 1916. War fervor among the civilian population provided enough volunteers in the first year-and-a-half of the war, but already in July 1915 Hayes could see mandatory service looming. Speakers in the streets harangued: "'If these ideals our fathers died for are worth saving, then let us fight to save them!'" Bagpipes played stirring martial music outside the sailor's home as pretty young women darted about pinning white feathers of cowardice on the coat lapels of "every likely looking young man." One recruiting sergeant called out to Hayes that he'd better go and save his nation.

"'I'm a Yank.'"

"'Tell 'em you were born in Canada!'"

Hayes thought the Allies would win the war but only at terrible cost even in victory: "The general impression is that Germany will soon collapse, but she is strong, stronger than most of us realize. She has been preparing for this day for more than forty years." To Hayes, the war looked entirely futile. Sadly, it appeared equally certain the high passions on all sides would have to run their awful course.

The best course for Hayes Perkins would take him right out of Europe altogether. But a tattered sailor with little money had few options. He would have signed back onto the *Southland* but the ship had gone into dry dock to fit anti-submarine guns fore and aft. Even staying at the sailor's home, "riotous living" by his necessary standards of economy, Hayes' purse wouldn't stretch until the *Southland* launched again. He contemplated trying for one of several ships bound for the US, but every contract stipulated sailing out and back. He wouldn't, in conscience, sign on intending to desert: "it isn't square."

Stopping round the offices of the American consul hurt more than helped. An angry official bawled Hayes out: "'Why did you not stay in your own country's ships? You'll get nothing from me, and I hope you do get subbed; get out of here and don't come back.'"

Hayes would not stay in his own country's ships, even had one offered in Liverpool, because, "[a] sailor on an American ship is the lowest slave." Working conditions on US "hell-ship[s]" lagged barbarously behind ships of other nations. Reliable gossip on the docks warned that the mate on an American ship had shot a seaman off the yard just before docking in Liverpool.

Broke and desperate to find a ship, Hayes nevertheless discharged a responsibility to the board of the Heart of Africa Mission: "The acts of Messrs. Studd and his stooge Buxton must be related to them." His financial circumstance precluded travel to London, so he penned a detailed letter from the sailor's home. The gist of the letter asked: "Why must men and women be deceived by these charlatans who pose as self-sacrificing messengers of the Prince of Peace?" How can they "be permitted to impose on a credulous public who have the interests of Africa at heart?"

A week later, separate replies arrived care of the sailor's home from board members Coleman and Ingram. Coleman took Hayes seriously, wanting to hear more concerning "Studd's doings." Ingram demurred, playing politics. The second response so discouraged Hayes – "everyone is false these days, no wonder there is war" – he considered disappearing to some South Sea island. But no, he rallied himself: "One must fight to win, even if he dies trying it is better than drifting with the tide. It would be moral suicide to shirk the fight." The fight referenced here was not World War I, but rather the fight to speak truth about the mission at Niangara. Hayes refused to abandon his moral obligation to speak out, even faced with corrupt institutions, unscrupulous men, and fickle public opinion. This would not be his last attempt to speak honestly and directly about the Heart of Africa Mission.

By July 1915, German submarines had been targeting Allied steamships for only six months, but to devastating effect. Just to sustain trade and supply, the Allied nations had been forced to drag sailing ships, long abandoned in favor of diesel engines, from mud flats where they'd been left to rot. At Liverpool, Hayes counted himself fortunate to land a place on a revivified British four-mast barque, the *Oweenee*, outbound for Australia

Hayes could size up a ship with some expertise: the *Oweenee* looked hungry. Jack Thorsen, a "sturdy Norwegian" loading cargo with Hayes, agreed. On a slow ship with a foul bottom, when food stores dwindled off the Australian coast, ship's officers would eat while the crew starved. If this case of potatoes they carried got diverted into, say, an empty bunk in the forecastle, a more equitable distribution might be affected in time of need. Hayes and Thorsen surreptitiously redirected several hundred pounds of potatoes into a private sailor's reserve.

Hayes' description of sailing by wind power on a large merchant vessel in 1915 evokes another era. He counted himself only a half-sailor to acknowledge the skill and independence full-sailors exercised in the most extreme conditions of water and weather over a lifetime at sea. Any momentary wartime return to sail power would not last. Hayes counted himself lucky to be even a half-sailor again: "It is unutterably sad, especially to a sailor, to realize these ships will soon be no more. With them will pass the rugged seamen of old. The places of these will be taken by men who have technical knowledge, or by men who can steer, but have no other work to do but to scrub paint, swing a paint brush and handle lines when mooring."

Hayes' encomium to sailing ships and sailors couldn't hide two first-hand realities. First, lots of heavy work, "hauling the yards round, making sails fast and loosing them again," by a lean crew working through South Atlantic gales, the northeast trade winds, across the equator and into the southwest trades. And second, quotidian danger: on August 23, 1915, Hayes lost the tip of a finger when "one of the green apprentices let go a halyard I was overhauling which drew my finger into a block and sliced the end off as neatly as a surgeon might have done." Hayes wrote nothing more about the finger other than to report the stub had healed cleanly some three weeks later. The spirillum fever still lodged in an arm painfully swollen, but not severely enough to keep him off the yards.

A furious storm hit the *Oweenee* on October 7, 1915. At the top of each giant wave, a third of a mile between crests, "the sails are hauling all they can and not blow away." When the ship fell into the trough between crests, all sails went completely slack. Hayes worried about all the stress on the old ship: "It is this constant tension that finds the weak spots in the ship's armor, and if there be any fault it will be exposed here."

Not long after the storm cleared with the *Oweenee* still intact, as Hayes and Jack Thorson had predicted their ship got hungry. Fortunately, they had the potatoes. A sailor's recipe for potato/seabird kugel: scour the black from potatoes with sand, don't peel, it's too wasteful; layer a stone pickle jar with potatoes followed by seabird, potatoes, seabird, until full; light a fire, making sure to give proper thanks to the skipper for stealing that coal on *Oweenee's* previous run; place the jar onto the stove, locking the door to the forecastle lest the skipper learn the use of his coal and his potatoes. Bake and share: "These bird pies are not so tasty, but are filling."

Off Woollahra, Australia, the skipper sailed the starving ship cautiously in thick smoke from bush fires ashore. Finally, after beating into wind and smoke for a week, on the morning of November 19, 1915, a tug dragged the *Oweenee* to anchor at Rose Bay. Only when offloading cargo did Hayes discover sailing ships carried non-perishable goods like wheat, timber, cotton, liquor – and gunpowder(!) A cargo the crew had "been carrying all this distance, unconscious of the sleeping volcano under us." Well, they were safe now; "Life is like that, death is always just round the corner"

No one in war-fevered Australia had any interest in eyewitness reports from Cairo: "I gather they believe every soldier boy sleeps with a Bible under his pillow and lifts his prayers to Heaven constantly." The citizenry had twice voted down formal conscription but social pressure bore just as heavily as in England: "All are war mad." No man would be offered work without producing a doctor's certificate of disability for military service. Of course, Hayes had no doctor's certificate.

The pressure to enlist in Australia forced Hayes to make a decision about fighting in the war. He chose to abstain on pacifist grounds: "I am not going into the war. I have defrauded no man, and see no place where I have been instrumental in bringing about this business of every man slaying his fellow. I refuse to kill a man who has not wronged me, or even one who has if I can avoid it." But what would he do? With no medical certificate, he couldn't work in Sydney. Having settled the big question about the war, Hayes wasn't worried: "Something will turn up."

Never one to idle around just hoping, Hayes went looking for his *Oweenee* shipmate, Jack Thorsen. Still dead drunk on the last of his pay from four months at sea, Thorsen was a man with an idea: steal a yacht from Port Jackson and sail north to the gold fields in New Guinea. Hayes needed about one second to consider that plan: "Jack is too hot for me." He left Thorsen to follow his own devices, should the seaman ever sober up enough to stand, and went to enquire with a swift American mail steamer.

No luck, but the quartermaster pointed Hayes toward the *Mindoro*, a four-mast schooner across the harbor in Blackwattle Bay, another slow sailing ship, and American, but what other route had Hayes off Australia? "The skipper, a ferocious looking old Dane, ordered me on board at once if I expected to make her to Frisco." Hayes came aboard rostered as Lars Anderson – a *Mindoro* crewman who overstayed his leave at the Sydney brothels. The old Danish captain, "Double Reef" Larsen, wasn't a waiting kind of man; the names could be adjusted at sea.

Hayes Perkins didn't know whether to be more afraid of the *Mindoro* or its captain. The ship leaked from wide bottom seams; sailors had to hand pump (on off-duty hours, pumping was not considered work) when fully loaded just to keep the ship afloat. The decks bowed as much as a foot off true, permanently warped by heavy lashings of timber. And the *Mindoro's* "rattlings," riggings sailors had to climb to work the sails in all weather, showed visible rot from much exposure to the elements without replacement.

On the other hand, Captain Double Reef Larsen, a naturalized American, had short lips, the grin of a bulldog, and "the pale blue eye of a killer." He stood for hours, his "ponderous belly" hanging over the rail, glaring at the helmsman. Fusillades of abuse rained on the pilot following the slightest mistake at the wheel. The blue air cleared only in a coughing-fit with blood hacked from a stomach ruined by drink. Hayes didn't need the crew to tell him Larsen "is a devil." But from them he did learn that Larsen owned a small share of stock in the *Mindoro*, incentive to maximize profit at the expense of sailors.

As Hayes had recently experienced on the *Oweenee*, British ships hired full crews, then starved them on short rations. American ships, like the *Mindoro*, reversed the British strategy: hired a short crew, far too few to manage the work, but fed them well. At first, the American arrangement suited Hayes. He had good food and light duty in fair weather off the east coast of Australia. In calm seas, Larsen had assigned Hayes "a strange duty." Every bolt showing in the hold needed fresh paint. Why? Because the *Mindoro* had to appear new, dry, and seaworthy to copra (dried cocoanut meat) merchants at Apia, Samoa.

Out from Apia, an exhausted Hayes decided it didn't matter if a British sailor collapsed weak from lack of food or an American sailor collapsed weak from overwork. In the rough seas between Hawaii and the US mainland, Larsen called all hands-on-deck whenever storms required the sails to be reset. A three-man crew simply could not manage the work: "Usually all hands are called if anything heavy comes, which is an every night affair now. Our senses are numbed, we no longer hear the constant damning and cursing devoted to us, our ancestors, our future state."

One man on every three-man crew had to pilot the *Mindoro*. Whoever manned the wheel had to look out for Double Reef Larsen as well as the stormy weather. The captain habitually knocked the pilot from the wheel, threw it over, then hard back to show the poor sailor he had been asleep at the wheel and a point off course. Larsen tried his trick one night while Hayes had the wheel. Hayes already had the *Mindoro* "as close to the wind as could be done." Following Larsen's bullying, the *Mindoro* nearly ran "aback," dangerously slacking the sails across heavy seas. Hayes could not suppress a slight smile, a grin that nearly cost him his life.

On the third night after Hayes had smirked at Captain Larsen, the *Mindoro*'s fore-topsail sheet tore away in a gale. The captain "made me clamber out on the gaff and reave [reef] another, the ship lurching in the heavy seas the while." The mate, usually cowed by Larsen, protested the order. Overruled. Now jump! A sailor may not disobey an officer. "It was the most difficult act I have ever performed at sea and all hands came on deck to watch me be shaken off." Any other captain would have lowered all sails until calmer weather. Double Reef Larsen had earned his name this way: ordering sails shortened in heavy weather, instead of lowering them entirely, to gain a little speed regardless of the danger to his crewmen. Hayes survived the individual challenge in the high rigging by skill and pluck – only to nearly die with the entire ship's crew on the night of March 14, 1916. A steamer nearly "cut down" the *Mindoro*, passing immediately to stern close enough to "hear the thump of her engines."

Eventually bad luck has to change, at least for ships that return to port. A lovely southwest wind rose, sending the crew scampering to set all sails as the *Mindoro* flew to within sight of Point Reyes, California. Two days later a northwest wind pushed the *Mindoro* straight into San Francisco harbor, kicking so hard a second crewman had to help Hayes hold the wheel. As with his first great circle, Hayes made no mention in his diary about completing his second circumnavigation of the globe. Maybe he didn't even notice.

Hayes ignored one last curse from Larsen, waded through customs, and "strolled down Third St. to a cheap lodging house in the worker's quarter near Howard St." Safe from the war; safe from the *Mindoro*; safe from Double Reef Larsen; in San Francisco and not broke. The thrifty sailor had saved $103 at $30 a month from Sydney.

Traveling from Liverpool to San Francisco, by way of Australia, on sailing ships, had eaten up almost a full year of the war. Hayes got his first update on the European conflict from "a gabby German deckhand" standing on a San

Francisco wharf: the Germans were "'beating back the allies on every side.'" The man happily predicted the imminent German success at Verdun would end the war with peace dictated on German terms. Hayes wasn't so sure. The American newspapers, with the exception of William Randolph Hearst's *San Francisco Examiner*, wrote much less enthusiastically about Germany and "Hearst has always been pro-German and anti-British."

Hayes ate up the next year of the war mostly knocking about the West Coast of the United States. While his bankroll from the *Mindoro* held out, Hayes could afford to putter around in the sunshine, selective about what work he took. On April 13, 1916. he had a novel experience: a ride by automobile stage, "the first time I have ever ridden on one." He worked a day on a road gang in the mountains behind San Diego but the advertised eight-hour workday turned out to last eleven, so he quit and rode the stage back to tour the museum at Exposition Park.

Finding no work in San Diego and feeling unwelcome in Los Angeles, Hayes set course for Eureka up the California coast where he knew the mills. Maybe he'd try up the Little River where he worked back in 1907. One thing he knew for certain: under no circumstances would he hire on at Hammond's big mill across the bay at Samoa, California. He knew a man's prospects at Hammond's: "If he can manage to save a few dollars there he is a financial wizard, so close do the companies henchmen shave their men's pay."

Two weeks later, unable to sit idle any longer, Hayes signed on at Hammond's mill, the only job in town. He worked a nominal ten hour a day, but every worker also donated (unpaid) patriotic hours, so Hayes did too. The lumber business boomed in wartime. After deducting room, board, and hospital fees, a newly hired employee at Hammond's earned less than a dollar a day – for standing thirteen hours grading lumber pulled from a double feed sticker.

According to California statutes, Hayes worked almost entirely surrounded by criminals. All the young millworkers had joined the International Workers of the World (IWW or Wobblies) agitating, by illegal association, to improve working conditions. Hayes' rhetoric aligned fairly well with the Wobblies when describing treatment of the workers at Hammond's: "men are helots, peons just as were the slaves of the ancient Romans or the Mexicans under the Diaz regime." But no, Hayes would not sign on with IWW; he was not a joiner.

With previous experience behind lumber mill machines, Hayes easily managed to stay ahead of this one, expertly stacking the greens boards the machine spit toward him. But if he could keep up, the mill could speed up. The second time company overseers installed a larger drive pulley on their feeds, he and an equally skilled "half-breed Indian" on the machine beside him announced that any further speed up would lose Hammond's its two best graders. Hayes had saved $24 for six weeks work when he quit Hammond's following installation of the third pulley.

Up in North Bend, Oregon, in June 1916, war work could be had for a man willing to run an air hammer. In fact, the 80-pound riveting hammer required three men just to hold its recoil. A machine so dangerous union stonecutters in Indiana called for its abolition.

Hayes wrestled with the air hammer long enough to earn a stake out of North Bend; then he hammered a little longer sending his last check to pay an outstanding debt. The generous goldminers, Charley Groves and James Giliot, each received $20, c/o mining offices, Moto, Belgian Congo. No bank in North Bend knew an exchange rate from dollars to Belgian francs but Hayes figured $20 would cover the 200 francs the two Australians had pressed on him in his hour of need.

Maybe he should return to Australia? "Only for the war am I here now." Easy enough for Hayes to find a ship in San

Francisco, the freighter *Waikawa* bound for Sydney would have signed him on. Why not go? "America has been unkind to me, so I will leave here once again."

Maybe the *Waikawa* reminded him too much of the *Mindoro*? Maybe he remembered Australia offered no work to an able man refusing enlistment? Whatever the reconsideration, by the first of the year, 1917, Hayes returned to North Bend, Oregon, and got his job back: standing beside two companions bucking an air hammer in the rain.

Only his Sunday school class teaching bible verses to young North Bend girls and two intriguing letters hinting at Africa prevented despair. One letter came from a missionary at the Africa Inland Mission, Charles Hurlburt's operation, from which the Heart of Africa Mission had splintered. Much bad blood remained between CT Studd and Charles Hurlburt. The Africa Inland Mission had heard of Hayes' work in Africa. The card invited Hayes to return to "some of the wilder parts of that continent to build stations for them." How depressingly familiar. Yes, a possible route back to Africa, but, "[m]y last experience with missionaries was so disappointing I am fearful of risking it." Nevertheless, Hayes did not discard the mission option out of hand, writing: "I'm always willing to take a long chance."

The second letter came from James Evans, the mining engineer Hayes had met while at the Heart of Africa Mission. Evans had mentioned a big Belgian/American diamond mine in the Southern Congo near the Angola border. Evans told Hayes they could use a good man with experience in Africa. Diamond mining might work; Hayes hoped so: "If I stay on [at North Bend] there is nothing else to do but marry and become a part of the body politic and that irks my every sense of life."

By March of 1917 nothing had come of either letter. Hayes still stood freezing six days a week at the shipyard in North Bend. His work had changed from running the murderous air hammer outside in the rain, sleet, and snow, to rigging ships outside in the rain, sleet, and snow: "We almost perish from the cold, for this work requires no physical effort and we are benumbed to the bone and chilled with the constant bad weather to which we are exposed."

The United States entered World War I in April 1917. Suddenly, the same war fervor Hayes had seen in Australia and England gripped North Bend. Some of the very same recruiting posters he'd seen exciting Aussies and Brits to war now plastered the entrance to the shipyard: a lot of propaganda about German war atrocities. Hayes had no doubt German soldiers committed atrocities; to his mind that is what war is. Nor had he any doubt Allied soldiers committed atrocities, to his mind that is what war is on both sides. No thank you; Hayes had seen enough atrocity at Gallipoli to know he wouldn't enlist, and at 39, he was too old for conscription. He wouldn't go to war but he had to do something to get out of the Oregon rain.

When a second letter arrived from the Africa Inland Mission (AIM) inviting Hayes to their headquarters in Philadelphia, he talked himself into taking the long chance: "I am not enthused with the idea, but it's an out from a place I don't fit in [the shipyard]," and an out from the rain. Africa, he reminded himself, offered much more than missionaries. If he could put up with a few bad apples, another mission might be all right: "I know the bush and know Africa, love it and like the natives. Maybe it will be better this time."

Quitting North Bend in May 1917, Hayes rode the train to Oklahoma City for a short visit with his mother on his way to Philadelphia. Their reunion brought Hayes mostly pain, a reminder of his estrangement from family: "My mother is old now, and it is not possible for me to realize she is nearer related to me than any other person I see in my wanderings." A visit to his sister Memrie in Waco brought more of the same: "My relatives are normal people who live the average life of all Americans. Everybody seems out of step but me, but they consider me the transgressor." Nevertheless, Hayes

132

pressed on, traveling with his mother to visit two other sisters, Virginia and Pearl, in Houston. Meeting two more familial strangers, then leaving all of them, occasioned about all the pain Hayes could manage: "It is better I stay away and never come at all."

Hayes' first impression of Charles Hurlburt in Philadelphia did nothing to alleviate his uneasiness with the whole African missionary redux: "His hands are as brutal and cruel as the club-like paws of Double Reef Larsen." Hurlburt grilled his prospective handyman at length concerning CT Studd and Studd's activities at the Heart of Africa Mission. Hayes undoubtedly answered frankly, to which Hurlburt made no comment one way or the other. Hulbert did, however, have much recent information from central Africa. Hayes' disdain for all things Studd probably loosened Hulburt's tongue.

According to Hulburt, CT Studd had thrown Roome out of the Heart of Africa Mission. (This indicated to Hayes that Roome must be "square after all, else he would have been kept on.") Hayes' "old friend" Renzi still lived. (Welcome news.) But Renzi's sub-chief, Bukoyo, had committed suicide. (Hayes doubted that explanation since suicide is "something a Negro rarely ever does.") And finally, on another note, Frank Bowen had escaped Belgian custody after arrest for robbing a Frenchman. (A charge Hayes knew could not be true because "whatever Bowen was he was not a thief.")

Hurlburt and his millionaire backers in Philadelphia struck Hayes as facsimiles to Studd and his board in London. Hayes fell in much more easily with an AIM staffer, John Stauffacher.

Hayes happily joined the Stauffachers and their two young boys at Hatboro, a few miles outside Philadelphia, where all worked, "cleaning, digging, and trying to shape up a place long neglected." This kind of work Hayes could join with gusto: renovating a decrepit mansion into a home for the penniless Stauffachers and other retired missionaries.

Miss Alta Hurlburt, daughter of Charles Hurlburt, visited Hatboro in mid-June 1917 just as the mansion and a beautiful garden began to shape up. Alta's endless stream of questions seemed a little odd to Hayes; he couldn't help but "[w]onder if there be anything behind this?"

Yes. Following Alta's examination, Hayes had an inkling his dismissal might be coming; nevertheless, the "short arm jolt" from Palmer, headman at Hatboro, made Hayes' heart skip a beat. Summarily fired, with "as much Christian charity in it as one would expect in a bartender's when chucking bums away from the free lunch counter."

The next day, while sitting for an hour-and-a-half outside Palmer's office to "bring me to a properly humble frame of mind," Hayes worked out that Palmer had, in fact, intended Hayes stay on with the AIM in Philadelphia. Palmer's straight arm jolt had been a feint designed to elicit the appropriate groveling for a job and the proper reverence for Christian missionaries. When ushered in, Hayes interrupted Palmer's chastisement to state that he had only come to clean up some final paperwork; there would be no groveling. Fine, if that was the way Hayes wanted it, Palmer refused to pay Hayes for both his month's work at Hatboro and the train ticket from San Francisco to Philadelphia. Good day.

Stiffed by the missionaries, Hayes could not afford train fare all the way back to the West Coast, so he paid most of his money for a hard seat as far as Walla Walla, Washington. That left $2.20 from which he purchased bologna and bread to carry him across country, plus an extravagant 2¢ for a newspaper: "I'm reckless and desperate, so don't care."

The federal employment bureau in Walla Walla offered only the roughest manual labor: pouring concrete on four great viaducts for the O.W.R.&N. railway outside of town. "'Lead me to it!' I answered. (There's less than a dollar in the exchequer now.)" At 30¢ an hour, Hayes doubled his bankroll after one morning pushing a "muck stick," as Hayes called a shovel.

After three days behind the shovel, Hayes got a dollar a day pay raise. The head carpenter for the O.W.R.&N. had learned his new man had experience high in the riggings on sailing ships. The carpenter pointed to a cable on a boom 120 feet above ground and asked if Hayes could see where it had snagged. Looking around, Hayes could see "everybody is afraid to go aloft." What could be easier work for a man used to running the ratlines? Hayes scampered up to affect a trivial repair.

In the two months Hayes stuck with the job on the viaduct, that boom crashed to the ground twice, killing him neither time because he happened to be elsewhere, doing other heavy work. No longer willing to push his luck scrambling around rotten rigging the carpenter refused to replace, Hayes let himself be fired at the end of August 1917, having saved $200.

With that much money, Hayes made it the rest of the way out to the coast to bounce around fruitlessly looking for safer work in Portland, Astoria, San Francisco, Eureka, Riverton, and San Francisco again. He finally landed a pretty good job outside San Jose at the construction site for a massive water reservoir. They needed a man to follow along tidying up after crews cleared the forest, setting massive slash piles afire. Working entirely by hand, Hayes pushed together hot logs in the smoky remains of hot fires. The food was good and he got plenty of fresh air.

When the reservoir job played out in January 1918, Hayes looked in San Diego, Los Angeles, and Aberdeen before sacrificing himself back to the air hammer in North Bend. Now that the US fought in the war on the side of the Allies, the shipyard had tripled in size and hopped with activity. The turnabout in war allegiance could not have been more striking: suddenly all the Finns, Swedes, Irish, and German immigrants lauding the Kaiser a year previously were "yelling their heads off for the French and British whom they formerly despised."

In March 1918 a second letter arrived from James Evans, the mining engineer directing Mr. Hayes Perkins to apply with the Guggenheim diamond mines on the Kasai River near the Angola border with the Congo. No ray of hope could have been more welcome; Hayes sent an immediate reply. About this same time Hayes received another letter, less of a ray of hope, from his sister Virginia. Likely Hayes did not reply; Virginia informed him she had enlisted in the Red Cross, and "she intimates that I am a slacker" for not following her.

Sydney H. Ball, head engineer of Guggenheim's, wrote asking for Hayes' references toward the end of March. Hayes mailed his references and decided to quit the shipyard on April 5, 1918, independently of any reply from Ball. The super-patriot workmen at the shipyard had organized a rally for April 6 at which every man would promise to stay on until the war had finished. Any refuseniks would have their names "inscribed on a yellow roll." For all Hayes cared they could put his name at the top of their list, because, unlike them: "I am not that keen on robbing my country for personal gain." But he quit instead.

Maybe the war fever would be cooler in California. To escape Oregon yet again, Hayes paid train fare south to San Francisco. After working a day sweeping for the Southern Pacific Building on Market Street, he continued on to a job in Crockett, California, north of San Francisco at a sugar mill. At least the small salary included room and board: "It is not a pleasant place but I will stick until this mining affair is settled."

The work in Crockett dragged Hayes near desperation: "The past few years have been so toilsome I almost despair of ever rising to something better." Only a "kindly" group of illiterate Italian men on the "'Bull gang'" at the sugar mill eased his desolation. A fair boss, square with his men, threw Hayes all the overtime he wanted. A vague letter arrived from James Ball, the Guggenheim man, telling Hayes to hold on, a few details to resolve and he'd be called to Africa. While holding on, Hayes paid for some unavoidable dentistry – after making sure he had a $90 bankroll, enough for rail fare to New York should Ball give the word.

Just when his teeth and his money were all in order, calamity struck: pickpocketed! The whole $90. Undoubtedly "some chap" in the jam entering the dining hall: "I felt myself especially jostled at the door." Furthermore, Hayes learned he was not, in fact, back to zero dollars – he was in debt! The Red Cross assessed every man at the mill $5 for the injured soldiers, without the worker's consent. Such low dealings: "They know I have lost all my money, yet put me down for five dollars." And now?! came the telegram from Ball: Come to New York soonest. Immediate departure for Africa.

How? Hayes couldn't even afford to reply to Ball's telegram. He located a couple of stamps at the bottom of his satchel and sent a letter to Ball at Guggenheim's, detailing his plight, promising he'd be on the first train to New York as soon as he made fare. With his long streak of bad luck, Hayes assumed Ball would read only that his prospective recruit had been on a drunk. Surely the offer would be withdrawn.

Chastising himself, "It is folly to fret," Hayes sent his sister Pearl (not his sister Virginia who had accused him of shirking), a quick beg for $30, then went to work like a madman. The Italians all pulled for him, the boss threw any extra work his way: twelve-hour days, worked one after the other, with the blessings and encouragement of even the dour master mechanic.

Fret crept back into Hayes' diary on May 26, 1918, after another theft: "Some lobster pinched my pants off the line where they were drying." He must have had two pairs; he worked twelve hours that day too: "I'm piling up the filthy lucre rapidly against hearing from Ball, hoping, praying all will be well."

On May 27, Ball sent a telegram instructing Hayes to wire Guggenheim's for money. He replied to Ball asking for a $50 advance; with the $60 he had coming for the last fevered week's work, he could cover the fare: "All may be well yet."

(Hayes didn't mention receiving or repaying any money from Pearl.)

Hayes wrote his diary entry on May 29, 1918, from the seat of a train pulling through Nevada. Ball had wired the $50 and Hayes "hopped it" as soon as he could cash out of the sugar mill. His Italian boss had done him one last favor: "pinned a tag on me representing me as having paid up the Red Cross." The tag passed muster in the mill office, saving Hayes a precious $5: "The stool pigeon in the office never looked it up."

Travel by train was the fastest way across the US: over the Mississippi, Dearborn Station, Chicago, Akron, Youngstown, Binghamton, and on into New York City, arriving on June 3, 1918. When he finally shook hands with Ball, the engineer advanced Hayes an extra $125, grinning when told the full story of the pickpocket and the loss of the second pair of pants. In the short time before departure, Hayes needed a physical exam, typhoid injections, and, for the first time in his travels, a passport – newly required by the US government since August of 1918. Ball's $125 would go toward gathering a proper outfit for African diamond mining.

In three comparatively calm weeks spent in New York before departure, Hayes visited with cousin Lydia Perkins. Then, caught a ball game by himself at the Polo Grounds where Walter Johnson warmed up but did not pitch. He had to dodge all the super-patriots. Emmeline Pankhurst acting the patriot surprised him; she was in jail being force-fed when Hayes had seen her in 1906 in London, advocating women's suffrage.

Wondering, yet again, why anyone would choose to live in New York, Hayes escaped the city on June 23, 1918, on the "Compagnie Generale Transatlantique's vapeur *Niagara*." Submarines still posed a threat in the Atlantic, especially to the *Niagara* packed full with soldiers. The nation's foulest city, jostling soldiers on deck, the privations of the previous three years—all but the submarines faded to trivialities as Hayes filled once again with the joy of returning to Africa. Surely all his hopes and dreams of the continent would be fulfilled mining diamonds for Guggenheim's.

8. Forminiere Diamond Mine, Kasai, Congo, 1918-1920

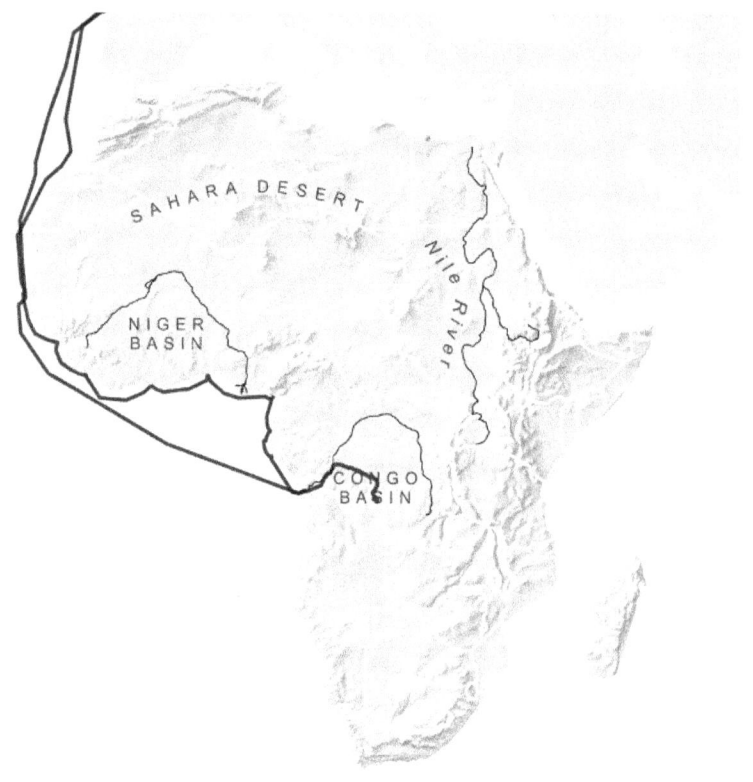

Americans working for the joint American/Belgian mining company, the Société International Forestiére et Mininiére du Congo, referred to their employer as the Forminiere. Forminiere mining engineers traveled first class. Ordinarily Hayes would have traveled third class, but in 1918 the French steamer *Niagara* left New York tightly packed with American, Polish and Czech troops "like sardines in a can"

outward bound to reinforce French battalions in the ferocious battles of late 1918. So many troops crowded aboard the *Niagara* not all could come on deck at the same time. Sagging hammocks held seasick sailors breathing increasingly fetid air below deck. To escape that enlisted man's horror, Hayes could put up with the officers in first class strutting around "to put Hannibal, Caesar, and Napoleon to shame."

At the mouth of the River Gironde approaching Bordeaux, wreckage similar to the ruined ships Hayes had seen in New York harbor testified to the real danger through which they had sailed safely. The *Niagara* steamed into port at Bordeaux on July 6, 1918, with all passengers safe, though one war-weary fellow nearly got himself thrown overboard by an enraged mob. The man had been accused of spying, "agitating" against the war among the Czech soldiers below decks. "The women on board were the epitome of rancor and malignity," but calmer hands among the crew sent the agitator safely along to the brig.

The chaotic throng of refugees from Paris that met the *Niagara* dockside could not obscure the unmistakably American dynamism at Bordeaux. Across the river at Bassens, the American Expeditionary Forces had built six miles of docks now teeming with activity. One soldier, from among the 200,000 American troops camped just outside the city, boasted to Hayes that his army had built twin rails to Paris that would speed troops and munitions to the front. All 200,000 of these proud, green soldiers would be boarding the trains as soon as officers could instill the discipline required to enter the trenches of WWI. Even at Bordeaux, Hayes could hear the constant roar of cannons: "So rapid and so great volume is the gunfire it merges into a constant roar like that of an angry sea." These young soldiers had seen their comrades return from the trenches gassed, maimed, broken, and dead – and still they went.

Ten days after arriving in Bordeaux, Hayes boarded the Chargeurs Reunis boat, *Afrique*, bound for Matadi (Matari) at the mouth of the River Congo in company with 1,500 Senegalese soldiers invalided out of the war. Courteous French officers at the front had given their African colonial subjects pride of place in the vanguard of infantry charges over the top – into barbed wire and machine guns. Every Senegalese man had some grievous wound, an amputated leg, sometimes two amputated legs.

French mercantile officers, bound for positions at African trading stations, filled first and second-class on the *Afrique*. French coquettes bound for café chantants, French music halls, in Dakar filled third. The wounded Senegalese men lay stacked in the open air on the well-decks fore and aft, shivering in thin clothing under a single blanket each. Blimps soared and planes buzzed overhead, scouring the seas for German submarines sure to be lurking off the mouth of the Gironde.

Bouncing down West Africa and the coast of the Gulf of Guinea thrilled Hayes as much in 1918 as it had in 1906. He still thought the Cape Verde islands misnamed, "for most of the year they are sere and brown." At Dakar most of the crippled soldiers and all the coquettes departed the *Afrique*. At Konakry the French had bridged the channel, bringing rail service into the town. Monrovia remained dilapidated, though of some interest to the war: Liberia had been forced to enter on the side of the Allies to secure two great wireless towers – which a German submarine promptly destroyed. At Grand Bassam the magnificent boatmen still ferried cargo and passengers across a pounding surf, occasionally capsizing, always singing. At Lome, a tin miner named Winsor offered Hayes more than the Forminiere paid if Hayes would depart with him into what had previously been German Togoland, now divided between French and British interests. No, Hayes told Winsor, his contract with the Forminiere bound him. At Koutonou the *Afrique* greeted her sister ship, the *Europe*, outward bound to France carrying newly conscripted colonial recruits toward the trenches. At Libreville on the north shore of the River Gabon, heat and mosquitoes made this beautiful beach among the least healthy for the European officers forced in and out on rotating three-year tours. At Cap Lopez, the *Afrique* unloaded more of its principal trade cargo: booze, "trade gin and rum for the natives, whiskies, wines, all manner of European beverages for the whites." At Lonaga the French planned to run a road to Brazzaville and build a proper harbor behind breakwaters.

On August 15, 1918, bathing aboard the *Afrique* while still out of sight of land, Hayes raised his bucket from the sea expecting salt water but splashed his face with fresh water instead. It could only be discharge from the mouth of the river Congo, not yet diluted to salt: "So large is the volume of the river its influence is felt for 125 miles at sea, and the ocean is colored by the river." By midday the *Afrique* anchored off Banana, a tiny post on a sand bar, on the north side of the entrance to the river. After those aboard cleared medical and customs regulations, the steamer continued, up a river stretching 10 miles wide in places, dotted everywhere with luxurious islands, puffing toward Boma, capital of the Belgian Congo, thirty miles upriver from Banana.

By the evening of August 15, 1918, the *Afrique* had reached Matadi, 90 miles upstream from Banana, head of steamer navigation on the Congo. Wild cataracts crashing through steep canyons blocked any further river transport for 270 miles between Matadi and Stanley Pool (Pool Malebo). The roar from Chaudron D'enfer, a great whirlpool just below Matadi where the river fought a massive mountain of rock, rattled the window of the small room Hayes secured for the night.

As the narrow gauge train (Hayes says 80cm) puffed dizzily up the M'pozo River gorge, in and out of the valleys of the Crystal Mountains, Hayes chatted with a representative of Lever Brothers, "the famous soap people who have large interests all along the main Congo." His seatmate appeared to Hayes a man of culture and education, a doctor expert in sleeping sickness, but also a maudlin fellow who shook in the first stages of delirium tremens.

Arriving at Thysville (Mbanza Ngungu) at the summit of the Crystal Range, Hayes happily left the semi-lucid doctor to find his own hotel. The Forminiere had arranged a room for Hayes at the A.B.C. hotel at Thysville. Better accommodations, he hoped, than lunch the company had arranged the previous day at Matadi. He was still retching violently from the ptomaine poisoning.

After a painful night at Thysville and a queasy day spent chugging past bamboo and pineapple groves on the train, Hayes collapsed into another A.B.C. hotel room in Kinshasa.

Kinshasa had been built some 6 kilometers above Léopoldville, the town at the western edge of Stanley Pool, established and named by Henry Morton Stanley. Léopoldville still had a shipyard, docks, and shipping offices, but the old town had been located too close to the first rapid below Stanley Pool. Just before Hayes arrived at Kinshasa, two steamers whose machinery had been unable to overcome swift currents near the Léopoldville docks had been swept into the Kintambo cataract with no survivors.

The steamer *Mfumu Ntangu* (Sun Chief) wallowed away from shore at Kinshasa puffing across Stanley Pool, a barge lashed alongside, heavily laden with freight. Native women sat atop the barge cargo, some of the new arrivals, a "comely" lot, sent forcibly back upriver by Belgian authorities. The flushed countenance of the *Mfumu Ntanga's* skipper betrayed him a drunkard, what Hayes thought of as "a typical river captain."

Above Kinshasa, the *Mfumu Ntangu* entered a section of river called the chenal by both the Belgians, to the south, and the French, to the north. High hills rose 500 to 1000 feet above steep canyons falling sheer to the river with little level ground.

Hayes had ready evidence that the two banks of the river belonged to different countries. For one thing, the south side had been nearly deforested to fuel the much larger fleet of

Belgian steamers. But more deeply revelatory, Hayes noted the difference in population density. Almost all the people Hayes saw along the chenal lived on the north, the French, bank of the river: "This speaks for itself which country treats its subject peoples best. Both conscript the young men as soldiers, both have the same loose attitude toward the women, but there is not the flogging, the forced labor in vogue among the French that makes the Belgians notorious." Hayes described the north bank of the River Congo as a 2,500 mile "welcome sanctuary" for "oppressed natives" on the Belgian side. No doubt Hayes steamed upriver on the *Mfumu Ntangu* with some trepidation; he knew he had hired on to a job on the Belgian side of the river.

The River Kasai entered the River Congo at Kwamouth, "a tiny sleepy village where steamers land for no purpose at all." Here the Kasai ran narrow, only about a third of a mile wide, but very deep, with waters colored dark from rotting vegetation. The two rivers refused to mingle for miles downstream of the confluence; only the color separation, chalky Congo fighting the tea-stained Kasai, marked the entry of the Kasai into the Congo. The main Congo River carried so much water, the Kasai, a river draining more than 340,000 square miles, appeared to increase the volume of the Congo not at all. Continuing to the left up the Congo would have taken Hayes back toward the Heart of Africa Mission. Instead, the *Mfumu Ntangu* turned right, up the Kasai River, toward the Forminiere diamond mines.

Next, in this land of many great rivers, the Kwango River entered the Kasai River. Small steamers plying the river out of the "pretty post" of red brick at Dima worked up the Kwango and Kwilu rivers bringing palm nuts, rubber, casks of palm oil, and a fair bit of ivory from the south, headed toward Kinshasa.

Hayes laid over two days at Dima, end of the line for the *Mfumu Ntangu*, before he departed aboard the river steamer *Madeline* on Sept. 1, 1918. No meal on the *Madeline* differed from any other for the American engineer: "boiled buffalo meat, sour bread, and sweet potatoes." The Belgians aboard had a much more varied diet consisting, as far as Hayes could see, almost exclusively of intoxicants: "Unfortunately for me I am an abstainer, so starve."

Finally the *Madeline* pulled ashore at Djoko Punda just below Wissman Falls, head of steamer navigation on the Kasai. Here a man named Wilson, a "fat Sierra Leone Negro" reasonably well educated, especially in "words seldom used in common conversation," promised Hayes to provide porters. To pass the time waiting for his carriers, Hayes called in at a recently established Mennonite mission. Then he took a hike down to Wissman Falls, really just rapids, he thought, festooned with fish traps by the "ever-hungry natives."

A miracle: Wilson came through with the porters almost immediately. When Hayes wrote in his diary on September 10, 1918, he had already been on safari for two days, walking with goods and men along the course of the Kasai River. On the third day out from Djoko Punda, he twisted an ankle, resulting in a bad sprain. His men offered to carry him by tepoy, a seat on stout poles resting on the shoulders of two or more men, as they did for many Europeans – injured or not. Hayes mostly refused: "It seems a disgrace for a man to ride a chair carried by other men as long as he is able to walk." However, when passing through villages his carriers insisted Hayes ride: they would be disgraced if seen walking with an empty chair alongside a limping musungu.

After three weeks, and nearly 600 miles by riverboat and safari since departing Kinshasa, Hayes arrived at the headquarters of the Forminiere at Tshikapa, some forty miles north of the Angolan border. The post housed "three white women and a half dozen white men." Two Americans, Oliver and Pattison, directed affairs for a vast territory covering, Hayes guessed, as much as 200,000 square miles. Hayes described Oliver and Pattison as cynics, who saw good in nothing and believed every man a rascal until dead. The two had adopted Belgian management style. Native laborers failing to trot toward morning lineup got a touch of the Kiboko, the hippo hide whip. "This does not please me for it is inhuman." Nevertheless, Hayes admired the cleanliness of an alert and efficient post; even the large manioc plantation, the staple for the hundreds of African laborers, appeared well tended.

At a dinner hosted by Mrs. Oliver, Mr. Oliver relaxed his despotic African overseer persona slightly when hearing that Hayes hailed originally from Coquille, Oregon. Oliver's family ranched no more than a hundred miles from Coquille near Roseburg. "He knows many men whom I have been with about the world, but no real wanderer is otherwise in this."

After a week at Tshikapa, Oliver and Pattison sent Hayes forward to the fully operational Mpeso mine, in the bush along an old riverbed of the Longatshimo River, overseen by a Belgian named Gervisse. Hayes planned to stay for only a few days at Mpeso to learn something of the diamond mining practices of the Forminiere and a bit of Kituba, the local language, before pushing further on to his own prospecting site.

Mpeso had a rich diamond deposit. In September of 1918 its pits were more than 25 feet deep, mainly an overburden of soil above a gravel, diamond-bearing layer. Most of the 350 impressed workmen Gervisse commanded spent whole days removing overburden, baskets, balanced on their heads, leaking mud the length of their naked bodies. Shovelmen, with slightly higher social standing than basket-carriers, carefully scooped gravel from where the diamonds collected at bedrock. Gravel runners pushed small cars of gravel to a washing plant to be picked by meticulous eyes and hands. "Capitas," burly African men under the direct supervision of Gervisse, held the highest positions in the labor hierarchy at the pit. Capitas carried kibokos, the hippo-hide whips. Any dawdling workman stepped livelier after a quick touch from a kiboko. Gervisse, himself "an image of fury where the natives are concerned," screamed and slashed with his own hippo hide whip to set the proper example for his capitas: "It is bedlam during the long days, for he is trying for a record surpassing that of every man on the field."

On Sunday, September 22, 1918, Hayes made the mistake of attending a "house party" at an exploration near the Mpeso mine run by a Belgian named Deprez. Hayes listed, by name, the attendees: two government officers at the Kalamba post, four Belgian Forminiere men, including Gervisse, and five Americans also with the Forminiere. Horrified, Hayes managed to stay for the early portion of the party during which, "Deprez, a powerful Belgian peasant, drank them all under the table and boasted of his prowess." But later, when "came on the native women," Hayes alone excused himself, begging duties at Mpeso. What kind of party had that been? "No good books, no interesting conversation, nothing but sex and whiskey."

According to Forminiere guidelines, native workmen should have worked five eight-hour days per week, a half-day on Saturdays, and Sundays not at all. But what were guidelines to Gervisse when the Mpeso mine could set a new record? At morning muster, Gervisse established daily goals impossible to complete in under ten or eleven hours. The men usually ended up working Sundays as well. By midmorning, the Mpeso pit sweltered under an equatorial sun superheating the workmen. Late every afternoon, pounding thunderstorms flooded the pit, drenching naked, sweating men with chill rain. At day's end, whipped men, cramped and tired, dragged themselves to their village nearby, often collapsing, too sick and exhausted to eat.

Capitas and diamond pickers received top pay: 7.50 francs per month with a food allowance of one franc weekly. Less skilled positions paid less and got only half a franc weekly for food. With a full franc a workman could buy enough food for five days – after walking ten to twenty miles – if any could be found at all. Hayes compared the exhausted workmen at Mpeso to horses he had seen abused at jobs around the world;

at the end of a long work week, hungry men "only [kept] to the collar" with the encouragement of the kiboko.

On September 25, 1918, Hayes recorded the ghastliest acts of violence he ever witnessed directly. Twenty men turned up for sick call that morning. Gervisse, an assistant named Stassen, and five sturdy capitas met them with whips. Hayes gave an excruciatingly precise account of how each man received his 20 lashes, some resisted and got 30, some cried, some prayed. Peals of laughter rang from Gervisse and Stassen as capitas dragged the last man from a blood-soaked pen.

Later, writing in his diary, Hayes said he should hate God for allowing such evil to exist. In the immediate aftermath of the whippings, he stumbled off into the bush to vomit.

So, he prayed and he vomited, but why did he stay in Africa, on this job, when he had just witnessed the horrors in which he would be complicit? Hayes does not answer explicitly, but his actions over the next two years demonstrate what he might have been thinking. Hayes believed he knew how to work better than any other man. If he could just get out into the bush on his own, he could demonstrate to the Belgians that a just overseer, who treated the workmen fairly and humanely, could achieve far greater production. Surely, in their own economic interest, the Belgians would follow his lead. How naïve. A workman named Killindini would eventually speak so directly to Hayes that the idealistic adventurer had no choice but to see the hubris in thinking one man could reform an international system of exploitation and murder simply by setting a good example. But for now the optimistic adventurer vomited, prayed, and carried on.

Four days after the hideous whipping of sick men, Hayes wrote that he was "straining every nerve to get a camp of my own set up and get out of Mpeso." He'd moved into an abandoned hut in a nearby native village, empty after Belgian authorities had removed every able-bodied inhabitant at gunpoint to forced labor on the roads. Even away from

Forminiere headquarters, bunked at the empty village, Hayes could think only of Gervisse's cruelty.

Where they could, when they could, many of the native men and women not yet forced into labor resisted Belgian plunder. From the very beginning Hayes admired their courageous rebellions large and small. In Lubembe tribal country, Gervisse's assistant, Stassen, had casually killed a goat when its bleating interrupted his sleep, then offered to "purchase" the carcass at an arbitrary price. Lubembe men with spears chased Stassen back to Mpeso in the dead of night. Hayes thought it was "too bad they didn't kill him." Gervisse redressed this insult to his right-hand man by asking Belgian officials at Kalama to requisition goats for the Forminiere post. Angry villagers, forced to comply, ran the goats so hard all the way to Mpeso, two fell over dead from exhaustion.

Toward the end of the first week of October 1918, Hayes thankfully departed Mpeso to an exploration on a high hill overlooking the valley of the Lubembe River where he could do things his own way. All went well from the very beginning: "For some reason the blacks have taken a fancy to me, and men are pouring in here as fast as I can take them on." Could that really have been surprising to Hayes? Men impelled to work in chains by the Belgian military or under the kiboko for the Forminiere would escape to a worksite with a humane overseer? Hayes immediately began hiding fugitives from other Forminiere camps in the tall grass whenever capitas arrived demanding their return.

On October 8, 1918, the rains, daily this time of year, came in the morning. The men at Hayes' camp, many recovering from injuries inflicted at other sites, huddled comfortably in their huts, warm in front of fires. A little news from the Great War in Europe leaked even as far as Hayes' hill overlooking the Lubembe River. The Allies seemed to have the upper hand. Very good, but his recent experiences with Belgians made it impossible for Hayes to stomach references in the accounts he read in scraps of newspapers describing them as, "'Our gallant allies.'" The Belgians! Gallant? "As far as I am concerned the Germans may take them over and give them a taste of the same medicine they are giving these charges of theirs in Africa."

In the floodplain of the Lubembe River, running 300 meters wide at the foot of the hill below Hayes' camp, his workmen had to wade to their waists setting up three empire drills. No digging a pit yet; Hayes and his men were prospecting. Test holes must be drilled down through the overburden to bring up some of the gravel at bedrock for examination. The many hippos that waded about these water-soaked flats pushed postholes into which men constantly stumbled. Worse, large leeches attached to the men's legs apparently injecting "some pain deadening fluid before they slit the skin, for the wounds bleed freely after the leech is removed."

Sunday October 13, 1918, every man at Hayes' camp rested. Work ended for the weekend on Saturday afternoon in compliance with Forminiere written policy. Hayes' workmen had successfully gathered "an abundance of food" by returning to their own villages; this within five miles of Mpeso "where Gervisse's crew is famine stricken." With the war in Europe, Hayes had little of his customary food supply, no "flour, sugar, butter or just about everything else edible." He subsisted on strange-looking fish from the traps his men set in the sloughs about the river and an occasional chicken one or another of the workers would sell him.

In Mpeso, Gervisse had remarked that Hayes was the first man ever to arrive in the Congo already speaking the language. In fact, Hayes arrived at Tshikapa speaking Bangala, not the language of this region, but one understood by many of the African workers. Hayes writes that he worked night and day learning Kituba, a separate language, not so different from Bangala. His men repeated Kituba phrases patiently as he

151

struggled with correct pronunciations and scribbled into his journal for study by lantern light.

On October 30, 1918, Hayes began his diary entry with a description of the well-organized crew under his direction. These men "with every incentive to work" sang at their tasks. His only complaint: the men liked their palm wine fermented a day or two – to give it a stronger kick. The cider Hayes drank the same day his man Mompasa drew it from the tree tasted sweet and refreshing. But, a day or two later, the wine became "intoxicating to a high degree." Hayes tired of constantly stepping in to separate brawling knots of workmen drunk on palm wine.

After a single paragraph describing his own well-ordered camp, Hayes wrote three much longer paragraphs relating, in close detail, the horror he witnessed on returning to Gervisse's pit: "Like some gruesome tale out of the Dark Ages, and hell did not seem far away." Hayes sat for an hour overlooking the Mpeso mine watching as Gervisse ineffectually tried, with a club, to regulate the violent, chaotic scene in the mud below.

Sitting with his legs dangling over the edge of Gervisse's Mpeso pit, Hayes couldn't help but reflect on the reason for all this violence: diamonds, no more than trinkets to adorn cuffs and necklines back home in civilized Europe. If Hayes protested Gervisse's methods directly to the Belgian overseer's face, he made no record of it in his diary. He may, though, have said something. The note Hayes received from Gervisse on November 1, 1918, two days after returning to his own camp, drips both charm and self-justifying triumph:

> Dear Mr. Perkins:
> Thanks for the money. I am sending you bananas and paipais. My production this month is a little over 8,200 carats. Record!
>
> Yours Very Truly,
> (signed) A. Gervisse.

Word came through Thieman, commandant at the Belgian post, that Bulgaria, defeated, had withdrawn from the war. Austria too would surely crumble soon.

Hayes did not write in his diary again until the middle of December 1918. It had been a busy time "and with all, happy with everything but the Belgians." He got on increasingly well with his work crew, "for I like them and they like me." As more and more men streamed to Hayes away from the whips and clubs at other sites, some of the Belgians began to retaliate. One in particular, Deprez, drinking champion of the house parties, snatched Hayes' Tshikapa runner, Katende Kabondo, and whipped him so severely the man had to crawl twelve miles to return to Hayes' camp. Hayes registered a complaint, probably futile, with Oliver, the top Forminiere man back in Tshikapa.

The worldwide influenza pandemic of 1918-19 came late to the Congo. Originally spreading in the trenches in France, the contagion came to be called the Spanish Flu, probably because Spain, neutral in the war and with a relatively free press, first reported on it. In a two-year period, this N1HI virus would infect about a third of the world's population, killing an estimated 20 million people.

Hayes first mentioned influenza in late January 1919. The virus had not yet reached Forminiere exploitations along the Kasai, but Hayes wrote that the contagion bore down on them, sweeping across the African continent, felling whole villages. Gervisse, now half-blind from an unrecorded cause, had called Hayes to Mpeso. Gervisse needed an honest man to count the diamonds he could no longer see.

While Hayes was at Mpeso, orders arrived from Oliver at Forminiere headquarters relieving Gervisse and reassigning Hayes. A Scot named Bews would be arriving to take over the Mpeso pit from Gervisse. Hayes would depart immediately with Thiemann of the Belgian military to impose quarantine on a fifty-mile stretch of the Kasai River. The company man and the government man would impound every canoe they could find in an attempt to stop influenza crossing the river.

Any attempt at quarantine probably would have been ineffectual against the Spanish Flu, but the Belgian officers seemed to mock any real concern: "They delight in making a holy show of my efforts to make the quarantine effective." On one Sunday off, Thiemann and Le Roi, accompanied by their "gaudy harems," crossed the river for the regularly scheduled house party with Deprez.

With all the Belgian shenanigans and the extra work impounding canoes, diamond prospecting might understandably have fallen off – but not at Hayes' camp. In the month before Hayes himself contracted the flu, his drilling crew established a new drilling record: 1,200 meters, surpassing Moody, previous crack driller, by 500 meters. Just a slight modification to the drills: Hayes replaced the heavy drive chains with light cables. The drills were six-inch pipes threaded together as they were driven into the mud and through the gravel layer. The drills must have been hand driven; Hayes mentions no other power source. Every test hole his men sank here turned up a few diamonds but not enough to meet the quarter carat per cubic meter required for a payable exploitation.

Eventually though, the contagion got the upper hand. C.H. Davis, an American employee of the Forminiere, nearly died of influenza March 2, 1919. On March 6, 1919, a soldier died at Kalamba. A day later, several of Hayes' men were down and influenza had crossed the river. Acting quickly, Hayes impressed every able-bodied workman to secure his drilling equipment in a shelter they'd erected for just this contingency. By noon only half-a-dozen of his men remained standing. Hayes, not yet sick, would not let them lie on the ground, forcing sick men onto rough cots where he could tend to them as possible: "Matters look bad in my camp, but as Madika the sentry says, 'Bwala Na Nzambe' - It's God's affair – and we will have to let it go at that."

No one died at his camp until Hayes himself took ill on March 15, 1919. Feverish men, left to follow their own instincts, lay on the cool, damp ground, took chill and died. Others ran off sick into the bush. From his cot Hayes ordered those men still standing to dig graves. The men considered it none of their affair to bury a dead fellow – unless well paid. So Hayes paid them well. He could do no more: "My right lung feels as if boiling water had been poured on it, and a high, steady fever rages."

Hayes lay fully ten days on "the brink of the dark river," passing in and out of consciousness. He writes that he would have surrendered to death but for the responsibility to his men. Emerging briefly from the fog of delirium, he remembered hearing the sounds of his cook dying in horrible pain under the twin influences of influenza and syphilis. In the quiet, after hours? days? of listening to the man scream, Hayes had to crawl from his own sick bed to supervise the cook's burial. His few able men refused to handle this body riddled with great holes, no matter the pay offered. Unable to stand, from his knees Hayes directed the men to roll the body onto a makeshift stretcher using sticks. Madika "evidently a Catholic convert sometime in his life" sprinkled a little sand and mumbled a few words over a shallow grave. Hayes gave Madika, and the others, a full day's pay and handed each a bar of soap with instructions to wash thoroughly, then collapsed back onto his cot to lay semi-conscious for several more days.

By April 7, 1919, Hayes had the drills going again despite lingering pain in his lungs. News of the end of WWI had arrived some days earlier, causing something of a shakeup at the Forminiere. Many company men would be returning to Europe with the cessation of fighting. Germany, the last of the Central Powers to capitulate, had signed an Armistice on November 11, 1918, but a formal state of war persisted for seven months following the cessation of fighting. Now that Europe looked calm enough for homecoming, many of the men would go. Deprez planned a "big blowout" for the fellows leaving the Congo. Hayes felt no slight at not receiving an invitation; Deprez knew him by now.

With the Belgian exodus, Hayes got promoted to headman of an established mine. Van Deventer, the previous overseer, had been skipping around, sinking holes looking for the richest deposits, but had not successfully increased diamond production. Barely 150 starving men, weak with lingering flu, stumbled about a rundown camp on Ngombe Creek. Hayes would have to rebuild their huts, resurrect their plantation, and establish a regular mining plan.

A slaughtered ox doesn't go far to feed 150 men, but it was a start. The crew managed 250 carats their first week under Hayes' direction. The second week was a little better, 342 carats. Men looking for work poured into Hayes' camp so fast he couldn't keep ahead of the house building. All the best grass had burned in the annual fires accompanying the dry season, but he was making do. The men complained to be working when so much meat lay about for the taking in the wake of the fires: "Snakes, lizards, insects, everything that walks, flies, crawls or swims is meat in Africa." Hayes promised they would have Sundays off to gather meat.

After three weeks at the Ngombe mine, Hayes had directed the planting of "many hectares" of manioc. Small boys, eager for work but too small for diamond mining, kept the manioc rows tidy with hoes. Ever more men streamed into Hayes' camp ahead of the floggings elsewhere, but none came from Gervisse's former camp. The new man, Bews, put down the kiboko and now had men streaming into Mpeso as well. As for the production record Gervisse bought with so much blood? Bews shattered that record his first month at Mpeso and "kept his men's goodwill doing it."

Hayes' production for the month of May totaled 1,617 carats, double Van Deventer's mark. But something wasn't right. Oliver, Forminiere's Congo headman, was "handing out a lot of soft soap, urging me to increase the crew as much as possible." The increase posed no difficulty as men poured in, with more than 300 already "broken" to the work, but Oliver could not be trusted. He was "one of these men who has practiced double dealing so long it stands out in every action he makes. He would sell his own soul if it advance his worldly interests."

A week later, June 8, 1918, Hayes's crew had grown to 370 men and he now understood Oliver's "pats on the back and desire for the camp to be set in best condition." Oliver could see the excellent work Hayes had done: ditches deepened so they no longer ruptured, plantation in steady production, and fine houses built for the men. As a reward, Oliver announced Hayes would be transferred to a new camp, where the excellent American workman could do it all again.

Oliver said a fellow named McMillan would come shortly to replace Hayes at Ngombe Creek. Hayes knew that name; he'd run into the fellow on the steamer out from Kinshasa. In such a vast and small world, McMillan, son of the headman at Hammond's Mill in Eureka, California, turned up. McMillan had gone out to fetch his "white wife" and now Oliver needed a soft spot for the McMillans. So, Hayes found himself reassigned to prospecting along Kopopo Creek. Hayes resented Forminiere deference to the son of a rich man, even if Hayes did, in fact, prefer prospecting to running an established mine.

At Kopopo Creek, farther up the Longatshimo River, with a shallower overburden, empire drills were not necessary for sampling. Instead, Hayes had 10-meter long trenches dug to bedrock diagonally across the creek: "Diamonds have a specific gravity of 5.5 while the country rock runs about 2.66." The creek washed diamonds into the trenches along with "numerous tourmalines, [and] the rubies and zircons that number in the millions, but are too small to be of value." Gravel scooped out of the trenches, shaken through screens and jigs, was picked by sharp-eyed natives who seldom missed a diamond.

After barely a month at Kopopo, Hayes thought he had come to understand Oliver's machinations. Other Forminiere field engineers, whether from Belgium or the US, couldn't get work crews together at any new site; the workmen all flocked toward Hayes. All right. Oliver could work with that kind of man. This talented American would be used to establish camps. A specialist. Once he had a site up and running smoothly, full of men, Oliver would bring in what Hayes called "one of these bullies" with a heavier hand and send Perkins further into the wild. Hayes' American assistant at Kopopo, ignorant and insolent, had not yet revealed himself to be a bully, but he was immediately at hand. Oliver assigned Kirk to take over at Kopopo and sent Hayes along to a new site up the Lubembe River.

If Oliver wanted that game, Hayes knew how to play. Hayes could do nothing about who succeeded him but he could find a workaround to keep experienced laborers. In order to establish new camps with an efficient core of trained workers, with a wink, Hayes fired all his best men at Kopopo, making sure they knew the way to the Lubembe site. Some of these men arrived singing beneath loads almost before Hayes got there. Other men arrived not long after, coming from the mine at Ngombe Creek.

The new Lubembe River site, "far removed from other whites," had something of a reputation. This was the region from which natives with spears had chased off the goat-killer, Stassen. Oliver sent Hayes into the area with instructions to flee if the locals became too fierce.

In his first few days up the Lubembe, Hayes had a slight "run-in with a witch doctor," but nothing he couldn't manage. For the most part he saw squatting men laughing and chatting around fires, women cooing at babies as mothers do the world over, and well-tended fields of manioc bordered by scarlet creepers amid multicolored flowers along the tall forest border.

At the Ngombe mine, Hayes had employed a very good man, a native carpenter named Mateo with whom he "studied problems out, each giving due respect to the other's ideas." Now Mateo arrived, bringing all his skills, to join Hayes at the Lubembe site. McMillan, who knew nothing of carpentry, had struck Mateo sharply on the temple when the African misunderstood an order, so Mateo walked out.

In this isolated corner of the Congo near the Angola border, Hayes hoped he would be left alone by both missionaries and Belgians. "No European has ever been permitted to stay here before." But, no, Belgian commander Le Roi led 200 askaris and as many carriers pillaging into the immediate vicinity. Heide, "a renegade Norwegian in Belgian service" led a similar force, marching overland from the Longatshimo River to the Tschiumbo River where it met the Lubembe just a few miles above Hayes' exploration.

On July 27, 1919, natives fleeing the coordinated Le Roi and Heide advance downriver gave Hayes firsthand accounts of the campaign: What little material wealth any village had, goats, fowl, manioc, was eaten or carried off, "swept clean as if locusts had passed by." Young men of the villages were impressed as carriers – humping their own stolen goods. The most "comely women" were taken for Le Roi's harem, other women distributed among the askaris. Chiefs marched downriver in chains.

Oliver sent Hayes a messenger, J.S. Hoffman, with a second note advising Hayes to flee any uprising Le Roi and Heide might occasion. Hayes told Hoffman that "the only danger I anticipate is from the Belgians not the natives." Oliver's note directed Hayes on two possible courses: yes, run if you have to, but, if not, see to establishing this young fellow Hoffman, straight out of school, in Iowa, at your current digging. Hayes himself should proceed into the bush – further into dangerous, disputed territory – and see if he could set up a new station. Hayes accepted another round of Oliver's game, saying of Hoffman: "It will require a couple of weeks to learn him how to look after a camp."

Despite his grumbling about Oliver "cunningly" sending Hoffman without prior warning, reassignment didn't entirely upset Hayes. In fact, the land Hayes could see across the river, where he would be heading, called to him; it looked populous, more beautiful and fertile than any in the Forminiere concession. The only glitch in the forthcoming adventure was that the many people he saw were Babinge, well known cannibals: "My men are reluctant but will follow me if I go."

By now Hoffman could be trusted to supervise the camp for a day or two while Hayes went to scout the next exploration. Taking a small canoe a few miles up Pumina Creek, a watercourse large enough to be considered a river anywhere else in the world, Hayes found a likely spot, "fired" his best men at Lubembe Creek, and gave them directions up Pumina Creek.

Even using the "firing" strategy that allowed him to start with a trained crew at each new site, Hayes complained that Oliver had no idea the difficulty of establishing a new camp: the skill to find a likely digging, securing clean water for sanitation, recruiting men, building houses, establishing a plantation. In hostile territory! There had been a dispute over a third hippo, one Hoffman shot, on Pumina Creek. Hayes "settled" the confrontation by waving with his Mauser, but not to everyone's satisfaction. One particular chieftain "Chikwanga, does all he can to impede my work."

Chikwanga actually had a deeper dispute with Hayes and the Forminiere. The new site on Pumina Creek interrupted Chikwanga's business as self-proclaimed "Mufumu Na Mai, or King of the Waters." Chikwanga's ferry service prevented, by force, any other canoe traffic for some distance up and down Pumina Creek. Any local person wishing to cross paid a uniform fare: half anything they carried. What for those approaching Chikwanga's ferry empty-handed? Hayes' houseboy knew: "Yo kushikama!" or in English "You sit down!" Hayes casually dethroned the King of the Waters. His Forminiere canoes began ferrying at the base of a waterfall where the river current slowed on entering the largest pool in the area.

Hoffman would get on well at the camp on the Lubembe when Hayes pushed forward to Pumina Creek. The Iowan already had a "slight hold" on the language and seemed to understand Hayes' counsel about indiscriminate flogging. And Hoffman would inherit Hayes' thriving garden: 500 bananas, manioc, hundreds of pineapples and papaya.

By October 16, 1919, Hayes had framed a house for himself and built huts for the men he took with him up Pumina Creek. More than a year into his contract with the Forminiere, in the midst of establishing his fourth or maybe fifth new camp, Hayes began counting the days until the end of his obligation: "Nine months more! It seems a long time to the end of my contract here but it will pass."

It would overstate the passage in Hayes' diary from October 16 to say Hayes expressed fear at Pumina Creek. But he did remark that Oliver may have been right, back in Tshikapa, to insistent Hayes carry the Mauser (as if his rifle hadn't already been of utmost utility). Up until now Hayes had been entirely confident in his methods: "I get on well with the blacks, for I try to give them a square deal and they know it."

But now even his workmen cautioned Hayes to keep the gun rust-free and beside him at all times. Some of these "wild blacks" bluffing bravery would listen to nothing but force, Chikwanga foremost among them. Hayes' men told him The King of the Waters had shot a hole through the helmet of a Belgian named Rettie a few years back. Hayes scoffed, still confident in his "treat them square" approach: "I don't blame any native for doing that. Rettie is one of the worst drivers on the diamond fields."

The crew and camp had been fully installed at Pumina Creek by the middle of November 1919 and Hayes already had the men building a new track deeper into the bush. He anticipated orders from Oliver to move on any day; the trenches dug at Pumina Creek showed a few diamonds but not in payable quantities.

Oliver would soon be leaving the Congo to return to Forminiere headquarters in New York; his successor, Donald Doyle, had already arrived for training. "Some sycophant" sent a petition around to every camp in the southern Congo soliciting funds to purchase Oliver an elephant tusk keepsake. How could Hayes refuse to kick in a few francs? In gratitude, Oliver reciprocated with a bottle of scotch for each donor, more than enough for a lifetime for Hayes.

To Hayes' mind, the Belgians simply failed in colonial technique. How much more they could gain by imposing a well-governed peace? Contented villagers, producing enough food to support themselves and an orderly workforce who could extract long-term mineral wealth, would far exceed the value of this shortsighted rape and pillage.

Far from imposing a well-regulated peace, the Belgians preyed on the peaceful themselves. Hayes predicted the Congolese would rise in concert to throw off the oppressor before long: "I am disgusted with what I see. They have not changed since the days of Leopold." Oh, what a paradise the Congo could be if only colonized properly.

Hayes' peaceful, well-ordered explorations at Pumina Creek came up dry. None of the trenches showed diamonds in quantity to justify an exploitation. Hayes and his crew would soon push further into the bush toward a new site at Lubwa Creek.

In the immediate moment, though, Hayes needed a dentist to attend an ulcerated tooth. A bad tooth could not have been a surprise to Hayes. Scurvy, at twenty, severe enough to loosen all one's teeth, has predictable consequences later in life. Tooth pain or no, torrential rains and raging rivers made the two-hundred-mile trek to the nearest dentist at Luebo impossible. Hayes thought he could tough it out, grimacing, "I'll get by."

Still nursing the tooth four days before Christmas 1919, Hayes stumbled into a native game trap, twisting an ankle. He would, however, allow neither tooth nor ankle to hamper relocation to the new camp at Lubwa Creek. The men had cleared five or six miles of wide path over which all "excess baggage" had been carried in advance. With a trustworthy African man left behind to guard the stores at Pumina Creek, Hayes limped forward to establish the diggings at Lubwa himself. Not a single workday lost. The transition went so smoothly Hayes gave the men both Saturday and Sunday off for the Christmas holiday.

Oliver, soon to depart Africa for New York and "lavish with the soft soap," invited Hayes to celebrate Christmas at Forminiere headquarters in Tshikapa. Hayes begged off: Tshikapa was too far, the party would be too debauched, and the invitation felt disingenuous – why hadn't Oliver invited Hayes the previous Christmas? Hayes did, though, regret missing a chance to get a read on the new man Doyle: "Well, Doyle might be worse than Oliver."

Hayes frequently described African men and women as having a "sixth sense" about anyone moving about in their immediate vicinity. A couple of his workmen foretold the arrival of Donald Doyle when the new head of operations for the Forminiere in the Congo was still a full day out from Lubwa Creek. Forewarned, Hayes hurried to meet his new boss somewhere along the path. As the two sat talking for an hour under the shade of a tree, Hayes formed a favorable first impression. Doyle, a tall, well-formed man with piercing eyes, seemed genuinely concerned for the wellbeing of his employees. An even better indication that Doyle would be "square" came from the workmen. Doyle had earned the Swahili name "'Bwana Mizzuri' which means 'The Good Master.'" The locals, Kituba speakers, had corrupted Doyle's name slightly to "Bwana Musodi, or Lizard Master." A complimentary name even in Kituba, and the African men all seemed to like Doyle. Hayes appreciated a good first impression and the name but withheld final judgment: "I rather liked him, but in the Forminiere it is best to keep one's likes and dislikes in reserve until the likee [sic] is dead."

On the first day of 1920, his ankle had healed but Hayes lay bedridden with the ulcerated tooth and a return of the influenza. Resting, but not so sick he couldn't work – at something. Earlier in the month Hayes had drawn a 16-foot, 1 to 10,000 scale map of a portion of the large Forminiere concession. Now, from his sickbed, he worked on several 1 to 1,000 scale maps, showing the river and his trenches.

By mid-February 1920, Hayes felt well enough for a Sunday jaunt down to visit Bews at a big new exploitation at Tshitundu, at the confluence of the Longatshimo and Kasai Rivers. The way to Tshitundu led past Gervisse's Mpeso pit, now mined out and completely defunct. Hayes swore, though, that he could still hear Gervisse screaming, the whistle of whips striking bleeding backs drifting up from the pit, so quickly overgrown with convolvulus and tall grasses. Memories of Gervisse's cruelty still tested Hayes' faith. According to Hayes' theology, God saw all, so God saw this; yet still it went on. Hayes objected, asking God, "Is there any justice, any mercy, and righteousness in this world?" God remained silent, leaving Hayes to conclude, "It is a beautiful place, but oh, so wicked!"

The good impression Doyle made on Hayes must have been reciprocal. On February 19, 1920, the new head of Forminiere operations sent a message asking Hayes to extend his current term of service, set to expire in August. Doyle offered to install Hayes, replacing Bews, as overseer of the pit at Tshitundu, second largest Forminiere mine. But that offer didn't sweeten the deal for Hayes; if he did extend the contract, he would prefer prospecting work.

After eighteen months on the job, Hayes had become deeply conflicted about continuing in the Congo in any capacity. On the one hand, he wrote, "I am aweary of these continual raids, of the slavery practiced by the Belgians and condoned by the Americans." On the other hand, "this job is the best I have ever had, and I will keep it if I can." Under what changes to his employment could Hayes consider staying? If only he didn't have to continually "break in" new men "and [I] particularly want no Belgian about me."

Sadly, as Hayes well knew, even had he been able to magically blink away the Belgians, colonial raiding and enslavement would have been no less prevalent in this region. African enslavers from Angola to the south worked across the Congo Border abducting young women for sale upriver to the Portuguese: "another of our 'Gallant Allies' [during WWI] who have been assisting us to save the world for Democracy."

Hayes wrote that he had appealed twice to Belgian authorities to intervene with the raiders serving the Portuguese. Preventing raids would cost next to nothing; no more than one White officer and a couple of askaris would be needed to safeguard the area from the marauders. Belgian authorities made no reply. Why would the Belgians care about raiders or African women? Maybe if there had been anything of value to protect, but Le Roi and Heide had already stripped the area bare – for the Belgians. Whatever scraps remained didn't justify any military expenditure.

To bring any peace to the area, Hayes decided he would have to take matters into his own hands. But just as he was dispatching one of his best men, Chilimbesi, a Badjok, to contact the raiders about a face-to-face parley, Chikwanga, self-styled King of the Waters, rose against Hayes.

Hayes had already crippled Chikwanga's ferry business with an order that any person wanting to cross be carried free of charge on either of the Forminiere canoes that had a little extra space. Now, the river had taken Chikwanga's only canoe, swept downstream in a torrent. In order to re-establish his trade, Chikwanga seized both Hayes' canoes.

Hayes wrote what might have been considered a "thrilling account" in an adventure tale of Hayes' time of the running three-day battle between his diamond workers and

Chikwanga's free men. One hundred men ran through "the tropic night," whips whistled, hostages escaped, antique fowling pieces misfired, and Mateo nearly died before old Kasenda rallied Hayes' workmen crying, "'If you are afraid to follow your white man you can't stay here!'" Victorious, Hayes had "an honor guard" deliver Chikwanga to Forminiere headquarters. The Forminiere handed Chikwanga to Belgian authorities who sent him 200-miles distant to Luebo prison.

In the first week of April 1920, Moody, now second in command behind Doyle, ordered Hayes to Tshikapa for reassignment. Lubwa creek wasn't showing enough diamonds to persist there. Moody wanted Hayes, Forminiere's top prospector, to open up a site on Mulundu Creek. The number two man sprinkled his order with flattery, a big show of assurance Hayes could succeed in a location where both Hayes and Moody knew every other engineer previously sent had been either killed or forcibly evicted. Hayes agreed that the diggings at Lubwa Creek showed no promise so, without much reluctance, "fired" his men, packed up the machinery, and left old Kasenda to watch over the abandoned site.

On his way to Mulundu Creek, Hayes had to pass through company headquarters at Tshikapa. Forminiere custom obligated employees, "returned to civilization" after long stints in the bush, to attend a formal dinner with Mr. and Mrs. Doyle. Hayes tried to resist: "I flunked it, hid away, but Doyle dug me out and I went through with it as best as possible in my tattered condition." At a more-than-merely-social dinner, Mr. Doyle pressed Hayes about a contract extension. The Forminiere could offer $50 dollars more per month if Hayes agreed to stay on for six months past the original contract, $75 more a month for a year's commitment - contingent, of course, upon excellent yields.

Hayes knew he could make the yields. In his first 18 months with the Forminiere, he hadn't made the 45% bonus offered for top production because that would have required "driving the blacks at top speed and groveling at the feet of

Bula Matadi." But he had averaged 22.5% bonuses and "even at that I beat the field."

The money on offer certainly got Hayes' attention, but that lucre had to be weighed against an increasing problem. With the war in Europe ended, more and more Belgians arrived with every steamer to staff Forminiere positions in the Congo. It seemed that the Americans – who, granted, could be as bad as Belgians, but weren't usually – would not be returned to Africa from their rotations home. How could Hayes in good conscience continue opening up new territory to have each site staffed with a monstrous Belgian as soon as Hayes had it up and running? "I will never make such good pay again but opening the country for Belgian and Portuguese misrule and pillage would make me quite as bad as themselves." Hayes left without giving Mr. Doyle an answer one way or the other.

After only two weeks on Mulundu Creek, with Hayes still struggling to get another new camp in order, Moody arrived with a young fellow named Clossett in tow. In Moody's mind, Hayes would train Clossett from scratch on how to establish a camp, then Clossett would take the reins prospecting at Mulundu creek. After all, Hayes would surely jump at the irresistible offer Moody now made: an offer/order for Hayes to take over the establishment of a new mine on the Tshikapa River at the richest diamond strike in the entire field.

Hayes had passed by that strike on his way to the Mulundu Creek site. Its current head, an American named Foote, was a lucky prospector but a college-trained engineer. He had no idea how to establish mining operations. Many men idled about as Foote dithered. Much could be accomplished at this rich site. Indeed, the idea of taking over there had been planted in Hayes' head even before Moody came with the formal offer. As Hayes had passed through, Foote had casually confided that he would soon be invalided out of the Congo with a persistent "social disease." Foote offered to "will" Hayes his Black wife and family when Hayes took over his position.

Consequently, when Moody arrived with the big, new job offer, Hayes had already thought through his reply: No to the wife. No to the family. No to Moody. And no to developing the richest diamond strike in the southern Congo. The Forminiere couldn't be more transparent in their machinations. With Hayes in charge, native workers would crowd to the new mine. But Hayes knew for certain that soon after he had the mine up and running smoothly, his 22.5% methods wouldn't cut it. Some Gervisse, or Deprez, or Clossett, or other Belgian would be brought in to ratchet production up to 45% bonus by using the horrific methods evidenced at every previous mine site.

He wouldn't do it.

But … he hadn't firmly decided to quit the Forminiere entirely. The siren of that big bonus for a contract extension still sang. Maybe if he just kept his head down as a simple prospector up Mulundu Creek he could protect his own small cadre of workmen and carry on at work he loved, in a place he loved, at a very high salary. He still, partly at least, deluded himself that he could be judged as a lone actor, separate from the company he worked for, demonstrating morally superior behavior. And maybe, just maybe, he whistled to himself, his extremely productive example would occasion broader reform. Surely a man with the high moral character of Hayes Perkins would not stay on just for the fat paycheck.

After a year-and-a-half in the Congo, in the privacy of his diary, Hayes had begun to root for the native resistance. Twenty miles from the site at Mulundu Creek, a great Badjok war chief, Kilindini, commanded 3,000 men. Hayes knew that Kilindini's men with spears and clubs could not ultimately prevail, pinched between Belgian guns to the north and Portuguese guns to the south, but Kilindini's ferocity held the ground for now. Not long before Hayes came to Kilindini's kingdom, two American engineers, Newport and Decker, had pioneered into this territory. Newport survived; Decker and most of the native crew with him died violently.

As head of the Forminiere in the Congo, Doyle had a two-part strategy for penetrating Kilindini's territory. The long-term strategy: get the Belgian military to pacify the resistance for good. Commander Brassuer already had a small band roaring around Kilindini's fringes. Heide, the Norwegian, formerly co-commander with Le Roi, would move in with force as soon as he'd gathered enough askaris. Hayes wrote: "I wish Kilindini … every success against them."

Doyle's short-term strategy? Assign Hayes Perkins to work the same magic with the savages on the Tshikapa River as he had on the Lubembe. Presumably Hayes wanted the short-term strategy to work; he accepted the job and had no death wish. Willfully suppressing every evidence to the contrary, he kidded himself that success by his peaceful methods might forestall the military option.

The initial diggings at Mulundu Creek showed promise: "diamonds, and there are lots of them." Probably in response to good reports from Hayes' first holes, Moody came round to reiterate the Forminiere offer of a contract extension. Moody claimed that he didn't care one way or the other if Hayes stayed on, but Doyle had authorized Moody to sweeten the offer for Hayes: a $75 bonus for a one-year contract extension and Hayes wouldn't have to supervise a mine to get the bonus; he could stay on prospecting just as he was.

Hayes listened to Moody but wasted no time quarreling with the Forminiere underling; he would speak directly with Doyle. Or, with his mind pretty well settled on leaving, "perhaps with some of the dignitaries in Europe or America."

March 12, 1920, Hayes wrote: "After due reflection on the subject I have decided the Portuguese have the edge on the Belgians for sheer brutality, but that is saying a good deal." Both colonial governments took prisoners for forced labor. Both worked the men in chains at the neck or leg. But the Portuguese lamed their men by beating the sole of one foot.

Who knows, though? The Belgians might catch up. Orders had just come from Brussels to speed up diamond production; the price of diamonds had spiked in postwar Europe. And for what? Hayes knew: "More stones wanted for the beautiful women whose vanity is largely responsible for the condition of these luckless people who have no knowledge of the value of the stones in every creek and river bed in this country."

A number of photographs of the Forminiere mines can be found in a book by Isaac F. Marcosson: *An African Adventure*, Plimpton Press, 1921. Marcosson, just two years older than Hayes and a strongly pro-business, pro-colonialism, financial editor at the *Saturday Evening Post*, had been invited (and Hayes asserted, paid) by the Forminiere to tour South and Central Africa. Marcosson's extensive journey took him up by rail from Cape Town, by tepoy to the Congo River, down the Congo, up the Kasai, and finally back out the Congo. The early pages of *An African Adventure* lionize the Brit Cecil Rhodes, head of operations at the Kimberly diamond mines in South Africa. Later portions similarly celebrate the American Thomas Ryan, head of operations for the Forminiere diamond mines in the Congo. Marcosson's book is dedicated to Ryan "who first beheld the vision of America in the Congo."

Hayes first mentioned Isaac Marcosson on May 19, 1920. A messenger from Tshikapa brought news of the arrival of a gang of fresh Belgian mining engineers to displace more Americans. Marcosson would be accompanying them on assignment to write a series of articles "on the life and methods in vogue in the diamond fields." Moody had intimated, some weeks previously, that Hayes might be assigned to guide Marcosson about the field. Hayes relished such an opportunity: "If he does get me as guide, he will learn a lot of things few men would tell or show him."

Evidently tour plans for Marcosson got changed; Hayes never got a chance to speak with the traveling journalist. More sober heads probably rethought the choice of minders for an American author who would represent the Forminiere to readers of the *Saturday Evening Post*, one of the most widely circulated and influential publications in the US at the time. Moody and Doyle personally supervised Marcosson's tours of Forminiere mining operations near Tshikapa. Hayes never even saw Marcosson in passing.

The Mulundu Creek test holes showed so much promise Doyle raised Hayes' pay $75 a month even without an agreement on the contract extension. And, he reminded Hayes, don't forget the 45% bonus if the Mulundu mine met quota; a man could get seriously paid here. Hayes had confidence in the mine, his crew, and himself – if his health held up.

Boring holes systematically near the mouth of Mulundu Creek, Hayes came to a section showing test holes previously drilled. Deprez had scratched around Mulundu Creek before Kilindini chased him back to Tshikapa for requisitioning three too many young women. Deprez' map, stamped "'eliminated area,'" showed only one diamond from two test holes drilled seven meters apart. Eliminated? On the basis of that slapdash examination? Hayes asked around among his workmen to determine who had overseen the test holes, Deprez or a capita? A capita of course, Deprez had been "too attentive to his harem" to supervise the drilling himself. Maybe Hayes would drop one hole here just to make sure.

One hundred and one diamonds in the first hole; 267 diamonds from 1.63 cubic meters of gravel in the next four holes; 183 diamonds from the sixth; 100 from the seventh; and 87 in the eighth hole. Diamonds glittered so plentifully, excited workmen picked some of the larger stones out of unwashed gravel.

Deprez had missed the diamonds collecting between boulders that dotted the streambed. His capita had neither the experience nor the resolve to lever big rocks aside to expose the rich diamond gravel deposited beneath boulders.

All Hayes' men shouted out in jubilation at those first holes, not because they understood the value of diamonds in Europe, but because a big exploitation on this long creek would mean a settled existence for them. Hayes shared their elation on the day of discovery but with a night to sleep on it, decided instead, "I am downcast."

Hadn't Hayes been at Mpeso and Ngombe? He knew what would follow his discovery: "Slaves will be driven to break records, those who profit by the diamonds will toss it away in Paris and Monte Carlo." The Belgians would steal any pittance earned by the miners "in the guise of taxes." And what were the diamonds for? Ladies' baubles. The whole Congo diamond mining adventure had lost its luster for Hayes: "I am almost sorry the diamonds are here." Nevertheless, he stayed and kept on diamond mining.

Total diamonds from the first ten days after the initial discovery topped 2,100 stones. The first two trenches proved 23,000 carats, about ten pounds of diamonds - more than that if the overrun matched the 50% average. By the first of July more than a million dollars (1920) had been proven and "[d]iamonds continue to come with monotonous sameness."

No true prospector ever rests. No multinational diamond corporation ever sleeps on a bonanza, no matter how large. Even as the diamonds poured in at Mulundu Creek, Hayes sent two of his men, Tambo and Somba, at the head of a nervous crew, to begin building a road out from Mulundu Creek toward the next exploratory site on the Luvoa River. Tambo and Somba's road led directly toward Kilindini and his 3,000 fighting men.

In his diary, Hayes admired Kilindini and his free men, writing: "My sympathies are with this war chief, who wants only to live in peace without being under tribute to the Belgians and Portuguese." Surely though, Hayes knew his actions countered his writing. He sent his most trusted man, Chilimbesi, who was himself the son of a Badjok war chief, out ahead of Tambo and Somba as peacemaker to Kilindini "but the latter is not receptive" to an olive branch.

The reply Hayes received from Kilindini, delivered by Chilimbesi, seems to have been the defining event prompting Hayes to cease dithering about personal riches and return to personal integrity. Kilindini said to Hayes, through Chilimbesi: "This white man has done well enough, but in the end he is worse than any of the others. He enters our country, pays for what he gets, does not abuse us and when we are lulled into a sense of false security, one who breaks every law of God and man follows. Then this white man penetrates further into our country and it is all done over again."

Doyle came to visit at Mulundu Creek for a couple of days in late July. Doyle reckoned Hayes had already proved at least 110,000 carats. Writing in his diary a few days after Doyle's visit, Hayes upped that figure to 200,000 carats. Still in its exploratory phase, the Mulundu Creek site already yielded diamonds at the level of fully developed exploitations elsewhere on the Kasai.

Doyle had a technological innovation to show Hayes, a method for managing quicksand in African rivers: three heavy curved plates that bolted together to make a meter-wide circle. Hayes let one of his crews try the new plates but he had already installed a solution for quicksand. Years ago, up in the Alaskan Yukon, Hayes had seen alluvial gold prospectors tame a river with a method called cribbing. The gold men set large timbers at right angles to the flow to hold the creek open at bedrock. Cribbing worked just as well for diamonds as for gold. In fact, Hayes' men behind his cribbing worked twice as fast as those inside Doyle's iron circle. After the demonstration, Hayes overheard Doyle muttering to himself, "'I wish to God some of these other fellows could use their own initiative!'" Workmen stored the plates away in Hayes' toolshed; they might be good for something.

In return for the plates, Hayes gave Doyle an earful about Belgian excesses: 1) when the Belgian officer Brassuer had passed through Mulundu Creek, Hayes had been forced to give his entire crew the day off just to prevent Brassuer impressing the lot; 2) a new Forminiere agent, Mercheirs, had established a camp on the other side of the river from Hayes and begun a "hostage system for both food and men;" and 3) a new man, the "nephew of Paul Hymans, Belgian foreign minister and president of the League of Nations," newly installed at a camp just below Foote's mine, had been addressing African laziness with 120 strokes of the kiboko "which is enough to kill any living man."

In response, Doyle temporized claiming: 1) he had no control over the Belgian military and admitted giving his own men a holiday when Brassuer visited; 2) he would keep Mercheirs to his side of the river but made no comment about the hostage-taking, and 3) he asked Hayes, rhetorically, what could he possibly say or do about the nephew of a high ranking Belgian politician? Nothing.

On August 7, 1920, news arrived from Hayes' old Lubwa Creek site: the Belgian overseer installed there had flogged four men to death in his first month. Meanwhile, the Belgian regional military commander, Brassuer, roared about Hayes' newly built roads toward Kilindini, employing a craven tactic that reminded Hayes of Mushkin, the Egyptian who had placed a man under each shoulder when fording a river as protection from crocodiles – only here, Brassuer used women. In the tall grass between villages, Brassuer surrounded his tepoy by village women so that any attackers "would be careful lest they destroy some of their valuable womenfolk."

Whips and rifles, not far off, syncopated the music of diamonds that continued to come "by hundreds and thousands" at Mulundu Creek. Entirely "[a]s I had expected, the finding of this rich diamond deposit has excited the cupidity of every European on the field both state and Forminiere."

If only Hayes could adopt the callousness of the rest of the Forminiere: "I could make a fortune here in a few years if it was possible to hide my eyes to these brutalities, but I won't."

Finally, the violence and greed chased him out. Hayes put in a formal letter of resignation on August 7, 1920, having fulfilled his two-year contract. However, Doyle would not allow Hayes to come into Tshikapa until the end of the third week of August. In part, Doyle wanted to wring every workday possible from his competent American pioneer – at the $28 per carat regulation price at the time, Mulundu Creek projected $4,000,000 in diamonds, with about a third proved by the time Hayes left. But also, Doyle had to consider Marcosson.

The articles and the book Marcosson wrote following his visit to the Congo counter the truth of the diamond mines of the Kasai as Hayes experienced them. Moody and Doyle had shown Marcosson a Tshikapa the journalist subsequently described as "Little America," bustling with industry and efficiency. Marcosson's readers met twelve thousand "grinning natives" working Forminiere mines throughout the Congo "and nowhere have I seen a more contented lot of blacks."

How unfortunate it would be for the Forminiere if Isaac Marcosson shared a berth on the steamer *Madeline* with Hayes Perkins. Marcosson departed on the *Madeline* one week before Hayes.

At Tshikapa, Hayes shook hands with Donald Doyle. The Forminiere boss said nothing across their clasped hands but gave Hayes a look that spoke volumes. Hayes believed almost all the Americans detested brutality toward the Africans, but refused to protest for the sake of their jobs. If Doyle took any action that slowed production, he would be ruined as an engineer: "The long hand of Guggenheim and Thomas F. Ryan would trip him wherever he went." The men on both sides of the handshake knew Doyle should be the one to speak and act but since he would not, Hayes wrote, "I will be the goat." The eyes of every man in the office bulged when

Hayes pulled from his pocket 50 carats of diamonds for surrender to the company.

As the *Madeline* bounced from sandbar to sandbar on a Kasai River low at dry season, Hayes wondered how her captain could still be alive. He could see how the man successfully piloted the boat: "too stupid to interfere with the excellent members of the crew who know every sandbar and current in the river." By "stupid" Hayes meant "half comatose" from drink. Only a robust constitution could survive such constant debauch.

Stuck for a week in Dima waiting for transfer to the *Madeline's* sister steamer, the *Mfumu Ntangu*, that would continue down the Congo River, Hayes admired the beauty of the vegetation: flame trees, hibiscus, orange trees, and mangoes. His fluency in the river languages surprised the local women with whom he conversed; he managed to decline offers of "marriage" without giving offense. Some Americans at Dima, going the other direction en route to jobs with the Forminiere, told Hayes Warren Harding had been elected 29th president of the United States, the first Hayes had ever heard of Warren Harding.

When the *Mfumu Ntangu* finally arrived, Hayes watched several tons of gunpowder unloaded for sale to natives up the Kwango and other rivers running out of Angola. Powder native men would pour into old "Dane guns" to shoot at Portuguese. Only a very tired and very cynical Hayes Perkins would have written, "Perhaps it is just as well."

As if refusing to take him out of Africa, the narrow-gauge steam train that pulled Hayes along the river from Kinshasa to Matadi had to back up for two, sometimes three runs to crest the higher hills past Livingstone Falls. Albert Thys, the rail builder, had laid out the line to avoid digging tunnels. Somewhere between the two towns, Hayes' baggage went missing. With something of a return of his customary wry humor, Hayes described seven days in the same underwear as "a record for the Congo."

The last words of the third volume of Hayes' diaries, written just before he boarded the *Albertville* bound away from the African continent to Antwerp, recalled one more old acquaintance in Africa, the missionary CT Studd. Some Swedish missionaries Hayes met in Matadi said they'd been "induced to leave all and enter Studd's mission, then were left stranded." The Swedes filled Hayes with tales of refugees fleeing Studd's mission. One Englishman in the group described Studd as "the most hated man in Africa." Something of an accomplishment considering where Hayes had just been.

9. In the Meantime: Island Paradise, 1920-1921

After leaving the Belgian Congo in late 1920, at age 42, Hayes traveled away from the African continent for only one year before returning, but he put on a lot of miles in that short time, circling the globe for the third time. Not that he particularly noticed he was sailing around the world; that's just where the winds blew him.

On the *Albertville* sailing out of Boma, Hayes' shipmates mostly spoke French. Some were Belgian employees of the Forminiere, some were Jesuit priests more interested in politics than matters of the spirit. So soon after the war, ship's officers, not yet "out of the habit," still imposed boat drills for all passengers and crew. Should hostilities resume, Hayes would man a lifeboat with "three Portuguese, twelve Negro deckhands, and seven bewhiskered priests." After lifeboat practice one afternoon, Braham, "a wealthy Jew" on board, kidded that Hayes would be "well provided for spiritually" if cast adrift.

Immediately upon arrival at Brussels, Hayes called in at Forminiere headquarters. The American, Oliver, formerly in charge in the Congo and recently furloughed to New York, happened to be in Brussels on his way back to resume command at Tshikapa. Together with Boice, Oliver, acting director of the Forminiere Brussels, greeted Hayes, Bews and two other Forminiere men – the latter three warmly, Hayes rather more "chill." Hayes took no particular offence at sitting in an outer office while Boice and Oliver saw to every welfare and comfort of Bews, Koslowsky, and Buckley: "This is to be expected, for any man who hints labor conditions are bad in Africa never returns."

The three men not willing to comment on working conditions in Africa got jovial slaps on the back from the bosses as they walked past Hayes, each holding his renewed contract. Oliver and Boice ushered Hayes into the inner office last, but Hayes knew "I was the one they wanted to see for the big Mulundu mine has their eye."

Talk of the Mulundu mine could wait. Hayes rather pointedly steered the conversation toward "the excesses of the Portuguese and Belgians." Both Forminiere headmen anemically claimed to "dislike" the abuses in the Congo. Boice, still calm for the moment, offered: "'We know it is not ethical to flog; but as most men can get better results by using the kiboko, therefore flog.'"

Hayes could only have heard Boice's business principle boiled down: do the monstrous sin to gain the greater profit. Where had Hayes heard something similar? Yes, Alfred Buxton had advocated "the lesser sin to gain the greater good." If Hayes couldn't stomach the latter, how could he go along with the former?

Yet, Hayes didn't immediately walk out of Forminiere Antwerp offices.

He still very much wanted to return to that good job in Africa. And the company wanted him back, too. Boice revealed that Donald Doyle, in charge at Tshikapa in Oliver's absence, had specifically requested that Hayes return. Doyle, Oliver, Boice, "all of them say I am not compelled to abuse the natives, they would be glad if all Forminiere engineers could be likewise."

Hayes stubbornly insisted that the Forminiere must outlaw use of the whip on moral, ethical, and, Hayes probably argued, financial grounds. If these two good, and educated, and culturally elevated businessmen, in this fine office, in the center of this civilized city, could muster the courage and foresight to outlaw whipping, men like Hayes would swarm to work for them. All would be better, for the native folk, for the

European workmen, and, most importantly, for the Forminiere.

The conversation must have gotten heated on both sides. Hayes did not record if he shouted or how long it took for raw, corporate power to annul ethical discourse. Boice rose, livid like "the wielders of the Congo whips," and shouted into Hayes' insubordinate face: "'The country belongs to the Portuguese and Belgians. The n------s are theirs, and what they do to them is none of your damned business.'"

Oliver, "the same half-fox-half-jackal he always was," stood in silent assent behind Boice. Hayes didn't say if he quit or if Oliver and Boyce fired him. In any case, he would not be returning to the Belgian Congo. Ushered out of the offices of the Forminiere, on the sidewalk outside, Hayes thought maybe he would travel back to Australia next. Possibly Samoa.

Sailing on an old tourist boat out from Antwerp, Hayes suffered from a head cold compounded by toothache. Two days into rough Atlantic seas, he and nearly every passenger taken on at Southampton, England, then Cherbourg, France, became seasick. Happily, a relatively fat bankroll, saved in the diamond fields, allowed him to sail first class. He remarked on how unusually pleasant for him was the luxury of lying sick on a bunk in a stateroom, rather than on "a wave washed forecastle on a wind jammer, or a dirty forepeak forecastle on a freighter."

The port of New York imposed extended quarantine before passengers could enter the city. Hayes endured the mandatory isolation; found it, in fact, about as pleasant as New York City, once allowed to enter. His lengthy diatribe concerning the nation's greatest city described New York as "a city filled with its own self, with no thought of the rest of the world, evidently self-sufficient in itself." Hayes dismissed its isolated citizens rushing to and fro, from work to work, snatching lunch with no time to greet a neighbor, as the "[m]ost ignorant of men, [who] imagines himself wisest."

Hayes left New York, "happy to be on my way out of this dismal place," on a train bound for Oklahoma City, where his mother and his sister May lived. He stayed three uncomfortable days with his mother, the deepening estrangement from his family echoing in the diary very much as on the last time through: "To me it seems strange anyone could be nearer me in any way than the man I meet in the street."

From Oklahoma City he continued by train to Waco, Texas, to visit his sister Memrie and her husband, Frank Wilson. A short visit in Waco, then Hayes climbed back on the train and headed south to Houston to call on his sisters Jennie and Pearl. Jennie, a nurse, arranged dentist appointments for Hayes in response to a letter he had sent complaining of toothache. Her far-wandering, not particularly gracious, older brother suspected Jennie had arranged the appointments so he would have to "stick here for as long as possible."

Hayes did catch up with one person that interested him in Houston. As a boy in Hico, "the little town in central Texas where I put in three awful years," Hayes had known Mabel Wysong, the "kid daughter" of the local doctor. The last time Hayes had blown through Texas to visit his mother and sisters, he had stopped in to say hello to Mabel, who, he noted at the time, "was growing up too."

During that previous visit, Mabel had raged at the gender injustices of the time: "'I pray God every night He'll change me into a boy, so I can travel around the world like you. Being a girl, I'm tied here, what can I do?'"

Riding around Houston in Mabel's very nice Ford motor car, Hayes learned what Mabel, hobbled as a girl, had in fact done in the intervening years. Divorced from her high school sweetheart, she had enrolled in stenography school. By age 27, she had saved $1,000. Seizing an investment opportunity, she gambled the entire bankroll on a wildcat oil well that returned

$100,000. Mabel, "a good scout," currently controlled all Ford interests in Houston.

Hayes and Mabel shared more than one car ride between dental appointments the week Hayes stayed in Houston. His sister Pearl felt it necessary to ride chaperone in Mabel's car to deposit Hayes on a westbound train. As the train pulled from the station, Hayes carped: "I never interfere with their men friends, why should they if I have a girl?" How intrusive to have sisters preserving propriety with the local women, housing an itinerant traveler, even arranging dental work! In fact, though Hayes found Mabel refreshingly iconoclastic, she had remarried "so no chance for romance, and neither of us want it anyway."

On the second day of January 1921, Hayes sat in the Los Angeles train station taking stock of his life. The trip home had been harrowing. Hayes liked his sisters, despite their faults, but wished they could understand his life and not try to mold him into theirs. A knot of college students, "who have never known hardship, care, want," jammed the LA station reminding Hayes of the formal education he'd missed. Still, even without a degree, hadn't he "climbed to the pinnacle I had dreamed of?" A well-paid mining engineer, working in Africa, respected by his colleagues and workmen; what more had he ever wanted?

More important to him than accomplishing his adventuring and professional aspirations, Hayes credited himself for maintaining his basic decency. As bitter as it was to walk away from his accomplishments with the Forminiere, he did not regret that decision: "…it is better than listening to the screams of tortured slaves whom I can never help."

San Francisco seemed "tame without booze." The 18th amendment to the US Constitution banning the manufacture, sale, and transportation of liquor, ratified in 1919, had taken effect in 1920. The city remained full of bustle, but "lacks something since the Barbary Coast has been shut down."

Hayes approved of prohibition but mourned the passing of the rough-and-tumble old San Francisco: "the forest of masts one used to see along the waterfront, the whalers lying in the stream, the sailors boarding house and the sharks who preyed on seamen for their livelihood."

Almost wistfully, Hayes guessed old Hermann and Sailor Brown, who'd shanghaied many a greenhorn in days-gone-by, "were enjoying their full reward in hell," right alongside Double-Reef Larson.

Hayes left San Francisco on January 15, 1920, on the steamer *Sonoma*. At Honolulu, native Hawaiian boys dove for coins thrown from the deck – then shot craps for the lot. While sailing between Hawaii and Samoa, sighting the Southern Cross, the iconic constellation visible only in the southern hemisphere, raised Hayes' spirits. Under southern stars, he wrote "I feel I am getting home."

Hayes passed through American Samoa in February of 1921 but did not stay. Somewhere steaming through the South Seas under the Southern Cross, he had decided he needed to see the opal fields of Australia first.

Disembarking at Sydney, Hayes gave thanks that he still had funds enough to relax for a few days without needing to hustle work. Soldiers returning from WWI had Sydney in disarray. Most of the men had lost the taste for work and loafed around Hyde Park under two great government tents when not ranging from house-to-house begging, "arrogant and insolent to all civilians."

The railhead *nearest* an Australian mine did not necessarily mean a railhead *near* the mine in 1921. Hayes walked the last 50 miles from Walgett to Lightning Ridge. By early 1921, anyone who had found a fortune in opals at Lightning Ridge had either taken the fortune back to civilization or spent the fortune on alcohol.

Only a couple hundred "old and grey" men remained of the 2,000 eager prospectors who once scratched for opals in this rich deposit. Those remaining on the Ridge lived in flimsy shacks made of tin cans pounded flat for siding; most had barely enough food to subsist. One young lad found a nice stone while Hayes was there, in some "noodlings," the excavated tailings from a previous dig. The £9 the boy's big opal paid kept everyone else's hopes alive for the next big strike: "All and sundry" went straight to the bar to drink to the young man's good fortune. Cheers all around until £9 had been rung into the bar till.

Hayes returned to Sydney after only three weeks half-heartedly poking around for opals at Lightning Ridge. He had a couple of fine stones in his pocket, "but these are hard to market by an amateur merchant in Australia." He had found those few stones, but not enough happening at Lightning Ridge to hold him in that northern desolation: "The enchantment of the glorious Samoan ensemble of forest and coral beach, of reef and bluest sea beckons, and surely will be a more desirable place of residence than the drab bush."

He chastised himself for not departing the *Sonoma* the first time through. But surely in those idyllic islands he could still find surcease from "the brutal slave gangs of Africa and the equally hard driving machine age of the U.S.A."

On May 5, 1921, back at Pago Pago, Hayes disembarked a big steamer from Australia and transferred onto the *Faleofani*, a tiny 15-ton launch "laden to the guards with freight" on the way to Apia, capital of Western Samoa. Heavy seas off Tutuila tossed the *Faleofani* so roughly even some of the Samoan travelers suffered seasickness.

Through one long, rough night, Hayes lay nauseous in a small ship's hatch cheek-to-jowl with a most interesting man, H.J. Moors. The American Moors, now in his fifties, had come to the islands at age 19. In the intervening thirty years, "[h]e has seen the various native wars in which Britain, Germany, and the United States took part, and has by selling gunpowder, booze, guns and whatnot acquired a fortune." Moors controlled 19 trading stations about the islands. Maybe he could scratch up a place for a good man if Hayes had any interest?

Savai'i, largest of the nine Samoan islands, lies just west of Upolu. Hayes sailed 45 miles in a launch from Apia to the well-stocked station at Palauli that Moors had found for him. The place had $9,000 worth of goods housed in an "excellent store" with a residence "far too large for one man alone."

The deal Hayes had struck with Moors pleased him: "10% of all I buy and sell, copra [dried coconut] being the sole source of trade." On the other hand, the chatter among the Samoan boatmen escorting him to Palauli did not please him, ribaldry along the lines of "where was my 'missis' and if I would be getting another." Their gentle kidding foreshadowed Hayes' principal difficulty in this South Sea "paradise."

In the first week at his station near the center of Palauli, Hayes sold some of his goods and took in 3,500 pounds of copra. To surmount the language barrier, he hired "an ancient crone" previously married to three "'white mans,'" Mary or Mele, who spoke "a fair brand of English - for the South Seas." In all trades, Mary gave "her own people the breaks not me," but Hayes did not begrudge Mary this slight disloyalty; she would remain here among these people long after he had moved on.

At first, the marriage proposals coming directly from the "pretty, bronzed-skinned girls" added to "the general enchantment of the place." Mary warned Hayes off the young girls; wasn't he the only single "papalangi (literally Sky Burster)" [this translation and the one below are Hayes'] on the island? The novice trader agreed with his interpreter: "I have lingering, perhaps unworthy doubts whether [their attention] is not caused more from the many bolts of bright cloth, the silks, the canned goods and paelos (barrels) of salt beef in stock rather than my own handsome appearance and manly vigor."

"It is a slack day when I get a half dozen proposals and sometimes there are twenty offers of marriage. Parents bring their beauteous daughters and urge them upon me." Hayes began keeping a pail of water under his counter "to dash over such as become too ardent in their proposals." He pelted women outside the range of his bucket with green lemons. In reply, "[s]ome strip off their gowns, usually a shapeless Mother Hubbard introduced by the missionaries." The women disrobed to insult rather than attract: "This strip-tease is to tell me they regard me as they would a dog, a pig, anything but a man."

In early August, Hayes and Mary had sold nearly all Moors' first $9,000 worth of merchandise. Despite the business success, Hayes had already wearied of this "paradise" and its occupants. Before Moors would accept Hayes' letter of resignation, he sent Kruezer, a keen-eyed German-Samoan, to take inventory. Hayes had no worries about his bookkeeping: "All has come out even; I knew it would."

By August 16, 1921, Hayes was back at Apia. On a short stopover, he visited a Samoan doctor for biliousness and received a prescription for kava. Hayes had seen the medicine used by Samoans, kava leaves chewed by young girls then spat into a bowl, "[t]his the honored men drink with relish but not me."

The kava Hayes drank had been strained by hand through fiber. It made him not quite intoxicated but jittery, "nervous and unstrung." His brain remained clear but he lost control of his limbs and suffered increased stomach upset.

Sailing out from Suva on the steamer *Suva* headed directly to Sydney, Hayes vowed, "[t]his will be my last trip to the islands." He didn't care for the ways of the islanders and deplored "big companies crowding out the small men by methods worse than a bandit uses in robbing his victims." Hayes sailed yet again from an "island paradise" that turned out to be neither idyllic nor unspoiled.

With his peripatetic travels, Hayes' magazine subscriptions had a hard time catching up to him. A few copies of the *Literary Digest*, a weekly news magazine featuring condensed articles from Canadian, US, and European publications, had reached him on Palauli, but most of the past year's subscription waited for him at Sydney. In one, Hayes read excerpts from an article Marcosson had published in the *Saturday Evening Post* about Marcosson's tour through the Forminiere mines.

Marcosson's corporate white-washing of conditions in the Congo infuriated Hayes: "Much is said of the American red-blooded manhood who are opening the wilderness there. But the part about the brutality to the wretched natives is carefully left out." In a heated passage in his diary, Hayes charged that Marcosson had plenty to drink during his stay in the Congo and wrote exactly what Forminiere staff told him: "This selfish corporation has sent Marcosson to Africa to conceal their activities there instead of to make all plain to the public, and he has done his work well." Hayes made a slight, anonymous effort to set the *Literary Digest* straight, dashing off a note recounting his firsthand experiences with the Belgian/American company – but he asked the *Digest* not to publish the note or use his name, for "[i]f they do, it means my days in Africa are done." It appears the *Digest* honored his request.

Nothing in Hayes' diary indicated he had any particular destination in mind as the steamer *Demosthenes* sailed out of Sydney headed west, around Australia. Following only two brief stops, for cargo in Melbourne, then at drab Fremantle, *Demosthenes* next made landfall in Durban, South Africa, arriving exactly one day after Hayes' connecting steamer departed Durban for Bombay. On the long sea voyage between Fremantle and Durban, Hayes had hatched a plan: first he would go to Zanzibar, the exotic island of his boyhood imagination, long in need of first-hand appraisal, then onto the African continent in the former German East Africa (Tanganyika, Tanzania) to follow up rumors of mines buried and abandoned following the war.

The next ship would not depart Durban for Bombay, by way of Zanzibar, for another three weeks. An extended stopover in Durban didn't upset Hayes. No need to hurry; he still had cash in hand from the Samoan trading post.

The hotel room he rented on one of Durban's lovely beaches had a stretch of sea fenced for some distance into the water to separate the many bathers from the many sharks. When not swimming or visiting the fine Durban Zoo, Hayes spent most of his long days sitting in Durban's splendid library reading geology textbooks, one of his favorite pastimes in one of his favorite places: "Such institutions have been a godsend to me, for in them I have gained most of the book learning I possess."

Two stops along the coast of Mozambique at Lorenzo Marquez (Maputo) and old Mozambique (Freitoria), confirmed Hayes opinion of the quality of Portuguese colonial rule: "Over everything the blighting rule of Portugal hangs like a pall." To Hayes' eye, the Portuguese remained as cruel and slothful as "when Vasco Da Gama first rounded Good Hope and visited various ports along this coast, burning, plundering, proselyting in the name of Christ." Only the "energetic British" showed any initiative in Mozambique. At Lorenzo Marquez, the Brits had constructed magnificent new docks for shipping gold out from the Rand in South Africa.

Hayes could not have been more excited to finally reach Zanzibar: "Fraught with romance is Zanzibar, a romance lost in the mists of the Middle Ages." All Hayes' boyhood heroes had passed through Zanzibar: "I can see them as I write … Burton, Speke, Stanley, Livingstone, Emin Pasha, Teleki, Joseph Thomson, Tippoo Tib." All the great adventurers, missionaries, explorers, and enslavers of the generation gone by, the men whose stories had kindled Hayes' youthful imagination, calling him to join them in the adventuring life. Hayes ached to get ashore to walk where his heroes had walked: "Now it is [my] turn to pass this way, but I live again with them on this dream isle lost in the far corner of the Indian Ocean."

10. Scouting for Abandoned Mines, Tanganyika, 1921-1922

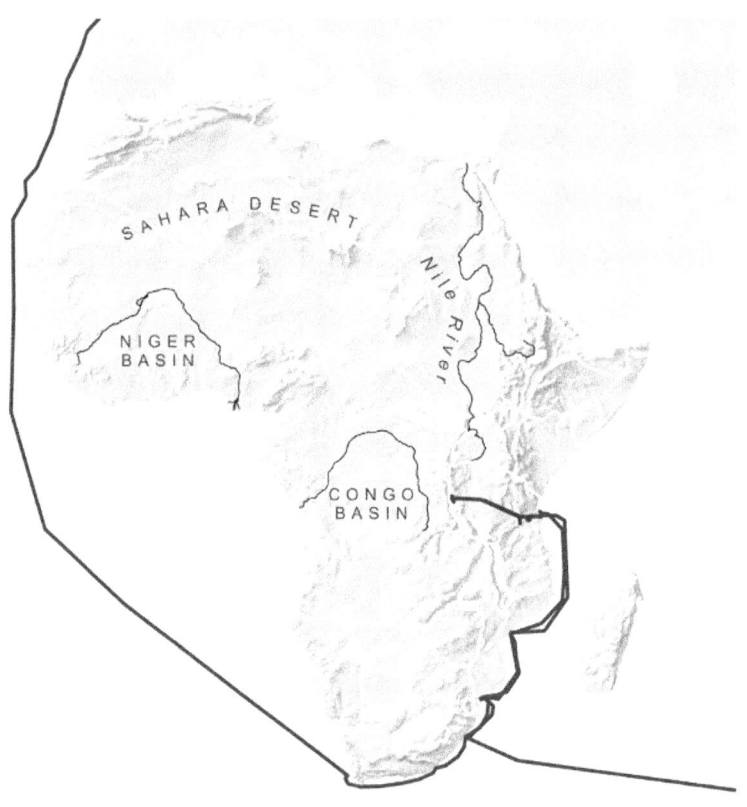

Zanzibar, a small island archipelago in the Indian Ocean just off the coast of Tanzania, has two main islands, Pemba and Unguja (informally called Zanzibar). Despite having a total land area about half that of Rhode Island, Zanzibar had been a cultural crossroads and trading hub for at least a millennium before Hayes passed through in December 1921. He gave a brief summary of various cultural incursions onto the island: "Arab and Persian contested for this island and the African coast for untold centuries. Persia declined then came the more vigorous Portuguese, brave, cruel, bigoted, and tried to oust the Arab, but never entirely. Then came the Briton and the German, and now the latter has disappeared from the scene, at least temporarily."

Hayes estimated the population of Zanzibar city at about 60,000, "but its space is not that of a town of a thousand in the U.S.A." In 1921, Zanzibar Island and its sister, Pemba Island, comprised, according to Hayes, "the kingdom of an Arab sultan who is supported by the British as long as he plays the game with them." Judging from the magnificence of his palace, the sultan's "game" appeared profitable to Hayes.

Strolling a wealthy section of the city, from among the many large houses Hayes eventually located an elegant white-walled mansion with a plaque on the door that read simply: TIPPOO TIB'S HOUSE.

No one in this city would need even the scant identification on the plaque; "Everyone in Zanzibar and on this coast knows of Tippoo Tib and of the great empire he builded [sic] up reaching from Lindi to Aden, from Zanzibar to Stanley Falls on the Upper Congo." To get an estimate of the size of Tipoo Tib's empire, Lindi is on the south coast of Tanzania near the Mozambique border, roughly 2,000 miles south of Aden in Yemen. Zanzibar lies off the east coast of Tanzania, 2,000 miles east of Stanley Falls on the other side of the continent. So, Hayes attributed to Tippoo Tib an empire on the order of 4 million square miles, slightly larger than the area of all fifty of the United States.

Hayes certainly knew the name Tippoo Tib before coming across a plaque on a house in Zanzibar. The ivory trader and notorious enslaved merchant wrote his name across several of the adventure tales of the early European explorers in the second half of the 19th century, the stories that so captivated Hayes and the rest of the Western world. An impoverished David Livingstone, wandering in the Great

Lakes region looking for the source of the Nile, starving and down to his last few porters, traveled for a time under the gracious protection of one of Tib's caravans of the enslaved. Henry Morton Stanley hired Tib on two occasions: once to guide his Congo River expedition, and later for the Emin Pasha Relief Expedition. In the late 1880s Tib served as Governor of the Stanley Lake district of the Congo Free State, appointed by Leopold following Stanley's recommendation.

After only two days in Zanzibar, Hayes took the night steamer to Dar es Salaam, capital city of Tanganyika (Tanzania). In 1921, Tanganyika existed as neither a colony nor an independent country; the British administered the former German East Africa as a League of Nations mandate following WWI.

On the fine, modern streets of Dar es Salaam, Hayes somehow got word that an old friend also happened to be working in Tanganyika. Ernest Bishop, the small elephant hunter, Hayes' companion down the Nile, had set up his itinerant trade at Kigoma, several hundred miles inland where the rail line ended at Lake Tanganyika. Of course Hayes would go see Bishop, that "good friend in those days when I needed one." But the train ran only once a week. Bad scheduling and customs delays prevented Hayes catching the train that left on December 9, 1921.

Stalled but not idle in Dar es Salaam, Hayes set about preparations for entering the Congo. He planned, even to the extent of changing his money to francs, to cross Lake Tanganyika after visiting Bishop on the near side. Evidently Hayes still had some thought of returning to the Forminiere. However, asking around town among the Belgians, he learned news that gave him pause about his Forminiere plan: Gervisse for whom "there is no love lost between us because of his flogging the natives so brutally at Mpeso on the Longatshimo River in Southwest Congo," had been promoted to head of Forminiere operations at Kisengwa on the River Lomami in east central Congo. Hayes didn't relish the idea of showing up unannounced to ask Gervisse for a job.

Happily, something other than the Forminiere came along. Rumors circulating about Dar es Salaam ever since the war hinted at secret coal seams discovered during German occupation. Talk on the streets seemed plausible enough to an international corporation, "Inchcape interests, here called Bird & Co," to warrant hiring an American engineer with mining experience to check them out. Inchcape wanted the coal for their steamers running between Bombay and Durban, but the company had other vast holdings requiring coal: plantations along the coast of Tanganyika; iron mines and steel mills in India; at least four steamer lines (British Indian, P.& O., Cunard, and the Union Line of New Zealand); "and many other things." Not only would their offer allow Hayes to give Gervisse a miss, this Inchcape company seemed well "worth hooking up with."

Before sending Hayes off in search of coal, Bellasis, the boss at Bird's, had a little side job for him. Bellasis sent Hayes 28 kilometers out from Dar es Salaam to Kisserawe, "a deserted station of pre-war days where the Germans had some rubber plantations." But rubber didn't interest Bellasis; he was after diamonds.

Sure, Hayes consented to go anywhere Bellasis sent him, but not without skepticism: "A man named Ross has found indications of diamonds there, so he says; but it does not look like diamond bearing ground to me."

On December 21, 1921, Hayes camped "alone" in the bush with a cook, "a typical mission boy," dressed in fine raiment, and "no man for the bush." On a more positive note, Hayes described his two Swahili carriers, Chanti and Orojami, as "the goods." Earlier in the day, rain had poured on their small safari, soaking all to the skin, so they didn't really need to bathe, but a half-hidden lake fringed with tall reeds and blue lotus invited a swim in placid waters. Long-toed birds walking on broad-leafed plants reminded Hayes of those he had seen on the Niger.

The entire country, though very beautiful, appeared to be loose alluvium rather than bedrock where diamonds collected. Hayes did, however, see "literally billions of rubies, garnets, and a few tourmalines, all too small to be of value."

Two days out and Hayes fired the cook for eating most of the food supply: "I wonder why it is a mission trained native is always spoiled?" Hayes, Chanti and Orojami washed gravel in the bed of Simbazi Creek but, as Hayes had predicted, found no diamonds: "Had there been anything here worthwhile the thorough going Germans would have discovered it."

Hayes marked a quiet Christmas 1921 in the bush, very like so many previously. On the way up toward Bagamoyo, an old slave port, Chanti flushed some Guinea fowl. He thought of eggs, crying: "'Maiyi!'" Orojami thought of eggs and young, echoing, "'Maiyi ya toto!'" Either, or both, would have provided a nice Christmas feast but they found neither and slept hungry.

On the last day of 1921, Hayes returned to Dar es Salaam to tell Bellasis any further diamond prospecting would be a waste of company money. That night, outside Hayes' cheap hotel, Greek New Year's revelers, "in an effort to drink each other under the table and this was not accomplished until daylight this morning," prevented anyone in the neighborhood from sleeping that night. In retaliation, Hayes rattled around his room making as much noise as possible on New Year's morning.

Finally coming around to the matter of searching for abandoned coal mines, Bellasis purchased Hayes another "shoestring outfit" in Dar es Salaam, then the two caught the train to Kilossa, 290 kilometers inland. Before departing the station, Bellasis bullied an Indian conductor into cramming all 35 loads for their safari into one small compartment, calling it hand baggage. Everything squeezed in except Bellasis' bathtub: too big for door or window, it went as excess freight, paid accordingly.

Hayes found Bellasis an annoying traveling companion who earned ill-will with whomever he dealt, "and it reflects on me." Imagine the shame had an Indian porter thought Hayes traveled with a bathtub.

On January 6, 1922, Hayes, Bellasis, and 35 cargo loads spilled out of a cramped train compartment at the Kilossa station. As previously planned, Bellasis marched off with the majority of their outfit in a direction opposite Hayes.

Pleased to be "alone" once more in the bush, Hayes unlimbered with a twenty-mile march out from Kilossa to a German experimental farm at a village called Uleia. A British Major Bradstock tended, or rather neglected, a variety of tropical plants brought here for acclimatization by the Germans, all of whom had been deported following the war.

Major Bradstock had his family with him at this "easy billet" including a daughter of twenty who gave Hayes much hectoring instruction about life in the bush: "She has a great reputation as a huntress and it has gone to her head." Hayes dryly indicated how deeply he appreciated her unsolicited counsel: "She told me more in an hour of Africa than I have learned in my years of wandering …. Now I see I am wrong, and will have to start all over again to know anything about the bush."

In the middle of January 1922, Hayes arrived at the camp of another Bird's employee, a New Zealander named Lloyd, a shabby site, "hidden away in a deep gorge in the Rubeno Ranges near the Ruaha River, chief tributary of the Rufiji, largest of the rivers of German East Africa."

Hayes immediately came down with dysentery and a fever at Lloyd's camp. (He blamed the "miserable outfit" Bellasis supplied.) When able to stand again, Hayes began to put Lloyd's "horrible slum" into some kind of working order. Lloyd's main problem? The man spoke no Swahili so he had a hard time acquiring food; both food sellers and their interpreters constantly swindled him.

Lloyd, a miner all his life at sites around the world, brought Hayes news of common friends in far-flung places but Lloyd wasn't much of a companion, for a "man often becomes irascible when he has too much of his own company." Nor was Lloyd much of a miner. At his camp on the Ruaha River, the lonely New Zealander had sunk a few test holes that showed "something resembling coal."

Hayes thought Lloyd's samples looked like some kind of rock older than coal, closer to graphite: "To burn it requires a blacksmith's forge." Nevertheless, Lloyd's not very promising find brought out Bellasis, Bradstock, Mennell (a mining geologist from Rhodesia), and Turnley (first prospector of this area) to have a look.

Some days later, still partnered with Lloyd, Hayes moved off to a new, more comfortable camp a few miles distant. Bellasis and Mennell had taken their leave toward Nairobi "for a social swim and big game hunt somewhere out of that business and outfitting center." Mennell graciously left Hayes some Chlorodyne and bismuth, with which to address the dysentery "that had dragged me down almost to a skeleton."

Bradstock and Turnley went on to a nearby village, Msombe, to supervise receipt of a shot drill arriving from Dar es Salaam

On February 4, 1922, Hayes' pagazis, his carriers, informed him, according to "that mysterious way news travels in the African bush," that Turnley had been badly mauled by a leopard at Msombe. Hayes hastened to the village to see if he could help Turnley and, if nothing else, to see to the disposition of the shot drill.

At Msombe, Hayes learned that Turnley had set a shotgun on a tripwire to exterminate a leopard that had been raiding about the village. The crafty leopard had reached around the length of the gun muzzle to swipe at a chicken baiting the trap – and just nudged the tripwire. The huge cat got a mouthful of black powder flash; the shot passed through its mouth, cheek-to-cheek, taking two teeth with it. The enraged beast ran, slashing an old man badly across one arm as it bounded the length of the village before holing up in a mealie patch.

Turnley and Bradstock approached, Turnley calling out: "'There it is! There it is!'" Bradstock tried unsuccessfully to restrain the overeager Turnley. As the big cat "rose in a graceful arch high over the corn, its tail straight out behind, its forepaws extended," Turnley managed to fire one shotgun barrel into the its snarling face. Hurt and angered by the pellets, the leopard leapt to strike Turnley full on the shoulders, knocking him to a sitting position. Turnley instinctively wrapped his legs around the cat's torso to prevent its raking his gut with powerful hind claws. Man and Leopard tumbled into a pit in that terrible embrace.

Later Mrs. Turnley would curse Bradstock for a coward and a poltroon. Hayes could understand the sentiment but dissented in this instance: "I do not like Bradstock at all, but he is at least brave." Approaching the struggle in the pit, Bradstock cried out "'Steady, Turnley,'" while waiting until enough leopard separated for a clear shot. A blast rang out and nine feet of leopard slumped against Turnley, who lay bleeding and cursing. Bradstock's single shot had pierced the huge cat's neck, killing it instantly.

Hayes heard the story of Turnley and the leopard only after the fact. By the time Hayes got to Msombe, all the bandages and most of the food intended for Hayes' camp had gone for doctoring Turnley. Hayes couldn't really quibble: "I would have done the same thing." But both Hayes and Bradstock did all they could to convince Turnley he must return to Kilossa and immediately board the train to seek expert care at Dar es Salaam. No, Turnley adamantly refused; he and Mrs. Turnley would press on to a Catholic mission in the nearby Rubehos Mountains.

The next day, having eaten nothing, and still weak from dysentery, Hayes carried one end of Turnley's sedan chair a dozen miles to Kidodia. Delirious with pain, the wounded man cursed his carriers with every stumble or bump along the way. After 12 miles of agony, lying quietly at Kidodia, his wounds broken open to relieve the pain, Turnley recalled himself enough to deliver a polite apology to Hayes and the other carrier for the imprecations.

Hayes walked back to Msombe to see about the shot drill. As a wry coda on the whole leopard affair, Hayes wrote that he had seen the chicken Turnley had used to bait his trap – short a few tail feathers, but otherwise unharmed.

As the days stretched by less eventfully, Hayes had an increasingly hard time getting along with Lloyd. The American ran the shot drill by himself just to stay out of the way of the New Zealander who busied himself sinking shallow pits and playing at being the boss. The rocks Hayes drilled were "older than the carboniferous, being back in the Devonian and Silurian, some in the Cambrian before coal was heard of." Even Lloyd's "near-coal" dwindled to thin seams of poorest quality. Only a "half promise" Bellasis had made to send Hayes forward prospecting along the shore of Lake Tanganyika kept him at this futile work alongside this irascible companion.

Surprisingly Bellasis delivered on his half-promise. In the last week of February 1922, Hayes bid Lloyd farewell and walked back toward Kilossa to catch the train east toward Lake Tanganyika. Because Bradstock's ill-tended horticultural station lay right along the path to the railhead, what would it hurt to stop and to greet the young lady hunter? She was well, but had no further advice to share.

The train from Kilossa to Tabora ran through "an endless stretch of scrub-covered steppes, chiefly granite country and sometimes almost desert." The Wagogo people made a precarious living here, often perishing in great numbers due to famine. No domestic animals could survive

198

this harsh land, only wild beasts: "giraffes, lions, zebras, koodoo and others find a living, and at the rare water holes sometimes people find existence."

Tabora, still 200 miles from Lake Tanganyika, came as a welcome relief to the parched traveler. Here, as many as 35,000 people lived at an elevation high enough to escape tsetse fly. Sheep, goats, cows, and many fowl all flourished. At Tabora's great market, under wide-spreading mango trees, Hayes delighted to find abundant food and anything else he could have wanted from Dar es Salaam.

Ever since he was a young boy poring over maps of Africa, Lake Tanganyika had been for Hayes "one of those half-mythical places" where his heroes had walked. Lake Tanganyika "became enchrined [sic] in my boyhood dreams when I read Burton's and Speke's expedition up from Bagamoyo."

Stepping off the train at Kigoma on the shore of Lake Tanganyika in 1922, Hayes exulted, his once half-mythical place was "very real now." Deflating the myths of his childhood never seemed to bother Hayes: "Now that I have reached it the romance has departed but I can still take an interest in its beauty." When the heat of the day had declined enough to make sitting possible, Hayes settled for an hour, looking west to where the Congo hills rose some 5,000 feet above the lake, writing, "[T]he water was a silvery sheen and on it was a path of gold reflecting the dying sun. The radiant coloring in the cirrus clouds displayed every color of the rainbow, equal to anything I have seen elsewhere." The beauty of Africa's far-away places refreshed Hayes' love for the continent as so often it had before.

Back in town, Hayes could see that the German colonists had started on a fine city at Kigoma, to be a trade center for the Great Lakes region: a modern railway station, fine buildings, and what was to have been a great hotel. The German crown prince had been scheduled to christen the hotel but, because of the war, never made it to Kigoma. Such a waste: "If Germany could have only left war alone what might they not have done?"

The Waha porters Hayes hired out of Kigoma would carry only as far as Ujiji, a small slave trading village, just a few miles south of Kigoma along the lakeshore where Stanley had famously greeted the "lost" Scottish missionary with the indelibly understated, "Dr. Livingstone, I presume."

As at Kigoma, the Germans had begun civic improvement at Ujiji before the war. They laid streets as straight as possible without destroying the "old Arab town with perhaps 6,000 people." Hayes identified oil palms German colonialists had planted here, the first he'd seen in East Africa. An old mango tree reputedly planted to mark the spot of the famous meeting between Livingstone and Stanley still survived, but barely. "The Germans placed a concrete curb around it, and this seems to have strangled it, for it is not flourishing." An inscription in the concrete read simply:

–Livingstone – Stanley–
1871

Heading out from Ujiji with new porters supplied by Mr. Langland, "the most courteous British officer I have seen in German East," Hayes' small safari came almost immediately to a vast swamp. Hayes had read of Stanley's grief wading waist-deep across this very morass, "and it brought it home vividly to wade it myself." Only the good fortune of meeting a "genial Greek planter," who gave Hayes a bit a meat, brightened a day spent crossing swamp upon swamp choked barely passable with papyrus. Hayes lamented the Germans hadn't had a bit more initiative: "Why so enterprising a people as the Germans undoubtedly are never built a causeway across these mudholes is more than I can imagine. We would have done so in the U.S.A. the first thing."

Following a long day, marching when possible, wading when necessary, with nothing to eat beyond the Greek planter's small scrap of meat, Hayes called a halt just south of the Malagarazi River, largest tributary of Lake Tanganyika. The small clearing where he pitched his tent hadn't area large enough for the carriers to camp too. When they asked to return to a village a half-mile back along the trail, Hayes consented, happy to camp alone.

Initially the lone camper worried about hippos grunting in the shallow margin of the lake nearby, then about crocodiles, and, as evening came on, maybe lions. He had certainly seen plenty of cat tracks in the path earlier in the day, but he reassured himself, "[o]ne lion can make a lot of tracks."

On that warm evening with no need for a fire, Hayes retired early to his camp bed, up off the ground inside his canvas tent, and "[a]ll went well until about 8:00 o'clock." The first "tremendous roar" sounded quite near, the next and the next nearer yet: "So near were the beasts I could hear the intake of their breath between roars."

Was the intrepid adventurer frightened? "If any man could listen to all this and remain unperturbed he is a braver man than I am." He had no gun and there were no trees about, either for climbing or to kindle a fire; so he did all that he could do. A match lit the lantern inside his tent, stones secured the flaps against exposure from the wind, and a shaky adventurer lay down on the camp bed to sleep.

Intermittent roaring and breathing on the other side of the canvas, sometimes very close, then further distant, kept him on keen edge well past midnight. Surcease came not from lions departing but from a dimly remembered bible verse – something about the lion and the adder trampled underfoot because he hath set his love upon me – from Psalms 21. Meditating on the Psalm, despite the lions drawn very near again, "I turned over and fell into a dreamless sleep."

The following morning, as dawn sent long streamers of light to illuminate the hills rising above the lake on the far Congo shore, the lions, still roaring, withdrew into some scrub-covered hills nearby. Hayes took a quiet moment with his diary to explain, perhaps to himself, the religiose outburst of the night before: "I am not a religious man, at least not actively so. But men who live near nature in the wilderness have a strong faith in God, and I have this."

Hayes reckoned he could probably do his coal prospecting for Bird and Company along the shores of Lake Tanganyika more easily from a boat paddling the lakeside. Accordingly, he sought out the local canoe maker. Under a spreading mango tree, the fellow had somehow acquired his impossible logs even though, "there are no large trees anywhere around the entire circumference of this great lake."

The ingenious boat-building certainly had to be admired: the man hollowed the length of his log, then poured boiling water into the cavity to soften the wood, so that braces driven in could spread and shape the canoe. The boat-builder increased the canoe's draft by sewing planks around the gunwales of the log with rattan. Startlingly beautiful, gracefully formed canoes advertised their origin: "Some of the trees are crooked, so the canoe wears the bend as the tree did."

Hayes, five paddlers, and a cook set off in one slightly crooked canoe south from Karago along the shore of Lake Tanganyika with no uncertain relief: "This canoe travel seems like heaven after wading swamps and long marches with sore feet." The crew had to paddle early in the mornings to avoid heavy squalls that stirred the lake to a "fury of white caps and great seas" pushed by gusty erratic winds falling into this lake deep in the Great Rift Valley. During moments on calm water, Hayes could see a hundred feet into remarkably transparent depths, but nowhere near the lake bottom: at "Kigoma soundings of above 4,000 feet have been taken. Tanganyika is one of the world's deepest lakes, being exceeded only by Lake Baikal in Siberia."

Hayes may have had a slight interest in the prospecting work for which he came to Lake Tanganyika; his diary for March 11, 1922, contains a passing geological note: greatly folded rock, the largest boulder conglomeration he had ever seen, followed by a note on how they might have formed and deformed. But the troop of baboons that came down a cliff side to drink at the river started a much longer reverie on the local wildlife. The big male sentry eyed the passing canoe without fear, more intent on watching for crocodiles. Little game could be seen in this country full of leopards and lions, but there must have been some kind of buck around for them to eat, and plenty of monkeys. Many birds worked the lake: terns, cormorants, kingfisher, osprey, and an eagle looking much like the American bald.

Finding nothing of mineral interest along the lake shore south of Kigoma, Hayes returned to reprovision. While waiting around Kigoma for a new boat crew, broke and unable to purchase first-quality food, Hayes suffered a return of the dysentery. The skinflint Belassis should have sent provisions or at least a directive, but no word came from that quarter.

On March 13, 1922, Hayes departed Kigoma, paddled north by men Bakari, the boat-builder, had assembled for Hayes: a "half-caste Arab crew, much more intelligent than the crude Karago gang," with Bakari himself at the helm. Compared with the shoreline south of Kigoma, that to the north was, if anything, "more hungry – which is saying much – and more dangerous."

As when he had traveled south from Kigoma, Hayes made one brief geology note in his diary: "the hardest sedimentary formation I have seen anywhere. A prospector's hammer makes little impression on them."

But enough about geology. His attention quickly strayed to what his Arab paddlers told him were two "sokos" ambling the lakeside. Hayes thought the pair may have been gigantic chimpanzees or perhaps gorillas strayed in from the Kivu district of the Congo. David Livingstone had recorded the term soko when first passing through this area, probably seeing large chimpanzees.

When Hayes directed his paddlers to approach closer, every man pulled hard in the opposite direction. The sokos would somehow get hold of them! Sokos attacked without provocation and, an Arab paddler assured Hayes, "[t]heir first act is to bite a man's fingers off."

Sokos did not frighten Hayes. He worried more about the gusty winds blowing fierce off headlands, rising 2000 to 3000 feet sheer from the water. Bakari, steering from the stern, scoffed at trivial concerns about the wind. "A good seaman," he darted into a cove whenever danger threatened from the lake – but would beach nowhere near a soko.

Hayes and the Arab crew spent ten days in the canoe on Lake Tanganyika. Bald eagles soared overhead, splendid waterfalls dropped sheer into pellucid waters, and an occasional rock merited tapping with a hammer.

Back at Kigoma, Hayes, footsore, his lips chapped and bleeding from the lake winds, delivered Bird's his definitive opinion: "There is no coal in this part of the country." A couple of limestone quarries the Belgians had worked during their years occupying these disputed territories near the Malagarazi River explained rumors to the contrary.

At Kigoma, Hayes spoke with a couple of men recently in the employ of Ernest Bishop and got a report on the recent adventures of the elephant hunter and Hayes' erstwhile companion up the Nile. Belgian officials on the Congo side of the lake had trumped up some charge or another against Bishop, really just a ruse to drive him out of the Congo and steal his trade goods. The men to whom Hayes spoke had broken Bishop out of jail, secured all his trade goods, and sailed a steel boat, in the dead of night, across Lake Tanganyika to the British shore. Conscientious British officials at Kigoma had looked into Belgian accusations against their countrymen but found insufficient evidence to comply with extradition demands. Hayes had just missed Bishop, gone up to "some new gold rush" at Lake Victoria just in case the dust needed a little more time to settle in Kigoma.

Hayes might have gone up to Lake Victoria to scout up his old friend Bishop but for the arrival at Kigoma of Bellasis with a geologist named Mendell in tow. The Bird's men wanted to verify Hayes' reports on the lakeside south from Kigoma to Karago. His reports were correct, but Hayes didn't mind going over the same ground again, especially since Bellasis had "a fine outfit," and, instead of walking, they would be taking the lake steamer *Fifi*.

The steamer *Fifi*, formerly a German naval boat captured by the British during the war, ran weekly between Bismarkburg (Kasanga) near the south end of the lake and Kigoma to the north. Hayes, Bellasis, and Mendell caught the *Fifi* headed south on April 1, 1922, and got off at the small boat's scheduled stop at Karago. Mendell proved himself "a fine chap … In fact, he is one of the best mining geologists in Africa, and I enjoyed his company." Bellasis proved himself just who Hayes thought he was: a petty bureaucrat "trying to make a big name cheap."

Bellasis finally conceded that Hayes' initial report had been correct: Bird's had come up empty prospecting on the lakeshore. So, what next? Bird's wondered if Hayes would like to take a train ride to Morogoro, three-quarters of the way back to Dar es Salaam? Bellasis had heard another rumor about yet another abandoned German mine.

His visit to this historic place, Kigoma/Ujiji, where his heroes Livingstone and Stanley had trod, had been one of the happiest accomplishments of all Hayes' travels. Nevertheless, he would be happier to leave it: "This is one of the most unhealthy parts of Africa I have ever seen." A day's rest on the train would help but this unhealthy place had worn him out: "I travel on nerve and nothing else."

As soon as he got off the train at Morogoro, Hayes wrote a thankful, loving description of all the food available at the markets. Riches! Health! He could buy meat every day, honey, fruit, and vegetables of every sort. Women brought him baskets of cucumbers daily. Not wanting to appear ungrateful, Hayes gave the first woman who approached a handful of salt and told her not to come again. The next day, she and all her friends returned laden with baskets filled with every variety of fruit and vegetable.

An agent for Bird's at Morogoro, just as parsimonious as Bellasis, supplied Hayes with a small amount of cash to outfit again for the bush. Hayes would have left Morogoro on April 15, 1922, but influenza and septic poisoning laid him low for four days.

On April 21, 1922, still sick with the dregs of flu, Hayes had been walking two days "through a land of marvelous beauty." Cold streams fell from high hills tumbling over great boulders to murmur in ripples and linger in pools under luxuriantly tangled jungle streamers. The next day rose even more beautiful, revealing a splendid German road "through dazzlingly white crystalline limestone covered with evergreen forest." Presently, the road dipped steeply into the gorge of the Ruvu River and let onto a wide, open-forested plain with a rickety bridge built to cross the river.

Just as Hayes began setting up his tent in the shade near a roadside brook, the sound of bugles shattered his evening idyll: "Two askaris, bearing one a huge banner, the other a naval blue ensign, hove in sight round a sharp turn in the road." The buglers marched along following the flag, then came "the great man with all the pomp displayed by Kaiser or Czar." A Brit whose name and rank Hayes learned later: Assistant District Commissioner Kenney-Dillon.

A small girl of some ten-years rode by next, and then a woman "clad in shorts and a blouse." Father, daughter, and mother all reclined in machilas, shaded hammocks slung on stout poles, carried by four men each. "After them came a motley array of askaris and servants arrayed like Solomon in all his glory." Hayes got a curt nod from Kenney-Dillon in response to what could only have been a mocking gesture, "this when I rose and saluted him." The child stared curiously "while her mother did not deign to notice me at all."

Not half an hour after the entire retinue paraded past Hayes' campsite by the brook, a "servant" arrived "courteous and ill at ease." Kenney-Dillon's messenger said he knew it was not customary for a White man to send a native without an explanatory note but the "Bwana" had demanded he find out who camped by the trail and "what I was doing in the country."

Hayes says he bit back an angry retort for the sake of his employers, and, mirroring the exaggerated civility of Kenney-Dillon's servant, politely directed the man to inform Mr. Kenney-Dillon he would not be calling due to illness. When a second messenger came later with an offer of medicines, Hayes declined, swearing, "I would rather have died than taken it from such a snob." Hayes continued on at some length in his diary about Kenney-Dillon, beginning at "swine," then "creature," arriving finally at, "[i]t was such swell headed fools who made the American colonies break away from the motherland."

Hayes took reluctant leave of the cool Uluguru Mountains on April 26, 1922, tarrying one extra day just to enjoy the luscious oranges selling a hundred for a shilling in these fertile mountains. Eventually, though, he had to get on toward the prospecting work.

In just a few hours the languorous wanderer descended the last of the hills and strolled the fine road lined with thousands of Borassus palms, "their bottle shaped trunks and feathery crests combined making a delightful picture." Riding across the combined streams of the Mvuha and Ruvu rivers by canoe, Hayes remembered to keep his hands well out of the water. At a riverside village, he had heard the residents "bewailing the victim of a croc," a cry he had heard "time and again" all over Africa.

Bird's had directed Hayes to this short-grass, lightly forested valley, "ideal game country," in search of another of their employees, Johann Berger. Berger, a South African Boer, ran a six-inch shot drill sinking test holes looking for coal. Hayes, now established with Bird's as a reliable coal expert, had instructions to show Berger where to drill.

It took Berger a lot longer to drill a test hole than it took Hayes to locate sites for drilling. To make himself useful in his down time, Hayes set about building Berger a proper house by the river. His timber crew had to go some way back up into the mountains and break through a thornbush barrier encircling the foothills to find suitable framing poles. The work progressed slowly; even so, how could Hayes chide the men for veering off-task to rob a beehive? His housebuilders wanted the comb and larva; Hayes happily took the honey.

Hayes had a congenial workmate for the drilling: "A nice chap Berger. Both of us have a great hate in common, Kenney-Dillon." The assistant district commissioner had been "high-hatting" Berger too, "and after we had shown him every courtesy."

When not carping about Kenney-Dillon, Berger pined for his lost love back in South Africa. "She is the moon and stars, the sun in the heavens, the elephant and the lion, his all-in-all." Hayes tried to help with Berger's lovesickness, pointing out that there is always a new crop of girls coming along. Bachelor Perkins went so far as to commiserate with Berger, telling his driller: "Like other boobs I too have fallen for girls, thinking I was some lady killer. The truth was, I was merely a fish well hooked." None of Hayes' kind sympathies seemed to ease Berger's suffering in the least.

Ten days after the first workman cut the first timber, the new house stood ready for occupancy. Bamboo from an abandoned Catholic mission had been repurposed for the rafters; long grass clad the walls and shingled the roof. How nice to share a dry, tidy hut after days working in a chilling rain.

Hayes pointed Berger to what, in his estimation, was the most likely test hole. Berger drilled straight to coal – the seam a quarter-inch thick – after hundreds of feet of coring. Success? Failure? It didn't matter because about this time, Hayes figured out Bird's true business in Tanganyika was a land grab: "Our company has 500 square miles area blocked out, though it is illegal."

Hayes feigned shocked outrage that graft might extend beyond the borders of his own country, even to the generally steady British, remarking that Bird's practices would have been right in step in San Francisco or New York. Still, "[t]his is one of the rawest cases I have met with in all my wanderings." Had he discovered such fraud in San Francisco or New York, Hayes would have resigned on the spot. So too in Tanganyika: "If I remain longer, I am consenting to it." His letter of resignation went out to Bellasis that very day.

Thoroughly disgusted with Bird's – and having no other recourse – Hayes planned to walk the sixty miles to the railhead at Ngere Ngere. He figured he could do it in two days despite a physical inventory that included self-diagnosed "dysentery, fever, blood poison, and bad food and exposure."

Two days and sixty miles later, Hayes sat in the rail station at Ngere Ngere bringing his journal up to date. Hayes fumed in the aftermath of a quarrel with the Indian stationmaster. British fare structure prevented any European from riding third class. The "Hindi" insisted Hayes pay second class, but, yes, he would be riding in an open freight car alongside native travelers who paid third: "I don't get the idea, but it's British justice and must be right." And, the stationmaster added, the train would not depart the Ngere Ngere station for seven days.

Heavy rains fell the night Hayes' open-air boxcar departed Ngere Ngere. The drenched second-class traveler shivered, "not far off from pneumonia," through the night toward Dar es Salaam. A couple of miles out from the capital city, a conductor jerked Hayes from among the third-class passengers, out of the rain and into a covered car. The conductor acted not out of any particular concern for Hayes, but in order to preserve the appearance of race propriety, and thereby "save his skin" at the station. Hayes, cold to the bone, registered no complaint at the preferential treatment.

At Dar es Salaam, Hayes got a deal on a last-minute ticket for the steamer *Karoa* bound for Durban, South Africa: "I paid 7 pounds ten shillings ... against fifteen pounds all the others paid, and there is much grumbling about it." The night the *Karoa* sailed, a couple of Hayes' grumbling pals tried their utmost to "get me spifflicated just for once." Of course, Hayes successfully resisted: "I have never taken a drink in my life and never will." He seems to have made good on that teetotalling prognostication written here in the 44th year of his 85 year life.

As Dar es Salaam dwindled off the stern of the *Karoa*, the same melancholy that always seized Hayes upon leaving Africa descended on the sober, solitary traveler. He knew he had to leave. How could he, in good conscience, stay on at Bird's? No, he could not participate in their corporate fraud – and, beyond morality, beneath his principled refusal to participate in Bird's swindle, Hayes' deteriorating health demanded a more congenial climate. Once again, an African adventure had wrecked his health.

But, he rallied, hadn't the experiences been worth the privation? He had seen Ujiji, stood where Livingstone greeted Stanley! As his two heroes would surely have attested, despite every travail, "[t]here is something tremendously fascinating about the bush. The hardships seem nothing once past, are the brightest spots in one's experiences."

11. In the Meantime: A Quick Circumnavigation of the Globe, 1922-23

To rest and recover from the rigors of Tanganyika, Hayes circumnavigated the globe between May 1922 and March 1923. He didn't acknowledge circumnavigations in his diary, but sailing west back to San Diego in 1922 marked his fourth full circle around the globe in the thirty years since striking out on his own at age 15.

San Diego always drew him back, but could never hold him. After he tired of the gentle breezes and soft sunshine of Southern California, his health recovered and feet itching again, he eventually sailed west, continuing around the globe, back to South Africa.

On the first leg of Hayes' long sea voyage toward San Diego, the *Karoa* weighed anchor at Dar es Salaam, Tanganyika, on May 31, 1922, to steam east toward Bombay (Mumbai). At a quick call at the Seychelles Islands, a few new passengers came aboard, one among them an interesting widow. Between the widow and Hogarth, "a giant Highland Scot," on his way home from Dar es Salaam, Hayes had congenial conversation partners for the long, easy sail down the east African coast past Mozambique, then Lorenzo Marquez, before arriving at Durban, South Africa. On one of the long, easy sailing days, the interesting widow must have conceived an incorrect understanding of Hayes' conversational gallantries. At Durban, she invited him to call at her home in Johannesburg. Hayes could tell by the look in her eyes that she was "keen on marriage." No, he confided in his diary, he would not call in Johannesburg. She had been an entertaining traveling companion for a week at sea, but "why should I look on her favor?"

At Durban, Hayes would very much have liked to catch a steamer for Japan, but ships sailed only rarely for the Orient and the port had none scheduled in the immediate future. Hayes couldn't afford a long layover in Durban. The Savoy Hotel was comfortable enough, but his health wouldn't improve in the poor weather. Furthermore, he had neither the stamina nor the funds to properly attend to "the young married women down to take the sea air [who] want men to escort them and pay the bills."

The only realistic destination out of Durban would have to be London; from there Hayes guessed he could continue on to New York. Hogarth would be along as far as London, a good companion for that leg of the trip.

On the deck of the *Gloucester Castle*, in rough seas off Cape Agulhas on the southern tip of the African continent, Hayes steadied himself to make a brief inventory of his explorations in Africa. Both a sense of accomplishment and characteristic melancholy tinged his reverie: "In my wanderings I have seen Africa's four most prominent headlands. Bon [north], Guardafui [east], Agulhas [south], Verde [west]. Her four great rivers, the Niger, Nile, Congo, and Zambesi. Yet there is much I have not seen, and likely never will."

At Cape Town, with an eye ever-attuned to natural beauty, Hayes admired the great flat Table Mountain rising 3,000 feet above the city. On the other hand, with a moral sense ever-attuned to exalted villainy, Hayes condemned rather than admired Cecil Rhodes. The itinerant American mining engineer from the backwoods of Oregon sailing sick, alone, and despondent yet again away from Africa, dismissed the architect of British Empire in South Africa and founder of De Beers Consolidated Mining Company, with its worldwide diamond monopoly, as an "alleged empire builder." No one could dispute the wealth, the power, or the lasting influence

Rhodes, dead only twenty years in 1922, had on the southern half of the African continent, but Hayes, for whom ends never justified means, could, and did, critique Rhodes' business practices that Hayes saw as identical to those he had witnessed in the Congo.

Out from Cape Town, the *Gloucester Castle* made next landfall at a lonely island Hayes had long wanted to visit. After the defeat of Napoleon's reconstituted army at Waterloo in 1815, British leaders sent the God Emperor to St. Helena, in the South Atlantic Ocean, 12,000 miles from the nearest landmass. From the docks, Hayes and Hogarth hiked the five-and-a-half miles to Longwood, Napoleon's last residence, "a building much like a Kansas farmer's home in my own country." Another mile brought the hikers to Napoleon's first gravesite, vacant now after the body had been transferred to Invalides in Paris "long ago." Hogarth offered Hayes a "chin-chin" as the two toasted "La Premiere Empereur" from a stream running clear past a simple plaque nailed to a large tree in a grove tended for more than 100 years after the British gave control of the island over to the French.

The *Gloucester Castle* didn't stop at Ascension but Hayes saw enough from the deck to give the island a coruscating review: "If one sought the whole world over, he could scarcely find a more unattractive spot than Ascencion [sic]. Hot, desolate, barren beyond words to tell, it is and always will be a place to be shunned."

Tenerife, in the North Atlantic off the coast of Western Sahara, pleased his traveler's eye more than Ascension. Wireless towers had been installed since Hayes had last visited, but no more need be said about Tenerife, since "[t]his place I have seen several times and have described it elsewhere, so will say little here."

Hayes dawdled in London only long enough to visit the South Kensington Museum of Natural History. Five days after arriving in England, he faced into the mid-Atlantic wind on the steamer *Aquitania*, making 23 knots toward New York.

Hayes had written previously about New York and he repeated more denigration here: "People don't live in a city, they merely exist." In fact, Hayes barely managed his own existence in New York. The compulsory smallpox vaccination he had received aboard the *Aquitania* had awakened his recurrent malaria. He lay eleven days thrashing in a cheap hotel room subduing the vaccine and the disease.

By the time he could stand again, Hayes had lost whatever physical recuperation the sea might have affected. He assessed his physical condition as about the same as when leaving Dar es Salaam: fever, sore arm, and his face covered by water blisters. Happy to see the last of New York, Hayes hobbled aboard the Pacific Mail steamer *Columbia* bound for San Francisco via the Panama Canal.

Colón, Panama, had the "the largest number of prostitutes I have seen anywhere." The working women seem to have been the main attraction for many of his fellow passengers on the *Columbia*, tourists out "to drink the breweries dry." Hayes avoided the prostitutes and the breweries but not a pickpocket in the tourist square. A savvy traveler, of course he carried only $2; nevertheless he objected on principle to being robbed.

At Cortina, Nicaragua, 800 caged, squawking parrots came aboard, bound for the California parrot market. Small nimble boats, Hayes called "lighters," came and went with other cargos at La Libertad, San Jose De Guatemala, Acajutla, and Champerico, various towns along a green coast fenced by perfectly formed volcanoes: "There are no words to describe this untellable, enchanting beauty, one must see it for himself to adequately understand."

Hayes gladly stepped off the *Columbia* in San Francisco on September 13, 1922, fifteen pounds off his normal weight following the malarial fevers. Some old friends in this familiar town suggested Hayes seek medical treatment in a hospital. He appreciated the concern, but "[t]his is an institution I have never graced, and hope I never do. Cash is too difficult to obtain to spend it for mere recuperating in one of these places." Instead, Hayes put himself to bed for 36 hours in "a low class Howard Street hotel."

Deciding that the soft air of San Diego would be more recuperative than the fog of San Francisco, in late September Hayes went south to spend a couple of weeks in balmy Southern California, enough time to kick the fever, regain ten of the lost pounds, and, at age 44, begin thinking about returning to school(!)

He followed the thought of scholarship seriously enough to enquire at the offices of the University of California about their geology curriculum. In reply, the University of California produced a stack of books, which, upon examination, Hayes announced he had already read. Hadn't he bought the books himself to meet the practical needs of his various mining jobs? Fine, he was told, three years at the University of California learning it all over again properly would yield the credits: "So I'm not going, life don't hold enough years for that."

Hayes always had mixed motivations about formal schooling. When returning to high school at age 27, he wrote of wanting a warm place out of the rain, downplaying his voracious curiosity and the desire to have his independent learning accredited. Some of the same motivations probably applied here, along with the fact that a credentialed engineer warranted a much higher salary than a roustabout autodidact.

By mid-October Hayes found himself back in Bandon, Oregon. He hadn't wanted to come, but succumbed to an internal sense of familial duty: "I don't want to go north. But go I will, for it seems my place, and if I fail to go I will not prosper." He received a warm reception from various cousins (undoubtedly including Minnie Donaldson whose son John, to whom Hayes eventually gave his diaries, would have been 22 at the time and attending Oregon State University).

Hayes intention to "stay here for a while" lasted all of November and December 1922. The Coast Guard station took him on again; his health continued to improve despite the raw, cold air of the Southern Oregon seas; and, still thinking about formal education, at the urging of some friends and relatives, he followed through with an application to the school of journalism at the University of Oregon.

Four days before receiving his acceptance to the school of journalism as a special student (at age 44), Hayes wrote a long African daydream into his diary. What, he wondered, would have happened had he followed his intention to go into the Azande country and start a war against the Belgians assisted by Renzi and Bukoyo? Mopoie would probably have joined in with his 20,000 warriors, but, no, "[i]n the end they would have done for us ...." Hayes tried to convince himself, "... it is better as it is." Maybe journalism school at the University of Oregon in rainy Eugene would be a better choice than dying in a blaze of glory leading an African rebellion?

Hayes stewed over the journalism school decision for three weeks as he watched the simple people of this simple Oregon coastal town, "take their adventure vicariously, watching moving pictures and racing around in cars." Journalism school would certainly secure him a position of prominence in this dull, domesticated society. That realization – that journalism school would secure for him a quotidian place in the society of his birthplace – settled the question.

On the last day of 1922, Hayes resolved to return to "the long trail," headed for "Tahiti, New Zealand, Australia, and elsewhere." Of course, the "elsewhere" would be Africa as it always was for him.

Rough seas at Coos Bay prevented any ship crossing the bar at the mouth of the Coquille River, so Hayes had to travel "overland" to San Francisco. A "cousin Mary" traveled with him the first 120 miles to Eugene. This was almost certainly my grandfather John Donaldson's sister Mary, my great-aunt, who, according to my mother, had a low opinion of Hayes. Mary disapproved of Hayes' practical joking.

On the steamer *Tahiti*, outward bound from San Francisco for the island of Tahiti, Hayes chatted politics with a Russian mining engineer named Archangel. Exiled to the islands by "minions of the Great White Czar," Archangel, who had made his way back to his homeland following the Bolshevik revolution, was now returning to his plantation of cocoanuts and vanilla on Tahiti.

Archangel supported the communist revolution in principle but granted that it could have been a little more successful in the concrete. Hayes quotes Archangel saying "'I never had a square meal during the eighteen months I stayed in Russia.'" Archangel said he'd thought seriously about accepting an offer from Trotzky [sic] to head up all mining in the Ourals [sic]. But no, plantation ownership on Tahiti suited him better than the chaos and hunger in Russia.

Hayes bid Archangel farewell at Tahiti with the two not quite in accord about Russia because Hayes did not like Archangel's "apologies for the slaughter of the Czar and family, it will always be a blot on Russia's escutcheon." Archangel, waving on his way down the gangway, tossed back: "'Any change that came had to be for the better.'"

Shipboard conversation on the *Tahiti* lapsed only briefly for Hayes with the departure of Archangel. As the Russian revolutionary departed, an interesting-looking fellow came aboard: Chadwick, a recent hire by the British African Eastern Trading Company (parent of the present-day Unilever Company), returning to oversee British interests in the Belgian Congo at a post in Coquilhatville (Mbandaka).

In fact, though new to this job, Chadwick was returning to the Congo. On his first stint up the Congo River, Chadwick had chanced across an old acquaintance of Hayes, the elephant hunter Frank Bowen with whom Hayes and Ernest Bishop had traveled to Lake Albert when Hayes left the Heart of Africa Mission in 1915. Chadwick rather insensitively delivered Hayes some sad news: "'You will see Bowen no more, unless you meet him in hell.'" Chadwick had only the haziest details about the death of a man he clearly considered a scoundrel – something to do with the Belgians.

The news of Bowen's death threw Hayes into something of a funk: "I miss him, bad as he was." Off the top of his head, Hayes listed the names of nine other adventurers he had known, ten with the addition of Bowen, departed down "the long trail that knows no return." He could think of only one, good old Bishop, remaining above ground. Hayes mused that the free adventuring life, lived large, is usually not long. (In January 1925, Hayes speculated he would be with Bowen, hopefully not in hell, "in a little while." For all his self-supposed clairvoyance, Hayes mis-predicted his own death by nearly 40 years.)

Hayes said only a brief hello and goodbye to a few friends in Sydney before transferring from the *Tahiti* to the *Sophocles*, departing the same day he arrived, his 45th birthday. Sailing on a third class ticket, paid through to London by way of South African ports, the aging adventurer mused: "Time slips by, I will soon be an old man." If only, he wished, humans could live 700 or 800 years – maybe one could realize a few more accomplishments in that span. But then again, "[m]ost of us would spend the time in pleasure and selfishness."

The great albatrosses constantly circling a ship so far out to sea looked comparable with the largest Hayes had ever measured, a full eleven-foot wingspan. And the whales. Where were the whales? By 1923, Hayes could already see their numbers vastly diminished from his earlier sea voyages. His disgust that these magnificent, mammalian seagoing companions had already been pushed toward extinction, consumed for oil and fertilizer, expanded into an eloquent, characteristically misanthropic, critique of humans in the ecosystem – written some eighty years before the introduction of the term Anthropocene extinction: "...the supply of whales is not inexhaustible. Few people seem to realize this, however, and man is running true to form. Such species of animals as are of use to him he protects and increases their numbers greatly. All others have to make room, the world is his and all that is in it. The standard cry is 'What use is that animal? Why perpetuate the species?' I wonder what these animals think of man, and wonder myself just what use he is, what with his poison gas, his many instruments for exterminating his fellows and at the same time some advocating mass marriages with a new child every year."

Tangled in these melancholy ruminations, Hayes stepped, with no particular fanfare, back onto African soil at Durban, South Africa, on March 8, 1923. What exquisite heartache, sickness, disappointment, and miracle, he wondered, did the continent of his imagination promise a now-aging, unfulfilled adventurer this fifth time heading for rough travel into the interior?

12. North from South Africa; Running Scared through the Congo, 1923

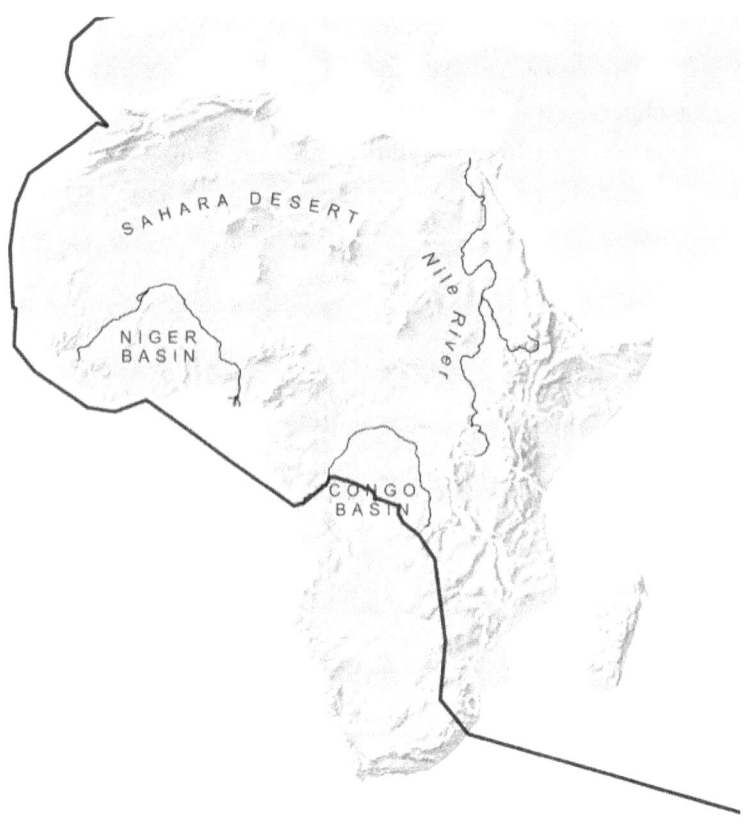

Wealthy South Africans thronged the dusty streets of Durban in March 1923, having come to the seaside for the crisp air and the horse racing season. The crowds still bustled, but Hayes could sense a definite change in a city "not so flush as last year."

Since Hayes had last visited Durban one year previously, European gold mine workers had revolted near Johannesburg, in what became known as the Rand Rebellion. Violent mobs protested diminished wages and the advancement of Black and other non-White workers to skilled positions previously reserved for Whites.

The Rand Rebellion had been a bloody affair that dampened spirits and emptied wallets even in Durban 350 miles distant, the main shipping port to and from the riches at Johannesburg. Hayes reported that 273 police and more than 600 striking workers had been killed. The mine owners had prevailed and, in the aftermath of the strike, wages had been slashed. But even a passing American could see the labor unrest hadn't really settled: "The trouble has merely been driven under cover, and will at the proper moment emerge the stronger for its rest."

Hayes had come to Durban with only the vaguest of plans, but his real objective seems to have been to return, by the long route, to the Belgian Congo. He thought (perhaps hallucinated might be more apt given the ruckus he'd caused on leaving the last time) he might scout around the Kasai, see about maybe getting back on with the Forminiere again. Sure, Boice and Oliver had been brutes at Forminiere offices in Brussels, but hadn't they said Donald Doyle, their man on the ground in the Congo, wanted Hayes back in harness? Sure, Hayes gulled himself, that might work.

On the weeklong, 1,700–mile train ride from Durban to Elizabethville, between March 20 and March 26, 1923, Hayes wrote extensive diary entries detailing the geography and culture of southern Africa. British colonial policy the world over followed a kind of economic play-it-safe character.

At the outset, before disputed lands, not yet colonized, had become profitable, the British chartered single private companies to initiate economic exploitation, supported militarily but not administratively. Later, with the money flowing from the private corporation, official British governance could be established. In South Africa, the British parliament granted Cecil Rhodes charter to the British South Africa Company north from the Limpopo River (the current border between South Africa to the south and Botswana and Zimbabwe to the north) in 1889 – with no clearly specified northern limit.

By 1923, the wars between British, Dutch and indigenous forces resulted in British colonial holdings in southern Africa extending 3,300 miles north from the Cape to Lake Tanganyika and 1,500 miles east to west from German South West Africa (Namibia) to Mozambique. Two of the large northern colonies, bearing Cecil Rhodes' name, remained under control of the British South African Company until the middle of the 1920s: Northern Rhodesia (Zambia) bordered the Belgian Congo, where Leopold's claims had stopped the company's expansion north; and Southern Rhodesia (Zimbabwe) that had incorporated Matabeleland.

On his first rail leg north from Durban to Johannesburg, the Dutch settlements reminded Hayes of any small town in Kansas or Nebraska. The Zulu settlements looked prosperous as well: kraals, grass-topped villages, herds of cattle, and fields of maize.

Nothing other than gold could explain the existence of Johannesburg on these upland rolling hills that now looked to Hayes so much like West Texas or New Mexico. A thirty-mile continuous settlement of mining structures traced "the reef" of the Witwatersrand. Great mounds of creamy grey tailings extended twice that distance, the full length of The Rand. Hayes considered "[t]hese mounds … as impressive as … the pyramids." Windblown dust penetrated everywhere.

Mafeking (Mahikeng), 175 miles west from Johannesburg, sat on the border of the great Kalahari Desert – sand and scrub stretching away to the north and west. Here shallow lakes continuously changed location as shifting sands altered the course of rivers that flowed in from more moist regions to the north, rivers coming to die in the Kalahari.

In Livingstone's accounts of exploring this region, Hayes had read that Lake Ngami in Northern Botswana supported hippos, crocodiles, and native fishermen. When Hayes came through, 80 years after Livingston, Lake Ngami was "a desert waste."

Livingstone also wrote of the abundant wildlife crowding this region when the Scottish explorer/missionary came through in the 1840s: millions of antelope, rhinoceros, giraffe, elephants, and lions everywhere. Hayes blamed Dutch market hunters for the extermination of this vast biome for meat and skins. Hayes saw not a single wild lion south of the Orange River; only the occasional springbok in all the Transvaal; and the "quagga and blue buck have departed from this world as completely as the dodo of Mauritius."

Dutch rifles also "killed off the bushmen as vermin, just as the American wiped out the native Indian and the Australian poisoned the aboriginals in Queensland for eating his sheep." Hayes wryly attributes this "progress" to "'civilization'" then brings himself up short with: "One might say a lot about it if he wished."

Hayes writes that Bulawayo had been laid out for a population of 300,000, but in 1923, he estimated no more than a tenth that number lived there. Here the dry lands of the Kalahari gave way to lush grass from good rains supporting many cattle. Inexpensive meat could be purchased at the Bulawayo market, a welcome circumstance as the train had dropped its dining car, leaving passengers to provide for themselves. A daily newspaper, excellent civic buildings, even a museum open to the public, marked the prosperous, up-and-coming city of the future through which Hayes briefly strolled.

Just over the border of Southern Rhodesia (Zimbabwe), crossing into Northern Rhodesia (Zambia), the train pulled into the small town of Livingstone. Hayes made the seven-mile walk to sit and write in his journal on the edge of the great cataract of Victoria Falls. "Of all the strange scenes I have seen in my wanderings nothing excels this in beauty and awe inspiring wonder."

He continued on for two full pages describing the fall of the Zambezi River 360 feet into a narrow abyss, its five columns of mist rising miles to form clouds in the blue sky. The mighty Zambezi, "about as large as the Columbia after all its tributaries have joined it below Portland, Oregon," was, according to the locals, running at a 23-year high in March of 1923.

Deafened by roaring water, Hayes watched the great plume disappear into a small fissure below. He could see rain falling in torrents just out from the falls, the mist returning to earth to fashion a small, verdant ecosystem in an otherwise arid countryside of acacia and tall grass. Rainbows played incessantly across the faces of these mist-clouds, ribbons of light changing with the drift of airborne water. In Hayes' mind, a name referencing a British monarch diminished rather than enhanced the beauty of the falls: "Would that Livingstone had left the native name on it! Mosi-o-tunya, or smoke-that-sounds."

In the late 19th century, British colonial interests, deeply influenced by the verve of young Cecil Rhodes, dreamed of a "Cape to Cairo" rail line, running the length of the African continent. Though the full line had (and has) yet to be completed, Rhodes did his part in the south. According to Hayes, Rhodes specifically instructed his engineers to build the bridge across the Zambezi where the trains, as they passed, would catch the spray of the falls.

Hayes did not mention a wetting from the spray, but said that passengers on the train got a good view of the falls after zigging and zagging forty miles along the "river a boiling brown mass of swirling water on which floats great balls of foam." Squinting carefully Hayes could not quite site where he imagined a powerhouse could be built, but the rest of a project to electrify this countryside seemed "comparatively easy" to him.

Just before arrival at Elizabethville (Lubumbashi), Hayes crossed from British Northern Rhodesia into the Belgian Congo, leaving the drainage of the Zambezi River and entering the drainage of the Congo River. Elizabethville did not "appeal to the eye at first sight." The central African town had none of the dash of Australian or Alaskan mining towns beyond a readily observable optimism that the ore would never run out – copper here, not nearly as exciting as gold, but Hayes had heard the 250-mile belt of ore assayed as high as 35%. (Top producing mines today barely reach 5%.)

Hayes wandered the streets of Elizabethville and its surrounding mines for three days before he realized something was missing: 40,000 African mining men and no whips: "Surely the high and mighty Bula Matadi has not forsaken the kiboko he loved so well!"

Why, if so, Hayes could go back to his well-paid job mining diamonds for the Forminiere. Everyone he spoke to around Elizabethville said whipping had ceased throughout the country. One man who had been in the Kasai told Hayes that his former boss, Donald Doyle, "a decent chap in many ways," ran the show at Tshikapa now. It sounded too good to be true. Hayes decided he would have to find his way up there overland and see for himself. He could ride the rail line a little further to Bukama, some three-hundred miles north of Elizabethville on the banks of the Lualaba River, 2,800 rail miles up from the Cape.

Hayes' small safari of five made 27 kilometers the first day out from Bukama in company with an itinerant Portuguese trader. Camped on a cool evening after a hot day, Hayes reveled to be back again in "the real Africa" away from the trains, the mines and the incompetent colonizers. How familiar it all was: the continuous hum of countless insects, jackals crying to the stars, a great lion with a strange catch in its voice seeming to double the volume of its all-night roaring, elephant spoor everywhere about the trail. In the morning, black and gold and scarlet shrikes warbled melodies across the cooing of a dove. The safari's exuberant leader pushed the small troop 41 kilometers the second day out.

A fourth long day's march across a grassy, water-soaked plain brought the company to a beautiful, though hungry, village. This close to a European post, the villagers planted only enough for their immediate needs: "They prefer to starve rather than to see the proceeds of their labor taken." The raids were bad when lead by a Belgian officer; worse if a lazy officer ordered out askaris unaccompanied: "for they rape the women, plunder the place for anything easily transported and wreck everything if there is a remonstrance."

Hayes paid a franc for the only food available to a weary traveler, manioc, "a ball of paste as large as my head." Fortunately, Hayes had carried a bit of meat from Bulawayo as he lost all appetite for the manioc upon seeing a seven-foot lizard loaded whole into the communal pot from which his paste had been portioned.

But the villagers kept the rest hut immaculately clean and a dance was on. While he wrote, about fifty women danced outside his door, their hair sculpted with red ochre and fat "like a plaster cast." As for the rest of their attire, "I could put [it] in my vest pocket." The men danced a short way back, looking wild in war paint and colobus monkey skins. Not entirely unexpectedly, Hayes heard the drumming cease as he walked to the riverside to bathe. All the dancers crowded around to view White skin on display: "One gets accustomed to a lot of things in Africa."

Unable to write on April 8, 1923, Hayes wrote instead on the 9th, labeling both "terrific days." The eighth started in a throwdown with one of his pagazis: "It was a draw, both of us got torn clothing and he drew a black eye, while I have a bad thumb …" Their struggle for leadership continued midday at the next hamlet where the man with whom he had fought proposed a halt for the night. Hayes reached for the nearest club to settle the matter: "One has to win his fights in Africa, else he has lost his prestige and has lost Africa. It is unlikely there will be further argument with this gentleman as long as our association continues." The small safari made ten more sullen miles that day, wading a swampy plain to a squalid village that rang with an eerie death wail "for someone lucky enough to die out of it."

Fortunately, the Lomami River, swift and turgid with a belt of thorn palm and papyrus swamp on either side, didn't have to be waded. Only thirty meters in width, a swinging rattan bridge slung between trees on either side easily spanned the river course. On the other side, the "usual neck-deep backwater" standing in "smelly bogs" where the incessant rain puddled between hills, repeatedly drenched the walkers throughout the afternoon on the way toward the rest house at Sultan Muleva's village.

The Sultan arrived clad in full leopard skin regalia to greet Hayes with a goat on offer, to purchase for dinner. And if the goat pleased Hayes perhaps this Inglese man could intervene with Bula Matadi? Muleva's village had been stripped of all able-bodied men and girls, his own sons held hostage. Hayes listened politely to the same story "too old to be rehearsed": hostages taken to secure carriers; women taken for harems of White officers; all foodstuffs confiscated. Hayes agreed: "Life is not worth living in the Congo." But what could he do? "Sorry I can't aid Muleva, but it's the old, old story I've heard a thousand times since my first time in the Congo nine years since."

Hayes stayed two days in the next rest house at Motombo Mukulu. The only work he saw any man of the village do adhered to a Belgian innovation: the chain gang of indigenous men, here overseen by other indigenous men, "for the imitative Negro at once copies every feature of Belgian rule he can."

The night before Hayes' little safari departed, the villagers gathered in the quagmire of the central compound for a Bakishi dance: "the men look weird and wild with white painted naked bodies." Young women, "whose beauty has not yet faded," stood in the background, the harem of Motombo Mukulu and his sons, all driven before the rhythm of an incessant drumbeat.

Just a few miles out of Motombo Mukulu the next day, an officious young Belgian officer stopped Hayes and his meager safari to check for proper authorizing papers. Hayes wasn't the only adventurer slogging around this part of Africa, most of the others "campaigning about … looking for alleged gold mines and other minerals, this without a license."

Finding Hayes' papers up to date, the officer, Du Vienne, remarked he had met Americans from the Forminiere before "and realizes we Yanks pay very little attention to dress in the bush." No insult either intended or received. Du Vienne went on to brag that by forced labor, he had constructed a fine road all the way to Kanda Kanda, four days march hence. Hayes welcomed the good path however far it lasted and excused Du Vienne's use of forced labor in the case of the men of Motombo Mukulu: "The women have to be the bread winners anyway, so it is well for these idlers to contribute something."

Du Vienne's road, "the finest bit of road I have seen in Africa," held up to within a mile of the Lubilash River (the upper stretch of the Sankuru River). But then, the safari had to wade a full mile of mud to approach the river proper. The channel beyond the mile-long slog ran as wide as the Lualaba (greatest source of the Congo River) and swifter. A ferry had been constructed here to accommodate automobiles!

Du Vienne's road continued straight and wider on the other side of the Lubilash. Hayes and his carriers warily boarded the clumsy ferry – three canoes lashed together riding low in the water to the point of floundering, to carry automobiles? – doing their best to ignore a gentle roar suggesting cataracts just downstream.

The far bank of the Lubilash marked a change in geography: rockier ground with less mud, the end of the dense jungle, and the beginning of abundant food. One can often measure how hungry a previous bit of Hayes' travels had been by the length of the list of foodstuffs he mentions at the end of the lean time: "Beans, onions, pumpkins, sweet potatoes, even European potatoes, bananas, plantains, chickens, eggs, and other edibles." With better food available, even the bully among the carriers left off his grumbling.

Outside Kanda Kanda, after crossing a raging Luilu River by wading to the armpits before floundering into a canoe, Hayes and the four new carriers came to the Catholic mission of Thielen Ste. Jacques "rising like a fairy castle in the wilderness." The architecture impressed Hayes far more than the work of the missionaries. Generally speaking, Hayes believed missions harmed more than helped their African converts: "Usually they are worse liars and thieves than before they renounced Paganism."

As if to prove Hayes' generalization, in the night, a young mission girl came to his room offering to "share my loneliness." Out of the question, of course, but not before Hayes had fully appraised the offer.

On April 27, 1923, three week's safari out from where he had departed the train at Bukama, Hayes made first contact with the Forminiere in the Congo. An engineer named Hill, whom Hayes knew from the Kasai, had been sent east from Tshikapa, here to Lukulenge overlooking the Bushimai River where "there are more diamonds … than at any other place known in the Congo." Hill had already proved 3,000,000 carats. So many diamonds of so little value: "None of these are gemstones, all are bort, or commercial diamonds fit only for abrasives, drills, and such."

Hayes found much to discuss with Hill: old times with the Forminiere; how to extract commercial grade diamonds; and how best to train up the ten "useless" Belgian assistants the company assigned Hill since "none of them know anything about the bush or of mining." Some of Hill's news sobered Hayes: a fellow named Mason, stationed near Hayes' Ngombe camp on the Kasai, had died recently from blackwater fever. But Hill also shared a bit of gossip that seemed more providential: someone had written up "the flogging business." The Belgian King Albert seemed to have taken notice and sent officers to patrol the mining camps specifically to guard against abuse of the natives. Hayes asked where Hill had gotten this information and "as it is the *Saturday Evening Post* it must be me." Speculating in his diary that he had authored an article halting use of the whip in all the Congo(!), Hayes surely did not speak his suspicions with Hill.

With three days to think it over, Hayes wrote, "I am almost surely in bad with the Forminiere." Hill very much wanted the experienced American to join him at the Lukulenge camp, "but says Doyle has the last word, I must see him." So despite misgivings about showing up at Forminiere headquarters, a man responsible for an international exposé about ongoing labor abuses at the Forminiere, Hayes set out west toward Tshikapa to speak with Donald Doyle about a job - with the Forminiere.

Not far from Tshikapa, on the doorstep of the main offices of the Forminiere, Hayes hated "to have come all this distance and not make good." But it did occur to him that a disgruntled worker who had borne tales to Forminiere offices in both Brussels and New York, not to mention writing an exposé to the *Saturday Evening Post*, might not receive a warm welcome back into harness. "But if it has stopped the slave gangs, the brutal floggings featuring the mines and the forced labor it has been worthwhile." Anyway, what choice had he this far along the trail? Nothing to do but press on and find out: "I wonder whether the Forminiere is going to kill the fatted calf or turn the bull dog loose for me." Hayes rather suspected the latter.

At lunch with a Belgian road worker the next day, Hayes learned Doyle ran the show at Tshikapa, overseeing sixty Whites – a good omen, Hayes assured himself, to have a friend in charge. Further on, still 200 miles from his old camps near the Angola border, many African men passing him on the trail, including one who had been Gervisse's cook, recognized Hayes. All reported "there is no more flogging at Tshikapa or on the field." So, that news buoyed Hayes' spirits further. Maybe this jaunt up from the Cape, "a venture at random," would turn out all right: with Hayes back in a lucrative job, vindicated in his convictions.

At Luebo, any budding optimism began to erode. On his way to a bunk at a large Presbyterian mission, Hayes passed by "a great cathedral where the Catholics have erected a vast church … this to show they are superior to the accursed heretics." Catholic missions always made Hayes gloomy, but the Presbyterian heretics, working under the very shadow of the cathedral, should have been better men reflecting, in Hayes' mind, the better doctrine of their denomination. While Hayes had been working the Forminiere diamond mines between 1918 and 1920 and afterward, Presbyterian Polity back home had been meeting with all the other Protestant missionary agencies to the Congo. With a united voice – from thousands of miles away – all, "greatly deplored the excesses of the Forminiere agents and others in the Congo, especially the brutal treatment of the natives."

Nevertheless, here on the ground in the Congo, Hayes could see that the twenty Presbyterian missionaries, all college-educated Southerners from the United States, must have been corrupted by the all-powerful joint Belgian/American mining company: every one of them had a motorized bicycle. From where else would each man get his motorbike, so helpful to spreading the Word? Who else but the Forminiere would donate 100,000 francs toward building a Presbyterian hospital?

In Hayes' experience, such donations never came without expectations. He wrote with certainty that these men's mouths had been "hushed with gifts, their eyes are blinded by courtesies they must in course return." Hadn't these men been preaching redemption through Christ all the while the Forminiere whipped its workers as a matter of company policy? Until Hayes alone had the courage to speak?

As always, Hayes had no patience for missionary hypocrisy, writing, "I would be ashamed to even mention the name of Christ unless I protested with all the means at my command at this abuse, as I have personally to the head officers in Brussels and New York and later to the publishers of Marcosson's propaganda in the *Saturday Evening Post* and the *Literary Digest*."

The Presbyterians further dampened Hayes' optimism with some unwelcome news: Boice, Hayes' bitter enemy, would be replacing Doyle at Tshikapa before Hayes could get there. To round out a thoroughly disagreeable visit to the mission at Luebo, the dentist in practice there, the one Hayes had detoured out of the direct path to Tshikapa to see about a nagging toothache, had recently departed with a colleague toward Forminiere headquarters. No dentistry for Hayes' aching jaw here. The mission supplied him five fresh porters and everyone in residence happily bid this acerbic wanderer farewell, out their door and on his way to Djoko Punda on the bank of the Kasai River.

As Hayes returned to the area of influence of the Forminiere, he began to see increasing evidence of Belgian depredations, notwithstanding reports he'd heard about no more whipping. Whole villages had been ripped up and transported here by the Belgian government to clear land for fruit plantations. Now the villages tended the plantations by "[f]orced labor, of course, with most of it returning into government coffers in the shape of 'taxes.'" More evidence a bit further on: big gangs of women impressed to work on the road stooped at their work, overseen by six Belgians "about equal to the black capitas I used on the Kasai, the only difference being the latter were more efficient."

Hayes had come to Djoko Punda to find Sommer, a missionary with whom Hayes had been friendly when he had been in this area three years previously. He quoted Sommer's initial, surprised, greeting at some length:

"'What are you doing here?' queried Sommer in wide-eyed wonder. 'Are you not afraid?'"

"'Of what?'" Hayes asked.

"'Of the Forminiere. Have you not heard your letters have been given publicly in the press, not only in the United States, but in Europe? We have just returned to Africa, and Boice came out from Europe with us. His is angry, says the company will keep an eye on you!'"

In fact, Sommer did put the fear of the powerful Forminiere into Hayes, but not immediately. The two sat up long into the night, Hayes listening to a long recitation of changes mandated at the Congo mines in the previous two years and why Boice held Hayes Perkins personally responsible: "Evidently my letters to both the *Saturday Evening Post* and the *Literary Digest* were taken to New York offices of the Forminiere, and these could not be repudiated by the company."

Or, Hayes thought but did not mention to Sommer, the press might have gotten hold of the story based on an interview Hayes gave to "a half drunk reporter who interviewed me at the dock in New York." Whatever its origin, press attention compelled the Belgian ambassador to the US to take the matter up with his home government "and it reached the ears of King Albert himself." Albert acted swiftly, sending officials to every mine and plantation in the Kasai, "to once and for all stop these abuses, and it has been done with an iron hand." Henceforth, no more whipping would be allowed in the Congo and an officer would be stationed in every village to ensure proper housing and humane treatment of the workers.

Hayes rejoiced at the changes but only briefly. Sommer had come to the frightening bit, telling Hayes: "'Boice is like an enraged mandrill or a grizzly bear in his desire to retaliate for being thus shown up.'" On Boice's order, no foreign correspondence from any Forminiere engineer could mention anything about the diamond fields until approved by officers of the company. Hayes could see that his very presence at the Mennonite mission made Sommer uneasy, "lest the weight of the angered Forminiere fall on them for showing me even this small kindness."

Later that night, alone with his journal, Hayes let his imagination run to the dire. How easy for the Forminiere, virtually without constraint in the Kasai, to trump up some charge. A long prison sentence? Or maybe they would "let me 'die of fever' being transported." It wouldn't be the first convenient death arranged in the Congo: "The askaris who escort such a man drown him on the way and report his death from malaria."

By midday, Hayes was halfway back to Luebo, running scared.

At Luebo, following a grueling seven-hour march, Hayes collapsed on the south side of the Lulua River, wary of crossing to the Presbyterian missionaries with their bicycles lest he endanger them with the Forminiere as well. To their credit, the missionaries invited him over but Hayes declined. He felt more at home in the village "among these publicans and sinners, for here there is at least no reserve, they treat me as one of their own." A Belgian man married to a "half-caste" girl put Hayes up for the night, including a generous supper that evening with Hayes seated among all the "mixed bloods at the table."

The Belgian family told Hayes a small auxiliary steamer ran up the Lulua River as far as Luebo. Should the boat ever arrive, Hayes could fly to Basongo at the confluence of the Kasai and Sankuru rivers and from there on to Stanley Pool. Rains poured without halt for four anxious days in Luebo as Hayes conjured imminent dangers: "Boice and Moody will trump up a charge and torture me if they could get away with it."

Fast time downriver putting Forminiere headquarters at Tshikapa farther and farther behind relaxed Hayes. He had time to look around at the natural beauty he must once again leave: green islands covered in flood, egrets, cormorants, geese, a sleeping crocodile, still many hippos, but their number vastly diminished from when Hayes traveled this way three years previously: "Pot hunters for the Kinshasa market have decimated their numbers, and there are now none where hundreds basked on bars or dozed in quiet pools at the ends of islands through the day."

His first night in Basongo, some disturbing news put Hayes back on the edge of fear. The first boat to Kinshasa wouldn't depart Basongo for three days and word around town had it that Donald Doyle, American head of the Forminiere in Congo, was following, quite by coincidence, on the next boat downriver from Luebo en route to the US. Doyle had once been Hayes' friend, the man Hayes thought might hire him back on at the mines, but now? "I think Doyle is right, but one never knows." Hayes hoped to get away before Doyle arrived to avoid any difficult confrontation.

Finally, the *Roi Albert* steamed up the Kasai to Basongo. Either Hayes' informant had incorrectly placed Doyle or the *Roi Albert* beat Doyle's boat to Basongo. Hayes made no mention of any encounter with Doyle on the *Roi Albert* down the Kasai, the river now three miles wide below its confluence with the Sankuru.

One day out from Basongo and Hayes wrote, "the *Roi Albert* is fast…." He referred not to the boat's speed but to her captain's ineptitude: the man had run his steamer full tilt onto a hidden bar. During the 24-hour wait until the steamer *Sambre* chanced along to pull them off the sand, Hayes collapsed with sunstroke. Cloudless hot air, sun striking off a mirror-like river, and the heat of the *Roi Albert's* boilers "was all I could bear," even beneath the brim of his helmet.

Underway again, a welcome breeze blew up the Congo River, or simply, "The River – as it is called by all people who live in this part of Africa," just below where the *Roi Albert* steamed out past the confluence of the Kasai River with The River. Lesser rivers in this land of rivers all feeding the Congo

River had distinct names. Hayes attempted to name as many as he could off the top of his head: "Luemba, Lubilash, Lubishi, Kalambai, Mulungu, Luilu, Bushimai, Lubi, Lulua, Kasadisadi, Lubembe, Tschiumbo, Longatshimo, Tshikapa, Lovua, Loange, Lubue, Lukendi, Sankuru, Lie, Kantsha, Kwilu, Kwango, and Mifini, … I have not named them all." Hayes estimated one tributary alone, the Kasai River, stretched as wide as the Mississippi at New Orleans.

As the *Roi Albert* tied up at the head of Stanley Pool (Pool Malebo), Hayes watched the sun set across the water on a rock formation Stanley's man, Frank Pocock, had dubbed the Dover Cliffs, shortly before Pocock died in the wild water below. Symptoms of the sunstroke Hayes had incurred on the river bar days previously persisted. Maybe sun delirium occluded his normal self-deprecating style. In his diary Hayes began comparing his own African adventures to those of Henry Morton Stanley: "My African travels are almost as great as his; but he was first and I am unknown." From marveling at the raw courage Stanley displayed in his early days of exploration and adventure in the 1870s and 1880s, Hayes soon progressed to critique his onetime "beau ideal." Stanley died in 1904, a world-famous explorer/adventurer. But in his later years, Stanley had become a willing collaborator in King Leopold's pillaging of the Congo, (and, Hayes noted with distaste for Stanley's lack of principle, the world famous adventurer/explorer was the only man known to have fought on both sides of the American Civil War).

By 1923, as Hayes sat on the east bank of Stanley Pool reflecting on his one-time hero, Stanley had been buried for nearly 20 years at Surrey in England. His headstone is inscribed Bula Matari, 1840-1904. In the 20 years since Stanley's death, Hayes had in fact traveled many of Stanley's paths – Congo, Equatoria, Tanganyika – a firsthand witness to the legacy of Bula Matari. To Hayes, a man on the lam, running before the limitless power of a multinational corporation for the crime of exposing some of its most inhumane abuses, Stanley now seemed to have been "a selfish adventurer who crushed all opposition in his effort to gain fame and wealth. He got them, but soon died unsung and unhonored, for he had saddled the Congo with a slave trade worse than that of the Arabs whom he sought to destroy."

The best Hayes could muster in defense of his childhood hero was: "Perhaps it required a ruthless man whose conscience had never been aroused to break the barriers and find his way down the trackless Congo." Even if he believed that about explorers and barriers, at 45, under the stern tutelage of a continent, Hayes had learned that he himself was not Stanley's kind of man.

Less than three months after leaving the Indian Ocean at Durban, South Africa, Hayes sailed on the *Thysville* from Banana into the Atlantic at the mouth of the Congo River having traveled some 3,000 miles north. For now, he wrote, "I do not care to cross Africa again. My journey has been profitless, and I am almost blind from sunstroke."

Of course Hayes sailed second-class on the *Thysville*, partly exercising his customary economy, but also because he presumed that Donald Doyle must be aboard this ship as well. The big man of the Forminiere would surely travel first class; maybe Hayes could dodge Doyle altogether.

Second-class on the *Thysville* turned out to have its own awkward encounters. CT Studd's daughter Pauline, whom Hayes had met in London when interviewing for the Heart of Africa Mission, and her husband, Norman Grubb, whom Hayes had not met, berthed second-class alongside the adventurer. Hayes spoke to Norman a couple of times incognito but avoided Pauline. He thought Pauline might recognize him: "Her eyes bore through me like those of one of Torquemada's familiars, and no doubt would love to have me on the rack now."

The ship's captain announced arrival at Assinie but Hayes knew they were actually at Grand Bassam. A mistake easily made: "All West Coast towns are similar to one another. Red tiled or corrugated iron roofs and white painted walls make up the houses." Light boats still ferried goods and passengers across the surf as in all Hayes' previous travels along the West African coast. The skipper allowed no sightseeing; only those departing went ashore. And, yes, Hayes confirmed through the grapevine, Donald Doyle was on board but had thus far been too busy with his reports to leave his cabin.

Not until Dakar did the "polished gentleman … courteous and thoughtful in every attitude," rise from his reports to take the deck air. Neither man feigned ignorance on meeting: "Our recognition was mutual." If strain had taken 20 pounds off Hayes' frame, it had put 30 pounds onto Doyle "and [he] does not look well." After a bit of small talk, "He deplores the excess weight," Doyle got down to the matter: "He tells me he sent three letters to me at Djoko Punda telling me to keep clear of Tshikapa, this because of fear of Boice." Frantic upon receiving no reply, Doyle then dispatched a runner who returned to him with news that Sommer's warning had been sufficient; Hayes had already fled.

If sunstroke had sent Hayes off the rails comparing himself to Henry Morton Stanley, it must have returned with a vengeance off the coast of Senegal. In response to Mrs. Doyle's dirty looks, Hayes compared himself to Jesus Christ. Oh, Hayes started, he knew he would have to endure much, "it is part of the game in the reform business, such men must learn to take it." He just hadn't counted on the duration of the suffering: "If one is lucky he dies. To live on is to be forgotten, forsaken of everyone who might have been a friend. I often think how fortunate Christ was, to have only three years hounding, then a short six hours of agony and a merciful death to end his sufferings." Overwrought comparisons aside, Hayes lived on for another 41 years through many more interesting adventures. He did die alone, misanthropic and forgotten at age 86, but stubbornly planted and tended more than a mile of floral beauty along the California coast with the last tatters of his optimism intact long into his final years.

On June 17, 1923, Hayes attended a shipboard salvation service directed in English by Norman Grubb. All the time Norman exhorted those present to change their ways and prepare to meet their God, Hayes feared "his wife Pauline was going to do a bit of personal work and drag me forth to the mourners bench." Hayes withstood her "eagle eye," all the while thinking that these missionaries would be better advised to renounce the evils and abuses of powerful men and corporations rather than "currying favor with companies like the Forminiere," if they really wanted to accomplish their stated work of alleviating the suffering of the natives.

Four days later, Norman Grubb finally confronted Hayes just after the steamer *Thysville* departed Santa Cruz de Tenerife. Pauline thought she recognized their traveling companion: "She remembered me from London." When Hayes confirmed his identity, Grubb inquired about conditions at Niangara at the Heart of Africa Mission in the earliest days. In reply, "I related my experiences with utmost candor."

Hayes claimed to take no offense at Grubb calling him a "damned liar" directly to his face. What else could one expect from CT Studd's son-in-law? The missionary was slated to take the reins at the Heart of Africa Mission when the old rascal shuffled off (not for another eight years as it turned out). Hayes did wish, however, that Norman Grubb had some experience of those early days upon which to base his denunciations. Ironically, as the conversation continued, it turned out that Grubb did have firsthand experience of the ways of his father-in-law: "[Grubb] himself admits Studd drinks, uses narcotics…"

Hayes evidently lacked the theological training necessary to untangle the sophistry that led from Grubb's initial admission concerning alcohol and drugs to the end of the same sentence: "… yet [Studd] is a saint." Hayes never could square the follies of drink and drug use in "a chosen apostle of God" as so many others around Studd seemed able.

Most of the "noisy French colonials" aboard the *Thysville* departed at La Pallice. In the resulting quiet, Hayes became reflective: "One takes stock of himself and wonders if he has been any use to the world he has been born into." He wondered if his travels had been any kind of accomplishment. By his count he had been "sixteen times across this ocean [the Atlantic], up and down the Pacific from Behring [sic] Strait to Cape Horn and Australia. All over the Indian, up and down the Mediterranean and over all Africa now, with other places as well." Many miles, but he couldn't decide if they had been of any worth. At the end of the passage, he decided he lacked standing to assess the value of his travels: "That must be left for God to sum up, and not myself."

Hayes always expressed heartsickness when leaving Africa, but this time his despondency weighed more heavily. The traveler seriously doubted he'd ever set foot on the continent again – if he would ever even want to. His boyhood fancies of adventuring with Stanley among "elephants and cannibals" had given way to a battered adult's inescapable knowledge of the real Stanley and the duplicitous missionaries and rapacious corporate miners for which the revered explorer had paved the way. He had no clear destination in mind. Back to the US to recuperate. Away from this Africa.

13. In the Meantime: Oregon Coast Guard; Touring the Far East; Southern California Edison, 1923-1927

The *Thysville* dropped the weary traveler in Antwerp, where Hayes had no intention of re-visiting Forminiere headquarters. Still moving fast, he caught the first available ship out of the capital city of diamonds, suspecting he might be unwelcome there.

The Red Star Liner *Zeeland* sailed from Antwerp carrying Hayes and a heavy load of eastern European immigrants: "Jews, Ukrainians, Ruehenians, Roumanians, Hungarians, Jugo-slavs, Russians, Galacians what-have-you." Each had a pitiful story; one woman of 37, to whom Hayes must have spoken, shepherded a blind husband and dependent mother. Hers was only one story among all those on board, all had gambled everything on admittance to America following the ruin of World War I in Europe.

In his journal, Hayes derided his shipmates as unwashed, grasping, and illiterate; he thought every one of them was "likely to be deported upon arrival in New York." But, despite that scorn, he went on to write that he would rather bunk among the dirty immigrants than the posh and wealthy traveling first class: "somehow I am glad to share third class with [the immigrants]. It is easy to make money if one don't care how he makes it."

Not for the first time, Hayes ruminated that had he been willing to compromise with the Forminiere as, say, his boss Donald Doyle had, Hayes too could be sailing first class on the *Zeeland*. But, as always, Hayes arrived at the same conclusion: better to share the occasional louse with an immigrant than rise in wealth and worldly esteem by unethical means. He congratulated himself on the stance regarding the whip in the Congo even if it had cost him his job and his good name with the Forminiere: "As it is, the natives may be a bit happier. If so, I am content."

After three days in "the hot, dusty city" of New York, Hayes gladly boarded a train south to the nation's capital. In Washington, DC, he took a quick peep in the National Museum, a quicker visit with cousin Adam, "and kept right on." Cinders blew into his face through a train window without screens all the way from Washington to New Orleans. In the Big Easy, forty ships built in wartime anchored in the river above the city, "and if [they are] like those I saw under construction in Oregon, unseaworthy." Fearing he might board a ship built at the San Francisco shipyard where he had watched riveters installing ornamental rivet heads, decorating but not securing ship's hulls, Hayes got on another train.

At Houston, sisters Virginia and Pearl warranted no more than a day's visit. Both had fallen on hard times. Hayes does not say if his sisters asked for financial help – probably not – being proud. Nor if he offered – probably not – being broke. He had next to nothing to say to or about his sisters – except to remind them that he had warned them that their prosperity would not last. This is the last time Hayes mentions visiting his sisters. His diary contains no mention of his mother here or later.

The weather in Los Angeles agreed with Hayes, but not the company; he simply could not escape the family of CT Studd. Sister Pauline (Studd) and Norman Grubb had accompanied him across the Atlantic, and now brother George Studd, stood shaking Hayes' hand on the street of the city that was supposed to be his refuge. Neither George nor Hayes shook hands with any particular warmth of greeting. The lack of fealty Hayes had just shown his own family in Houston sharpened the ironic barb due George: "He has to stick by his hypocrite brother regardless of the latter's wrongdoing."

While his diary doesn't specify who urged him to speak, Hayes agreed to address an auditorium in LA with tales of Africa on August 1, 1923. Maybe the distasteful encounter with George Studd a few days previously put him in a particularly frank, tell-all mood. Hayes knew from experience it would be fine for a speaker to paint Black Africans as fierce, exotic, and primitive, but woe to the truth-teller who spoke about the actions of the "'superior' whites."

At the outset of his talk, Hayes warned his listeners "it would be hot." He then went on to tell precisely what he had seen in Africa: corrupt missionaries, homicidal diamond miners, rapacious elephant hunters, all of it. At the end of his talk he wound down a little bit, surprised that he hadn't been thrown out; they even paid him.

He accepted the money, writing, at 45, for the first time an expression of concern about the retirement of an aging world-adventurer: "I would like to have a small competence to tie me over in the decline of life, but care for no more." After a lifetime of reckless self-sufficiency, striking out who-knows-where, dependent only on his bodily health and physical strength, Hayes now glimpsed the shadow of a time when neither would be dependable.

On the more regular employment front, a letter arrived for Hayes in Los Angeles from Clarence Boice in Bandon urging Hayes to return to his job with the Coast Guard. Perhaps he would travel back up to Oregon; the rain wasn't too dreary in August. Not much going for full time work in Los Angeles, so he guessed the Coast Guard looked "as good as anything now, and I am minded to do it." Three weeks later, Hayes sat a lazy afternoon lookout tickled by a light breeze with a calm tide lapping sand at the foot of Bandon's cliffs. A line of steamers dotted the western horizon; picnickers waded in the surf.

Shortly after arriving in Bandon, Hayes wrote that he received a letter from George Lorimer at the *Saturday Evening Post*. Hayes must have sent correspondence to Lorimer asking about the release of his Congo exposé. Why else would a prestigious editor of one of America's leading journals contact an itinerant wanderer? Lorimer wrote that "he was not the one who turned my letters over to the press. What he did likely do was to send them to Ball at 42 Broadway [apparently Hayes knew this name and place], and perhaps to the Belgian authorities. Or was it the *Literary Digest*." Lorimer's hazy memory seemed a little convenient. Hayes concluded that one of the two magazines must have leaked his letters and, "If so I am glad, even if it has broken me. For it has surely broken slavery in the Congo."

During the nearly two years Hayes served the Coast Guard out of Bandon between September 1923 and July 1925, most of his diary entries were gossip about residents of the small coastal town. Bandon's most affluent upper crust made their livings as bootleggers. Shady men ran whiskey into the bay in ships of all sizes; the larger the vessel, the less likely the Coast Guard to intervene.

Hayes kept his distance from the other Coast Guardsmen at the Bandon station and further isolated himself by declining when "honored with an invitation to join the Ku Klux Klan." He didn't say who delivered the invitation to join the Bandon chapter, just that he didn't know much about the principles of the organization. He did "believe them to be a better influence in the community than the Catholics and Jews whom they seek to hold in check," but he wasn't a joiner and, besides, "they appear a trifle fanatical."

In November 1923, the steamer *Elizabeth* ran aground on the breakwater on the mouth of the Coquille River. Hayes got just four hours sleep in the next 60 hours, but, together with the other men of the station, got the *Elizabeth* off the bar without damage to the hull and with crew and passengers unharmed. The bars and the rocks off Bandon weren't always so generous. Just before Christmas, the steamer *C.A. Smith* broke to pieces, dashed onto the rocks at the end of the jetty during a failed attempt to cross the Bandon bar in heavy weather. Her crew of nine perished along with one other man swept off a tug attempting rescue.

On February 19, 1924, another ship in danger scrambled the Bandon Coast Guard into action. A call came in from the Coos Bay Guard Station, 25 miles to the north up the coast. The steamer *Columbia* had run onto the breakwater at the mouth of the Coos River. Could the fellows down Bandon way come help with the rescue?

Assisted by the steam schooner *Cleone,* the two Coast Guard crews anchored in the breaker line, "shot a line across and rigged a breeches buoy." Homer Winslow had painted the drama of a breeches buoy rescue in 1884. The wild wind and spray Homer painted may not have captured the height of the seas that day at the mouth of the Coos Bay harbor. Hayes wrote that "[g]reen seas were rolling thirty feet." As the combined crews of the two Coast Guard stations began zip-lining passengers and crew off the *Columbia* "the roll of our ship would toss them forty feet in the air, then sometimes submerge them as the lines slackened on the next roll."

At the end of two exhausting days, the entire ship's manifest of the *Columbia* had ridden the fragile, taut wire to safety. "Some were hysterical as we landed them on board, others crying, and few faces there were not blanched from fear." The captain of the *Columbia*, last off, had the closest brush with death. The main cable on the breeches buoy splintered when he was halfway across "and we dragged him 700 feet through the boiling surf." Hayes didn't name the captain, but remarked in admiration that the soaking-wet, near-drowned man "came on board grinning."

By March 1924, Hayes had saved $300: "Not so much, especially after the big money in the mines. But at least it is clean." By May, Hayes had increased his savings to $425. In July of 1924, the thrifty Coast Guardsman put $500 into the bank at interest. The shadows of his own mortality had him calculating a staid future: "If I could stick [the Guard] five years it would give me a modest competence, but is it possible?"

No, as it would turn out.

Hayes spent the relatively quiet year 1924-25 learning to type: "By hook or by crook I can learn, everybody has to start that way." Learning a skill filled the rainy off-shift afternoons, but also provided an economy. Up until then, when Hayes found time to compile his smudged and scribbled field notes, he made a tidy copy by "laborious hand printing." But he wrote other manuscripts that simply must be typed: job applications, exposés to the *Saturday Evening Post*, and other formal correspondence. Self-sufficiency would save in the long-run: "I have already lost far more than a machine would cost by paying for material being typed for me." Initially he borrowed a machine from a Coast Guard mate with a plan to purchase his own after gaining some competence.

Just putting his diary in order gave Hayes plenty of material for practice; in the years prior to 1924, Hayes had written and laboriously hand-printed some 450,000 diary words. But he typed letters too. More than one went out to inquire about one job or another, in search of some chance to return to Africa.

Hayes knew he wasn't too old but the companies he contacted disagreed as "every road seems blocked. Wonder if I'll ever make it again?" In October he crossed museums off his list. Administrative staff at the museums coveted any positions in Africa and, as they could "somehow get animals killed (by native hunters) and look after the skins themselves" they had no need for a "practical man" to accompany their colleting trips. Of course, Hayes had already crossed off any company handling booze and "most of them do a large business in liquors."

Toward the end of 1924 Hayes departed the Oregon Coast Guard, 25 pounds underweight and creaky with rheumatism brought on by the damp Oregon weather. But he had fully $2,000 saved. So, laughing at the shadows of age and infirmity, he pulled out the entire sum and spent the first of it on a long sea voyage. Surely, he thought, wandering the seaports of the Orient would return him to fighting form. He ebulliently sketched the vaguest of plans to continue west around the globe and return to Africa where he would "look up old Bishop there and we will set up a kingdom of our own."

At a stop on his way north toward Victoria, British Columbia, where he would catch the *Empress of Asia* for ports east, Hayes struck up a conversation in Tacoma, Washington, with a young man named Spiese: "I'm always running into some strange circumstances, but there have been few more peculiar than this."

Spiese, 22, had the missionary bug, telling Hayes God had called Spiese to East Africa and "unlike most wishful missionaries, he has plenty of money." Spiese had married well, though with something of an age difference, his wife "just 33 years his senior." On the basis of what could not have been more than one or two days' conversation, Spiese and his wife pressed $300 on Hayes, enjoining him to secure for them a station in Kenya. They would follow later. Hayes accepted their money; it would be fun to set up a station again, like he had for the Heart of Africa at Niangara, and he could always hunt up Bishop on the side.

Hayes never traveled overland in either Japan or China but he did bounce along their coasts. In order to get a firsthand impression of the region, he had booked passage on the *Empress of Asia* knowing her itinerary included stops at major coastal towns of both countries. His diary entries are long and detailed, the kind of travelogue familiar to his reader: the lay of the harbors and coastal geography, conditions of the working poor, and, as in every port, the circumstance of women in sex work.

Hayes first called at Tokyo, walking a city still in ruins following the Great Kanto Earthquake of September 1, 1923.

Kobe and Osaka, further to the west, had been spared the great earthquake. The stacks of Kobe's mills reminded Hayes of Pittsburgh or Chicago. Nagasaki, on the southwestern edge of Kyushu Island, closest to the Asian continent, "is one of the great coaling ports of the world." Hayes stayed a week in Hong Kong. The city reminded him of Los Angeles at the height of its boom, "one of the most rapidly building cities I have ever seen." The helmsman of the P. & O. liner *Sicilia* carrying Hayes out of Hong Kong bound for Bombay steered cautiously to avoid the fleet of junks and other small crafts dotting the harbor.

Departing the Far East, rough weather across the Bay of Bengal brought Hayes happily to Colombo – "improved with the passing of years, and is now a much finer city." Passing on to Bombay, now also a "splendid city," Hayes located a sailor's home, "cheaper and better than the Indian shakedowns catering to Europeans whose purses are not too heavy." After seven days "enforced idleness," Hayes departed Bombay sailing smooth seas aboard the steamer *Karoa* bound for Zanzibar.

Hayes wrote an ominous note on September 25, 1925, the first indication that sickness would scuttle any inland African adventure for him that year: "Fever laid me low yesterday." He didn't think much of it at the time; he'd been sick before. He thought mosquitoes at Bombay had borne him this particular malady.

The *Karoa* carried Hayes from the Seychelles across to Mombasa. The Kenyan port city appeared greatly improved since his visit fourteen years previously "but I do not like it so well." Ever romanticizing the "real Africa," Hayes recalled the days when Mombasa "had an atmosphere of glamor [sic] and romance about it that has departed as the old Arab buildings have been torn down to make way for more modern structures."

Three days further down the East African coast, the *Karoa* called at Zanzibar, a second town seeming to Hayes somehow less romantic than the old town of his first visit.

On the other hand, a day after Zanzibar, Hayes disembarked the *Karoa* into Dar es Salaam, a town little changed in the three years since he'd last walked these streets. Only the attitude of the natives, who seemed to him surly now under lenient British rule, marked any change.

Hayes didn't entirely ignore the charge he'd been given by young Spiese and his much senior bride back in Tacoma, Washington; the $300 advance he carried from them gave the task some gravity. At British colonial headquarters in Dar es Salaam Hayes put in for a concession at Mutombo in the Uluguru Range, but with little hope of success.

After a week with no administrative reply – "It is always difficult to do business with any government and that of Tanganyika is no exception" – Hayes resolved to travel inland to Morogoro to hasten the application in person. He got as far as choosing a seat on the train when, five minutes before departure, a "chit" from one Captain Berne arrived calling him back to government offices at Dar es Salam. Berne spoke frankly: "The British disliked the idea of a woman of 55 marrying a boy of 22, and besides Spiese had no education."

Berne did, however, suggest a workaround: he would be willing to sell a failed plantation to Hayes. What did Berne personally care where Hayes' $300 came from?

Quite on his own, Hayes decided to wash his hands of Spiese and the whole missionary game before he became entangled, once again, with "arbitrary people who dictate when they have no experience and will not listen to those who know the bush." He had already had a lifetime's experience of that working with CT Studd and Alfred Buxton.

Hayes mailed the $300 back to Tacoma and set about looking for some other way to sustain himself in Africa. Mining? He had a connection with the old Inchcape interests. Peeling tanbark (harvesting acacia bark for tannins used in curing hides)? A genial non-drinking planter invited Hayes down the coast to join his operation. Gold prospecting? His old pal Bishop had struck it rich up near Lake Rukwa. Prospecting for coal? Rumors still circulated about those lost mines in Tanganyika. So many options.

But none of them panned out. On October 15, 1925, Hayes wrote: "Will have to acknowledge that I am beat." Rheumatism had combined with the malaria from Bombay to sicken him beyond his natural recuperative limits. He had traveled in Africa enough to know that pressing forward when so sick would be a path to death in Africa. He sold a bush outfit he had purchased in preparation to leave upcountry for two-thirds the price he'd paid for it and boarded the German liner *Adolph Woermann* on October 20, 1925, "before I am broken physically, it is not so far away now." With any luck, the twenty-four-day voyage from Dar es Salaam to Cape Town would cure his ills.

Beira, Lorenzo Marquez, Durban, East London, Port Elizabeth, and finally Cape Town drifted curatively past the *Adolph Woermann.* The stop at Durban had allowed Hayes to renew some old friendships and call in at the library where he had a chance to read Isaac Marcosson's *An African Adventure* (John Lane Company 1921, reprinted by Wentworth Press "Scholar Select" February 2019) for the first time. Marcosson's whitewashing account of happy native laborers tended by kindly European and American administrators at the Forminiere so infuriated Hayes he dashed off another article to the *Literary Digest*, even though he assumed "[i]t will likely fall into the jaws of a yawning wastebasket."

A seaman's strike threatened to strand Hayes in Cape Town. The sea voyage hadn't been as curative as he had hoped. Poor health dictated a hasty departure from Cape Town but, if marooned by the strike, he had a lead on a job in the diamond mines, something "that will take up the slack" on a gently flattening purse.

In the down time, waiting for either a ship or a firm job offer, Hayes dashed off a 22,000-word typewritten article "telling of the Forminiere activities in the Congo and Angola." He gave the document to the ship's doctor aboard the *Adolph Woermann*; the Germans were much interested in dirt on both Belgians and Americans in Africa. Toward the end of his life when thinking about whether or not to publish portions of his diaries, Hayes cited this exposé as one of the principal arguments against publication. Attention to Hayes and his adventures might bring to light that this essay had, as Hayes believed, gone all the way to Hitler. What seemed like a principled humanitarian gesture in 1925 might look more like providing the Nazis with useful propaganda after 1945.

The strikers allowed a ship to sail out from Cape Town, a White Star liner, the *Vedic*, before Hayes had gotten a firm job offer. So, he boarded the *Vedic*, again suspecting he would never return to Africa. As always, Hayes mourned departing the continent he loved: "Leaving Africa is like parting at the grave side from a dead friend."

Only a chance meeting of one decent man aboard the *Vedic*, a "love ship par excellence," brightened the whole sorry crossing. Frank Preston, "an Englishman who lives in Pennsylvania," whom Hayes met in a deck chair on the *Vedic*, would become a lifelong friend and advocate for Hayes. In the late 1930s Preston, a Corning glass engineer, would employ Hayes briefly as a landscaper and zookeeper at Preston's private labs in Butler, Pennsylvania. Preston advanced Hayes' admission to the Royal Geographical Society, and, in the early 1960s, shepherded Hayes' diary and some other writings into print. But for now, in December 1925 aboard the *Vedic*, "it has been a great treat to find a man who could converse on some other topic besides sex."

Escaping the crowded wharf at Sydney, Hayes sought out friends he knew in the Australian town. He didn't have to spend the dreary holidays alone, but he was glad when "Christmas and its good fellowship and hypocrisies have passed." In the new year Hayes sought out a Jewish friend, a "woman whom I know here and who has a remarkable reputation as a seeress." According to his fortuneteller, Hayes' destiny held a sea voyage to three islands, a long happy marriage, and much cash earned in the employ of a wealthy man. The first should have been pretty obvious if she knew Hayes at all and the second obviously wrong if she knew Hayes at all, but how could she have known so far in advance about William Randolph Hearst?!

Hayes boarded the steamer *Makura* on January 30, 1926, with a ticket through to San Francisco. Stops on New Zealand, Rarotonga [sic], and Tahiti fulfilled that part of the prophesy of the Jewish Australian seeress. Hayes celebrated his forty-eighth birthday quietly on the first day out of Tahiti with only the melancholy observation that "[t]hey seem to come oftener these days, a year slips by so quickly."

The *Makura* entered San Francisco Bay in a high gale on the morning of February 19, 1926. Immigration officers passed Hayes for entry into the US on the strength of a birth certificate and discharge papers from the Coast Guard. He had intentionally skirted renewing his passport at Sydney as a small act of protest against the whole idea of passports, which he saw as just another bureaucratic scam to milk a traveler.

During the unsettled month of March 1926 that Hayes spent in San Francisco, Frank Preston caught up to him and the two toured about the city "in style." Clarence Boice and most of the old Coast Guard crew from Coquille now quartered at Fort Berry on the Marin Headlands. Hayes mentioned his former mates but had no thought of rejoining them in Coast Guard service. Instead, he dashed off a quick application to the "Firestone interests" asking about employment at their rubber plantations in Liberia. Among some sixty replies to letters Hayes had sent in previous months, replies that now waited for him in San Francisco, ("But why write so many? I like to write.") came one from Ernest Bishop urging Hayes to return to Tanganyika: "Come to the mines and bring a lot of tools and steel for drills and bars." Hayes didn't say why Tanganyika didn't interest him; maybe Ernest Bishop was too much of an idea-guy for Hayes to take a risk on one of Bishop's schemes. Another letter came to San Francisco from Hayes' cousin Lewis urging Hayes to come to the Sierra Nevada Mountains. Lewis had a great job there building a power plant and could easily get Hayes hired on.

Hayes suspected Firestone would turn him down because he had listed the Forminiere as a reference. The rubber company must have checked his references; they wrote informing Hayes they would not be needing his services. So, Hayes went from San Francisco up to Bandon. Why back up to Oregon? Hayes admitted his motivation was "[p]erhaps a girl."

In April of 1926, Hayes sent letters to every scientific interest he could name, trying to catch on with one African expedition or another. None had a place for an aging adventurer. Even his old circle in Bandon "pulled my leg for what they could." Just good-natured teasing implying that Hayes fabricated most of his stories, and hadn't they all heard every one before? Feeling like a failed adventurer, Hayes convinced himself "[i]t is as well to get a job and stick to it, no other way out of it here." He wrote cousin Lewis he'd take that job at Big Creek in the high Sierras –where the Southern California Edison Company had mapped out vast hydro-electric plants – were it still available.

Yes, Lewis replied, come to Big Creek.

Once on site, Hayes earned $3.50 a day plus room and board. Southern California Edison even provided its workers a $1,200 life insurance policy. Hayes felt like he had signed on for life "but if I know anything of what is what it won't last."

Hayes stayed on at the massive works – "some $275,000,000 has been spent in developing this power, and that is real money anywhere" – for a year and a half, from May, 1926 through September, 1927. As always when sedentary, his diary entries became sparse. Complaints about every facet of the work – food, housing, administration, machinery, ignorant co-workers – alternated with wonder at the exquisite beauty of the California Sierras. Occasionally Hayes mentioned the rheumatism still lingering off and on from Tanganyika. He tried not to fret about his infirmities but doubted he would ever make it back to Africa.

In January of 1927, while drilling holes in granite to set 12x12 timbers to secure a bridge to the side of a mountain, Hayes' back gave way. When he tried to quit his contract, Southern California Edison referred him to the company doctor. Hayes wanted no part of Edison's in-house physician: "no sane man cares to entrust his life and limbs into the keeping of this chap, whose sole qualification is he stands well with the company."

He would, however, accept reassignment to lighter work and a week later claimed to be "going strong again." The company refused to let him quit, even sent a car to take him for examination by an independent doctor at the hospital in town. Hayes suspected any kindness, reassignments, or examinations Southern California Edison extended him stemmed from their "fear [of] a damage suit if I have been seriously injured by heavy lifting." His back got better and Hayes stuck the job.

The final break with Southern California Edison came following one more unreasonable task the company loaded on Hayes' shoulders. A couple of Italian immigrant anarchists, Nicola Sacco and Bartolomeo Vanzetti, had been executed for murder in Boston, Massachusetts, on August 23, 1927. The Sacco and Vanzetti case had dragged on for seven years, amid mounting national and international cries for justice and worker solidarity, before all appeals were denied and the two men killed.

According to Hayes, Southern California Edison feared one of the many ill-treated workmen the company had swindled might seek violent revenge as part of the widespread labor unrest following the highly-publicized executions. Plenty of dynamite lay around a dam construction site, ready to a disgruntled hand. As a precaution, an overseer assigned Hayes to keep constant watch on the dams day and night: "Of course it is impossible, but I am told to." He continued: "It is little wonder men turn to the I.W.W., to Communism, to any radical organization when such conditions apply."

At 49, and with a definite sense of melancholy, sick and tired from the punishing work on the big dam, Hayes rather perfunctorily hit the "long trail" again. Nowhere in his diary did he mention a destination; he just set off cross-country, as if without volition, drawn across the United States, across the water, once more to the continent now barely recognizable as the Africa of his boyhood fancies.

14. Shooting the Aruwimi for a Dental Appointment, 1927-1928

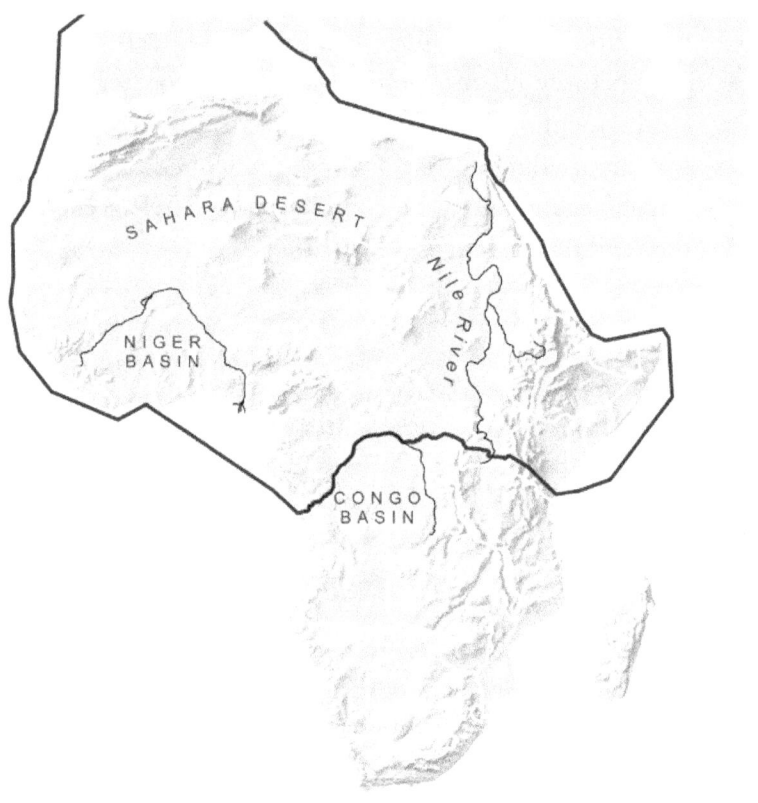

On his first four trips to Africa, Hayes had worked as a logger, a mission handyman, a diamond miner, and a prospector. On his fifth trip, he had intended to find mine work again before the Forminiere scared him off the continent. On his sixth trip, crossing east to west from Mombasa to Kinshasa, he started out with characteristically vague plans: revisit the Ituri forest then turn north into French Equatorial Africa; maybe he would find prospecting work in the Tibesti Mountains of present-day Chad.

All the museums and scientific organizations he hoped might have financed a sixth trip rejected his applications – too old and not well enough connected. So, to get back to Africa, Hayes took his savings from a year and a half at the Southern California Edison hydroelectric project and paid rail and steamer fare to get back on the "long trail" again. The first of several steamers Hayes caught toward Africa got away from New York on October 10, 1927 – according to his own count, his 123rd sea voyage.

The day after Hayes purchased a ticket in drab London to board the Dutch/German liner *Njansa,* bound for Mombasa, Kenya, rumor of a rich gold strike in Tanganyika swept the docks. His travel plans entirely fluid, Hayes wished he had chosen Dar es Salaam. But Mombasa would have to do; he'd already paid for the ticket.

Sailing near the Italian coast, a natural beauty relieved Hayes' roll call of dreary cities. When passing Stromboli Island, the *Njansa* sailed near enough that passengers aboard could see flames shooting 200 feet in the air from the active volcano. The awesome spectacle cheered Hayes but only until he noticed smoke from the volcano rolling off the summit to cover concentration camps where "the just and beneign [sic] dictator has his political enemies on ice." He referred to Benito Mussolini, in power in Italy since 1922.

Without dawdling at Mombasa, Hayes paid fare on a rail ticket to Kampala. The Uganda Railway, built by the British using Indian laborers between 1895 and 1901, ran mostly through Kenya – from Mombasa, Kenya to Kampala, Uganda on Lake Victoria. During its construction the British politician Henry Labouchère nicknamed the project the Lunatic Line, mostly because of cost overruns, but also because of the many wild animal attacks on workers. Hayes certainly would have heard tales of the Tsavo Man-eaters, a pair of maneless male lions haunting rail work camps during the first nine months of construction of the line. (Since 1950, half a dozen movies, including *The Ghost and the Darkness*, have retold this enduring horror story.)

At a secondhand shop in Nairobi run by an old Spaniard, Hayes "managed to get a fair outfit together that will carry me anywhere." All the big game hunters outfitted in Nairobi, so an experienced man could find whatever he needed, slightly used, at bargain prices. Furthermore, Hayes believed "less is better in the bush" because happy porters carrying lighter loads would travel farther and more reliably. Hayes purchased exactly enough gear to load five men with 45 pounds per man, nine pounds less than "a standard government load of 54 pounds." Still 400 miles from Kampala, porters at the Nairobi station loaded Hayes' outfit onto the Lunatic Line for transport to the capital of Uganda on the back side of Lake Victoria.

Motor transport radiated out from the end of the rail line at Kampala: 600 miles north to Gondokoro, 200 miles northwest to Lake Albert, and 200 miles directly west to Fort Portal at the foot of Mt. Ruwenzori in Toro country just below Lake Albert. British colonial administrators prohibited travel with porters where motor transport existed. So, rather than lifting his loads onto their heads, porters at Kampala loaded Hayes' 225-pound outfit onto to a lorry piloted by one of the many "bright boys" taught to drive by efficient British colonialists.

On the first day out from Kampala toward Fort Portal, the excited driver beside Hayes lapsed from English into Swahili, calling out "'Barafu! Barafu!" Hayes, who knew the Swahili word for snow, looked up as clouds parted to reveal the shimmering peaks of the Ruwenzori range seen through the pitted windshield.

At Fort Portal, the end of the line for truck transport, Hayes followed his standard procedure for assigning porters. First, he lined the bags up before his five men, then he let them choose. In the ensuing scramble the strongest man always elbowed his way to the lightest load and Fort Portal was no exception; the brawniest porter grabbed for Hayes' suitcase. When Hayes had distributed his gear, all the loads weighed roughly the same amount. However, anticipating the grab of the brawniest porter, Hayes had left some empty space in his suitcase. In the night he would repack, shifting some weight from the weaker men's loads into the suitcase and making sure a reliable man carried Hayes' typewriter.

Walking eighteen miles down an escarpment and across the Semliki plain the next day, Hayes' mind wandered. How long before cultivated fields of cotton or rice would supplant the waterbuck and kongoni staring with wide eyes on raised heads? Well, in the present moment, at least this first batch of porters was good; a shame he would have to replace them after crossing the Semliki River from British Kenya into Belgian Congo, but petty international regulations could not be ignored.

Porters eventually came to Hayes on the Congo side of the Semliki River on December 15, 1927. They had walked from Boga to carry Hayes' five 45-pound loads back to their village on the edge of the Ituri Forest, in the Belgian Congo but still on the Nile side of the continental divide. A couple of White men acting as agents for the Belgian government and for the mines at nearby Kilo greeted the wanderer at Boga, offering a clean rest house and plenty of inexpensive food. Hayes, content, rhetorically asked his journal, "What else does one want in Africa?"

After Hayes' small safari crossed to the Congo side of the divide, rain fell much more heavily. An annoyance to Hayes and the carriers to be constantly wet but, in compensation, food was much more plentiful here, "so all are content."

A day's walk along the forest margin, delightful in the shade, blistering in the sun, brought the safari to Irumu, seat of Belgian government for the District D'L Ituri. In this nicely situated if a little tumbledown village, grass had overgrown the few good buildings. Some twenty Belgian officers lived, "without books, newspapers, or other recreation than drink" at Irumu. Several had Belgian wives keeping house. The bachelors, outnumbering the married men, "find surcease from utter boredom in the arms of black fairies." Only the gold mines at Kilo-Moto just to the north sustained this outpost, soon to be reclaimed by the jungle.

Hayes had to dismiss his carriers at Irumu. As in Kenya, Belgian authorities forbade employing porters anywhere trucks and roads permitted motor transport. The first 46 miles of the road to Stanleyville (Kisangani, 400 miles west) had been completed: "By forced labor the Belgians are carrying out a plan of road building all over the Congo." A Belgian officer told Hayes workmen earned 25 francs a month but, speaking directly to a road builder, Hayes learned that the actual rate was 7 francs a month, minus 7 francs a month for his tax medal.

Motor transport 46 miles along the completed stretch of road would cost Hayes 552 francs, "or about $15.50 American money at the present rate of exchange." He would be free if he pleased to resume travel by porter beyond the end of the road. Hayes didn't carry that kind of money, but fortunately, the Branch De Congo Belge [bank] at Irumu could cash a traveler's check. Hayes withdrew some funds and wrote a small product endorsement in his journal: "American Express checks are best, everyone wants them no matter where one goes."

Upon entering the Ituri Forest, Hayes had begun a strict quinine regimen to prevent malaria: "I take fifteen grains every eighth day. As malaria requires nine days to incubate in one's blood, by this method the fever is forestalled just before it breaks out. I have one bad night and am free for seven days after." On December 21, 1927, his first good day following the bad night induced by the quinine, Hayes enlisted two guides to direct him to a camp in the forest nearby of people he called "pygmies".

Hayes had briefly encountered these nomadic hunter/gatherers when passing through the region a dozen years earlier on his way out from CT Studd's Heart of Africa Mission. One suspects that Hayes' sixth trip, back into the Ituri Forest in 1927, had been charted to revisit these wandering people.

At first contact with the band, only a friendly greeting from one of Hayes' native guides prevented the entire band from fleeing into the forest at the approach of a White man along the jungle path. News of his coming had traveled ahead of the traveler, but their advance man didn't yet know if Hayes was Inglese or Bula Matadi. The guide called out to the sentinel, "trembl[ing] like a shaking leaf," to identify Hayes as Inglese. Reassured his band needn't flee a Belgian, the sentinel ran to fetch his "sultani" to come greet this (American) Englishman: "Their attitude was one of friendly courtesy, as is the custom among all pagans. These people have their code and live up to it, differing from the more hypocritical European."

Hayes wrote with admiration about the hunting prowess of these forest dwellers. From among a crowd of more than sixty jostling around the Inglese, their many hands pushed forward one shy fellow who could not have weighed more than eighty pounds. His elephant spear measured five-feet in length, including an eight-inch blade, double edged and razor sharp. To kill an elephant, a lone hunter smeared himself with elephant dung to mask any human scent, then slipped beneath the belly of the beast to drive the spear home: "The unlucky beast will in its terror founder about, driving the spear deeper into its vitals until it succumbs." The eighty-pound man had recently survived a successful one-man elephant hunt. No braggart, the man deflected attention from his own accomplishment by telling Hayes his chief had once killed two elephants in a single day. After a kill, or two kills, elephant meat could be traded in villages nearby for manioc and plantains with plenty left over for their own feasting.

These experienced hunters considered buffalo more dangerous than elephants. The men hunted buffalo from trees with bows and poisoned arrows, shooting from safety with poison, then tracking until their dangerous prey lay dead. The poison from their arrows didn't appear to taint the buffalo meat. Hayes discussed a wide variety of game – Okapi, bongo, giant forest hog, red river hog, several species of antelope, monkeys – "all hunted by these tiny Nimrods of the forest." They appeared to fear only chimpanzees: "It is said they attack by biting off the fingers of every man they catch."

The band would stay at this place little more than a week, until exhausting the small game nearby. Then women of the band would pack up what few goods they owned and move onto a new forest residence, constructed in a day, wherever nuts and roots could be found to supplement the fresh game.

When it came time for Hayes to return to the deserted road camp at the end of motor travel toward Stanleyville where his luggage sat waiting for porters, Hayes rummaged in his satchel for gifts. The last night on the *Njansa* had seen a big blowout, a celebration of arrival at Mombasa, complete with "paper caps and other adornments." Hayes had carefully gathered the party favors for just such an occasion. With a little paper crown, Hayes held an impromptu coronation: "I crowned the chief with one of these caps, and he was an object of much admiration from his people." Many of his new friends escorted Hayes far down the path from their encampment. Some shook his hand in parting. Others, still shy, smiled at the Inglese, then all "faded away into the forest shades."

Three days before Christmas 1927, while sitting typing in the Ituri Forest, not quite halfway across the African continent east to west, Hayes first mentioned the dental troubles that would plague the rest of his sixth African trip. He approached the subject casually, certainly not of pressing importance yet. Before talking about the tooth, he estimated the size and economic value of the forest, arriving at somewhere between

150,000 and 350,000 square miles with at least eight large trees to the acre, "hardwood of excellent quality." Then he wrote a complaint about a native man stealing his helmet and "I have been generous to him too." Then an account of meeting an Englishman named Catchpole who'd been out hunting elephants but passed on 350 (large, but without tusks) right in his sights. Then about his dinner, a monkey shank Catchpole generously shared and "I feel like a cannibal, but I'm eating it." Finally, after relating all the important events of the day, Hayes eventually got around to the tooth, writing cursorily, "I tied eight-ply linen thread around [the tooth] and hauled it out myself."

The last days of 1927 passed happily for Hayes. He wrote long passages in his diary, often surrounded by the children of successive villages as he pecked away at his portable typewriter, describing the routine beauty of the African forest and its inhabitants. More fertile soils supported clearings where bananas, manioc and sweet potatoes grew, cultivated by the forest people. Hayes learned the people he called pygmies called themselves Bambutti. None of these did any cultivation: "they devote themselves to the chase and let the Negroes toil for their daily bread."

On New Year's Eve, 1927, Hayes began his diary entry: "This has been the longest day's march I have ever put in in Africa." The previous day his porters had tricked him, telling him they were at day's end two hours before reaching another rest house. Those two hours had to be tacked onto the walk on December 31. Writing by lamplight in a rest house at a "hungry, dirty camp" at the crossroads of the Andundu-to-Pengi road with the Irumu-to-Wamba road, Hayes waxed nostalgic, recalling a strange New Year's Eve he'd spent in Williams, Arizona, in 1897-98 where "coyotes took up the refrain of the celebration and howled the live-long night through."

Here, deep in the Ituri Forest, rather than coyote howls, elephant and human screams split the night. The pachyderms

263

screamed as they crashed through the bush, raiding native gardens outside the village. The villagers screamed and lit fires to protect their livelihoods. Taking flight from nostalgia about his own past, Hayes went on to romance himself into faraway times: "A gibbous moon lit up the forest with a weird light, and one could easily imagine himself back in the Pleistocene when cave men fought with wild beasts for their very lives."

Two days walking through "moldy, pungent smells" of the forest – "but it is all a joy to me, I am willing to take it as it is" – brought the safari to another hungry stop. Hayes had considered turning off toward Pengi but his men warned him there was no food at that village either. An hour scavenging ground cherries in an abandoned garden provided the only dinner to be had. Despite the hunger, later that night Hayes celebrated coming this way because they had camped in a forest glade where the local Bambutti men and women had come to dance.

As darkness fell, an outer ring of men chanted ceaselessly as they circled a central fire. The women danced inside the circle of men as the children gamboled closest to the fire with "[e]ach individual simulat[ing] a forest animal, and some I could recognize because of the accurate portrayal of the species." Though they must have known he was watching, all danced as if unobserved. Hayes understood this as "part of their hunt, their religion, their daily lives," work to be performed diligently and earnestly. Hayes felt privileged to witness this real work: "It is seldom an European gets to see a real dance, for these given for visitors are put on to get salt and cloth."

By 1928, CT Studd's Heart of Africa Mission had established a half-dozen stations south and west from the initial site at Niangara where Hayes had worked from 1914-15. When his safari of five porters and a cook walked up to one of these Heart of Africa satellite missions just outside Wamba, Hayes couldn't help noticing "a certain undefinable lack of welcome from the three missionaries, a man named Evening and the Steedmans."

Maybe Evening and the Steedmans had heard of Hayes 12 years after his departure from Niangara? Evening had come to Africa in 1922, Mrs. (Williams) Steedman in 1923, and Mr. Steedman in 1924. More likely though, the young missionaries were in a dither about the imminent arrival of the great man himself; CT Studd was due at Wamba the very next day.

News of Studd's arrival threw Hayes into something of a dither too. He had dismissed the five carriers with whom he had arrived. Lack of replacements foiled any quick departure. At the very least, Hayes had to forewarn Studd of his presence at Studd's own mission in Wamba. Hayes immediately dispatched a messenger up the trail toward Studd "telling him if he had ways I did not approve of doubtless mine were as objectionable to him. I would be glad to see him again and sink old quarrels." What else could he say? Perhaps the gesture would be enough to head off an ugly confrontation.

After the messenger hurried off in the direction of CT Studd, the Heart of Africa missionaries at Wamba fell to gossiping. They told Hayes Studd had not been out of the Congo in eleven years. But the partnership with Alfred Buxton had unraveled. Buxton had left the Heart of Africa the previous year "and has founded a work of his own, together with Rhodes, a former colleague of Hurlburt's in the Africa Inland Mission." As they talked, Hayes eventually recognized Mrs. Steedman. He had met the American woman in Matadi some years back. Nice to renew old acquaintances, but he never warmed to her or the two men.

Hitching up the loads the next morning, Hayes led the new carriers down the road west out of Wamba, passing right by the Heart of Africa satellite mission. If Evening and the Steedmans had been chilly before, now "if I had been a murderer they could have been no less grim." Hayes must have spoken with one the three at least briefly. He learned that Studd had returned the messenger Hayes had sent up the trail with word that any planned visit from CT Studd had been canceled.

At Wamba, Hayes had regretfully determined that his next destination had to be Europe: "I wanted to go on north into the French Sudan, and if possible to enter Tibesti as a prospector for the French." No, he couldn't go north, he needed a surgeon to pull the rest of his teeth: "The lower jaw is very sore, an entire bridge being affected." On the bright side, his route to the Atlantic led down the Aruwimi River to the Congo and "I want to see the Aruwimi, so it is not a displeasing circumstance."

At a gold prospecting camp run by the Forminiere (branching out from diamonds) at Gundadi, on January 10, 1928, Hayes learned of company developments at Tshikapa far to the south in the Kasai. Donald Doyle had fallen ill; no longer fit for the tropics; the competent American had been put out to pasture in Brussels. The Belgian administrator now in charge at Tshikapa had hired 120 non-American engineers to staff Forminiere headquarters. In halting English, a Belgian gold mining officer at Gundadi went on to assure Hayes the previous American management had carried too few men. Hayes privately disagreed: "Fact is, a Yank can do as much as a dozen Belgians in the bush."

Hayes saw no whips evidently in use in the Forminiere gold mines proper. But his sharp eyes picked out a chain gang working the plantain and banana plantations on the steep hills about Gundadi: "These men were so utterly broken from flogging and starvation, so the use of the whip has not been disconnected where Bula Matadi feels safe from prying eyes."

Passing on from Gundadi, Hayes chastised himself for having written "enough gloom." The music of running water at a quiet camp beside a rippling brook breaking from green hills raised his spirits as much as the chicken spitted over his fire. With a little rice purchased from the Forminiere, his tiny safari had food for another day. Hayes wrote that he would have dawdled to enjoy Africa in all its beauty and cruelty if not for his teeth: "Were it not for my septic teeth I would travel slow in this country. But it is a difficult matter to stave off gangrene, and I must hasten. The pain is constant, I sleep little." And he knew he had two more long days' marches before reaching the Aruwimi River at Bomili.

The Aruwimi River is one of the main tributaries of the Congo, flowing east to west from Bomili, above which it is called the Ituri River, to Basoko, below which it is called the Congo River. Hayes knew of the Aruwimi River from his readings of the exploits of Henry Morton Stanley. Stanley's Emin Pasha Relief Expedition had come through this way in 1886, taking the long route up the Congo to Equatoria in the Southern Sudan.

Hayes need not risk the overland route, so deadly to Stanley's expedition. The relatively nimble canoes piloted by natives familiar with the river could manage the rough water that had stopped Stanley's steamboat. At Bomili, Hayes negotiated, in Swahili, to pay 238 francs ("not eight dollars") for passage through roughly 400 miles of successive rapids from Bomili to Yambuya by pirogue. The fare seemed too cheap, especially when compared to the 552 francs he had paid for motor transport 46 miles out from Fort Portal,"[b]ut if they can stand it I can, and besides I want to see all the Aruwimi."

Hayes' spirits rose markedly the first day on the river. His ten boatmen "singing merrily and paddling lustily," inspired Hayes to poetic celebration, reciting four lines from Tennyson's "Haroun Al Raschid," apparently from memory:

> "'On many a sheeny summer morn
> Adown the Tiguis I was borne
> By Baghdad's shrines of fretted gold,
> And showy gardens, green and old.'"

Hayes' crew of ten handled the first three minor rapids themselves. But just before noon, their bowman directed the big canoe ashore as they approached "[t]he bad Matako Rapid." This one required the addition of "a special crew who live at the rapid" to guide them through. Hayes very much wanted to "shoot the white water" with them but the boatmen refused to carry him. Initially, Hayes refused to exit the canoe; he knew the risk and sought the thrill. His river guides had to explain to Hayes who would be taking a risk if they carried him: "'If we are lost, then Bula Matadi cares not,' they said. 'But if a musungu dies, then we must answer.'" Bowing to the boatmen's more precise understanding of the logic of Belgian colonial rule, Hayes stepped ashore and hiked around the Matako Rapid.

Halfway round the rapid along the riverbank, Hayes realized he had left his luggage aboard the canoe. He should have at least grabbed his money and his papers: "If they are lost – I don't care to consider such a happenstance."

Well, too late now. He hiked on to the bottom of Matako Rapid anxiously scouting for the big canoe to round a bend in the raging white water. "********** Well, thank God, here they are!"

Relief at the recovery of his possessions immediately gave way to awed admiration for these men who performed this dangerous work with such great skill: "One cannot but admire the effortless grace with which they guide the boats through the white water … Rocks are on every hand, but they guide the craft just aside and forget them. The rapids roar tremendously, every man is tense. Then, when safely through, every man yells his best to the spirits who safely guided them, the calls echoing and re-echoing up and down the river above the roar of the fall."

After their triumphant shouts, the boatmen pulled ashore to offload the local expert pilots and to load the musungu back on board. All the tension of the rapid receded in a long calm stretch of river. Soon the men were singing, joking, chatting, and slapping flies as they dawdled along between the two walls of green.

At the next bad rapid the whole unloading of the musungu and loading new experts was repeated, except this time Hayes saw to better care of his few possessions. A woman from the river bank village, "a young Amazon" so strong Hayes thought she could have as easily carried him too, threw his suitcase on one shoulder and took off around the rapid with Hayes jumping and panting to keep up.

Tired from walking around rapids, Hayes happily rested at a boat-building village that evening. These people, "a healthier looking lot than those in the forest," called themselves Barbaro, a name Hayes had not heard before. They were just finishing up a canoe "with splendid lines," fifty-six feet in length, a four-foot beam, carved from a single majestic log. Hayes had never seen a finer canoe.

River mist still blanketed the entire forest when Hayes' big canoe got underway at dawn the next morning. The Aruwimi ran fast here past many jagged pinnacles, but none so treacherous he couldn't ride – and none so treacherous he couldn't type. His grinning boatmen improvised a wild chant concerning this strange man sitting in their boat pecking at his strange machine. The first stanza told of the big matabish he would give them at Panga; the second described how mean he was should he fail to deliver.

Below Bangboso, the water ran swift, occasionally white, but the boatmen considered this stretch calm enough for their passenger so Hayes "enjoyed the thrill of dodging rocks and listening to the songs of the reckless crew." Any false reaction "and all would be lost" but Hayes trusted these men, raised on the river since small children.

Waiting below Djambi Rapid, Hayes saw something of the trip his men would have to make with the canoe returning back upriver: "It must be a tremendous strain to drag these heavy canoes up against the current, but it is being done constantly by the men placed at every rapid by the Belgians." Djambi would be the last rapid before Panga, where a waterfall halted even canoe transport. His current ten boatmen would haul their canoe from Djambi back up past the rapids, paddle in the calm stretches, again and again, all the way up to Bomili to await another passenger.

On the first rest night at Mankopie, "not a bad camp, although a hungry one," Hayes had to "take the head man by the neck" to get any food, "for he was spoofing me about elephants eating up everything." Hayes had in fact seen evidence of elephants along the river; one stretch of beach had been churned into mounds as if worked by placer miners where elephants dug for salt. But no experienced traveler would fall for "this old alibi among these river people."

After the exertions before dinner at the rest house, Hayes met Vasco Da Gama XVII, "seventeenth in line from the Portuguese navigator who blazed the road to India long ago."

Anyone familiar with Hayes might have expected incredulity, but he wrote of the meeting without irony. Vasco Da Gama XVII had a pretty wife, "a product from one of the packing house fortunes in Kansas City." The wife of Vasco Da Gama XVII carried Vasco Da Gama XVIII on one hip, much worried about his health and the dark skin inherited from his father. Hayes could see through this old story: she had married for the title, he for the fortune. Both seemed content enough, for now, to be adventuring on the Aruwimi, but how could it last when she spoke so wistfully of "grand operas, the dinners, to wear diaphanous gowns and be admired of men."

Initially slightly charmed by the unlikely couple, Hayes soured on the Da Gamas when Vasco started boasting about killing animals, seven gorillas in Cameroun, elephants all about the Congo: "He glories in murdering these fine beasts, his every word drools of their death and his joy in watching them die." Da Gama simply could not understand how Hayes got anything out of Africa without a gun in hand.

After waving farewell to the Da Gamas on the riverbank at Mankope, a quiet day on the water delivered Hayes in a leaky, old canoe to the village of Bululu. These boatmen!

Accustomed to "bluffing people new to Africa," the head boatman and a companion waltzed into the rest house at Bululu ready to spend the night alongside their passenger. Hayes threw both men bodily from the hut and, when their luggage landed in the dirt beside them, "they understood" he was no tourist ignorant of their tricks.

At Banalia, Hayes had a choice. An occasional motorcar came through this pretty village. He could ride the smooth road 124 km to Stanleyville (Kisangani), rest overnight at a fine hotel, and catch a steamer down the main Congo River to Basako – or he could continue on with new boatmen by canoe down the Aruwimi all the way to Basako to catch the steamer.

Automobile? Canoe? As if that required any thought. Of course Hayes was "keen on seeing what lies below Banalia, and besides it's cheaper." He calculated the cost at roughly $5 to go by canoe versus $43 by car, not to mention hotel fare. And besides, "there is no romance in chasing about in a car."

Two days out of Banalia, on January 22, 1928, Hayes wrote that all the talk of "bad water" between there and Yambuya had almost frightened him out of making the run – taking the car instead. But, so far, he didn't understand the fuss; he'd only had to walk around one "rather tame rapid at Dibune, and if there is not too much swift water tomorrow we should arrive at Yambuya."

Right on cue, the river "rose to one tremendous effort" just before Yambuya, throwing up five major rapids: "Metero, Yonga, Ikilo, Luko, and one whose name I have forgotten." Best of all, it was raining, making his reckless crew hurry so much they didn't bother putting their musungu ashore: "I stayed by the ship while we roared through rapid after rapid." One imagines Hayes joining in wild shouts of exultation blasting out the last chute of each maelstrom.

With no more rapids below Yambuya, Hayes could have chosen to continue on to Basoko aboard a small steamer that plied the 100-mile stretch of calm water between the towns. But, of course, he went by canoe, savoring the last days of his "real Africa." This new lot of boatmen, that he initially thought of as "looking scabby," turned out to be as good as any he'd had on the Aruwimi. Their task considerably lighter here on the calm river, the men chatted and ate, barely keeping the boat headed downstream. On this quiet river, with the excitement of white water no longer distracting him, the spur to Hayes' hasty departure resurfaced: "My teeth ache badly, they have all the way." The need to find a dentist before gangrene set in was becoming increasingly urgent.

Hayes distributed a little medicine at Mongandjo, even though he had only Band-Aids for people horribly diseased: "lepers, elephantiasis cases, plenty of syphilis and its near cousin – yaws." As his canoe pushed off from the shore the next morning, a man from the village came running, calling out, holding a couple of eggs. Hayes "grudgingly" had the canoe return to shore and reached for his purse. No, these were a gift, a thank you, for the medicine. For a brief moment Hayes recanted some part of his cynicism. He wished he could hold onto those two small eggs, "just as a remembrance of a native's appreciation."

The Aruwimi spread to a mile wide where it slowed to meet the Congo. Hayes' last crew had to paddle for ten miles. Whatever their exertions, they would have complained about the scant matabishes Hayes distributed, but all smiled in parting so Hayes knew they were satisfied.

The great Congo River flowed with a strong current, due north and fully seven miles wide at its confluence with the Aruwimi. For the Belgians at Basoko, Hayes might as well have materialized out of thin air. Europeans arrived at Basoko from Stanleyville aboard the steamer, not from Yambuya in a canoe.

Hayes had to find an English speaker at the Banque Du Congo Belge to interpret before he could calm officious government authorities concerning his uncanny materialization, but after that "everything ran smooth." Hayes found pleasant lodging with a local trader and purchased a ticket on the steamer *Tabora* bound for Kinshasa two days hence.

Hayes was surprised to find a plate on the bow of the *Tabora* that said the ship had been made in Pittsburg, Pennsylvania, USA. He described the steamer as "of the Mississippi type," meaning a sternwheeler powered by a large paddlewheel on the stern. Fare to Kinshasa converted to about $41 American. Four dollars a day, exclusive of food, but all was "clean and wholesome," so Hayes couldn't complain.

The entire upper Congo seemed to be infested with missionaries. At Coquilhatville (Mbandaka), seven hundred Europeans quarreled over sectarian approaches to souls as state-sponsored Catholicism elbowed with several Protestant denominations for primacy.

But Hayes got some good news in keeping with all the religiosity at Coquilhatville, a resurrection of sorts. The report of Frank Bowen's death given Hayes six years previously had apparently been exaggerated. A couple of English gentlemen at the African Eastern Hotel said a white-haired old Bowen had escaped his Belgian judge. In fact, the gentlemen went on, the aging elephant hunter Hayes had known in Uganda sneaked back into Coquilhatville now and then, dodging Bula Matadi, whenever he wasn't "hippo hunting on the Kasai, chasing elephants in French territory and generally hustling where he can." It brightened Hayes to know Bowen still lived even if he also believed "… Bowen is outdated. He is too rugged a character for the Africa of today."

Hayes probably thought of himself equally outdated as Bowen; hadn't the once-young adventurer, now nearly fifty-years old, been nursing infected teeth across half the continent? Hayes called at the offices of an American dentist in Coquilhatville to learn that, yes, his teeth were septic and advanced beyond anything a simple mission dentist could handle. Hayes had anticipated that diagnosis: "So there's no out, I must leave Africa." Forced from the continent once again by poor health, Hayes tried to look on the bright side: "Anyway, I'm having a glorious trip across Africa."

Past Kwamouth, where the Kasai River joins the Congo River, some passengers coming aboard told Hayes the Belgians had imposed a five-year ban on hippo hunting up the Kasai. Maybe hippo populations could recover in that short time? Hayes doubted it: "Man declares open war on every animal he may not fit into his scheme of living." In fact, Hayes knew more precisely which men were responsible for the assault on nature: "It has been that way wherever the European has gone. The bison in North America, the kangaroos in Australia, the whales of every sea and the game all over this continent is about done." The year was 1928. Hayes continued even more pessimistically about the future: "I am glad to have seen so much of it; no one will ever do so again."

Kinshasa bustled with so much activity all the decent hotels in town were full, so Hayes celebrated his 50th birthday at a little place run by and for Portuguese travelers. The accommodation was fine, as nice as "the ABC where all the high and mighty stop," but its American inhabitant pecked despondently at his typewriter in his good-enough room, recording some hard reflections on a decade birthday: "I am fifty now and have not got far in life. Not too much money, an ulcerated jaw, on my way out of the Africa I have loved perhaps too well."

At the end of his sixth extended adventure in Africa, Hayes did not write the wistful melancholy he expressed when previously leaving the continent. At 50, jaded, tired, a mouthful of septic teeth threatening his life, he felt too old for the romance of adventuring. In his journal he wrote only perfunctorily: "We dropped down river and entered the Atlantic without mishap." Surely, he would never return to Africa. Surely, he would never want to return to Africa.

15. In the Meantime: San Simeon, Wyntoon, Butler, Pacific Grove, 1928-1952

In something of a hurry to get his teeth pulled, Hayes first had to bounce up the coast of West Africa. Little had changed: miles of wide beach, low-lying coast clad with evergreen forests, passengers and cargo rowed ashore in whaleboats at the occasional village, white-painted villas, singing boatmen.

Twelve days after departing Matadi on the mouth of the Congo River, Hayes stood on deck shivering in dense fog blown by a cold wind down the English Channel as the steamer *Elizabethville* pulled into Antwerp on Feb 28, 1928. He immediately bought a new suit, the best they had, at a favorable exchange rate. Then he toured the docks – ignoring the prostitutes calling out to him in English admiring the new suit. He didn't mention looking for a dentist in Antwerp; maybe when he got to England.

Hayes spent three days in London, mostly at the Kensington Natural History Museum. The Kensington appeared a little shabby after the fine examples of taxidermy Hayes had seen in Washington and New York. True, the Kensington had more specimens, more than anywhere in the world with the whole empire to draw on, but all were, "mounted to stand stiffly with no sign of life."

The transatlantic steamer *Antonia* Hayes caught out of London carried immigrants (still) coming to America: "Poles, Jews, and the polyglot of the Balkans and from Italy." Some twenty years previously, in 1916, he had traveled with immigrants in ships boasting accommodations "not a whit above that afforded cattle shipped live." In 1928 his third-class berth equaled anything that would have been considered first in the old days. On stormy seas, all aboard suffered both seasickness and homesickness.

Hayes didn't look for a dentist in Halifax either. Most of the immigrants got off there. Only the Irish stayed aboard "enroute to Ameriky."

Finally New York, but Hayes temporized about Eastern dentists: "My teeth are as sore as in Africa, but it is better to go West and get fixed up in my homeland."

Hayes rode by train to Chicago where all appeared cold and bleak: "There is no beauty about the great lakes of North America. You get there and there they are." Like London, Chicago too had a fine museum, the Field. Hayes walked "miles of halls" wearing out his feet but not his eyes.

April 5, 1928, Hayes had the offending teeth pulled in Portland, Oregon. Of the dentist he wrote, "I only hope he leaves me enough to eat with." While awaiting the molding of his dentures, Hayes took a job painting houses in the spring rain. When not painting, he had time to see a couple of baseball games; take a tour the Columbia River, "about the size of the Aruwimi;" and to deliver one talk on wild animals to a large crowd in a Portland suburb.

On May 11, 1928, he thought his new teeth looked fancy enough, but they hurt – and they cost a lot of money. Hayes groused that "[d]entists, doctors, and lawyers do not give a fair return for the services they perform, yet one must seek their aid at times."

Hayes had money on his mind in May of 1928. The worldwide economy showed no hints of the cataclysm looming a year and a half away; still, Hayes had pressing personal concerns. US President Franklin Roosevelt wouldn't sign the Social Security Act until 1935 (legislation Hayes bitterly opposed because it undermined dignity and personal responsibility). Hayes, fifty years old, essentially broke and completely estranged from his family, could rely on only his own resources in his aged years. "I knew it was time to accumulate a competence against the decline of life, and there were not too many years left to accomplish this."

So, where does an itinerant vagabond, broadly skilled, with an excellent work ethic, look for steady employment on the West Coast of the United States in 1928? Hayes went to San Simeon, California, where the architect Julia Morgan, working for newspaper magnate William Randolph Hearst, was already several years into construction on the extravagant Hearst Castle.

George Hearst (1820-1891), William Randolph Hearst's (1863-1951) father, had a flair for finding metals. George found: silver at the Ophir Mine in the Utah Territory, copper at the Anaconda Mine in Montana, and gold at the Homestake Mine in South Dakota. George Hearst's many acquisitions, purchased with the various mining fortunes, included a 40,000-acre ranch at San Simeon on the California coast.

George did not have to purchase the one newspaper he owned; he is said to have received the *San Francisco Examiner* as payment for a gambling debt. His only son, William Randolph Hearst, inherited George's fortune, including the ranch and the newspaper. With only this "meager" start in life, William Randolph Hearst built the largest worldwide media conglomerate of the 1920s and 30s (still extant today under the name Hearst Communications).

Following the wreckage of WWI, impoverished Europeans offered much of the treasure of the continent at fire-sale prices. William Randolph Hearst became one of their most avid buyers. He supervised construction of his "Enchanted Castle" at San Simeon in part to house his European booty. Orson Welles drew a cinematic representation of Hearst at San Simeon; the character Charles Foster Kane in the enduring classic *Citizen Kane* is a thinly veiled William Randolph Hearst.

Hayes' journal of his time at San Simeon, kept somewhat more loosely than his African diaries, details day-to-day construction at the castle from a workingman's point of view.

It is a fascinating commentary on the parade of rich and famous, actors and politicians, come to play at the partially complete, sumptuous (some say tasteless) San Simeon. Prohibition? Depression? Not at San Simeon. Hayes wrote mostly about his workmates, their tasks and their infighting, but William Randolph Hearst, Marion Davies, Charlie Chaplin, Jean Harlow, Winston Churchill, et al., float by, drinks in hand, chatting convivially across the backdrop of Hayes' workaday world.

Initially accepting the lowest employment, on the end of a "muck stick," as he called a shovel, Hayes stayed on at San Simeon for five years, from May 1928 until March 1933. Navigating the constant swirl of sycophantic political jockeying for favor with the great and capricious Hearst, on the strength of his know-how and hard work, Hayes rose, for a time, to keeper at the enormous zoo at San Simeon. The list of animals under his care in 1929 included:

On pasture:			In cages:	
Giraffes.	4	Africa	Lions	6
Yak	1	Tibet	Tiger	1
Singsing				
waterbuck	3	Africa	Cheetah	1
Ellipse	2	Africa	Leopard	1
Leucoryx	2	Soudan	Himalaya Bear	1
Beisa Oryx	1	Africa	Sun bears	2
Llama	8	Peru	Grizzly bear	1
Nilghai	4	India	Brown bears	2
Duiker	4	Africa	Black bears	3
Springbok	4	Africa	Coyotes	6
Blessbok	5	Africa	Wild cats	2
Ibex	4	Africa	Mountain lions	3
Reindeer	3	Alaska	Coati mundis	2
Sambhur Deer	3	India	Coons	3
Axis Deer	9	India	Badger	1
Mountain Sheep	1	USA	Chimpanzees	2

Goat	1	Mexico	Rhesus Monkeys 3
Mouflon	1	Corsica	Orangutans 2
Black Buck	17+	India	Birds 1,500
Sable Antelope	2	Africa	
Kangaroo	7	Australia	
Rhea	5	Australia	
Emu	4	Australia	
Cassowary	1	New Guinea	

White fallow deer 100+

Under care outside fences or cages, herds of:
Bison,
Elk,
Native Deer, and
Cattle

Later, Hayes mentioned a small elephant that butted Joan Crawford when the actress "leaned idly against the screen, her forehead on the wire."

Eventually Hayes fell victim to the rough and tumble politics on the hill. In November of 1930 his immediate supervisor, Baldwin (whom Hayes unfailingly called "Snakebelly"), "bulldogged" (wrestled to the ground by the horns as in a rodeo event) a white oryx that had wandered into the wrong enclosure. Nothing Baldwin could do would re-attach an oryx horn snapped off at the base. Hayes pushed Baldwin aside to clean the bleeding stump and seal the wound with tar. In thanks, Baldwin scapegoated Hayes: sacked him and hustled him off the hill before Hearst, who was away at the time, could sort out the facts of the incident.

Hayes liked Hearst, with his "infectious grin that instantly puts all at ease." Of course this is not to say Hayes condoned the long list of Hearst's libertine ways: his mistress Marion Davies openly in residence when Hearst's wife Millicent wasn't needed to keep up appearances for visiting dignitaries; his flouting Prohibition with literally tons of alcohol delivered to the hill; and the ceaseless bacchanal of young, hopeful women preyed on by the rich and powerful among Hearst's revolving door of guests. But, in all, Hayes found Hearst overly generous and ever gracious in conversation on those mornings when the two met walking the grounds of San Simeon: "He is the best boss I have ever known, and I'll forgive his sins if he will forgive mine."

Three months later, when Hearst returned to San Simeon and found time to sort out who had actually injured the oryx, the great man gave Baldwin a stern admonishment but, overly generous, did not fire him. Furthermore, Hearst ordered Baldwin to find and re-employ that African traveling fellow, what was his name?

Steady jobs were hard to come by in early 1931; Hayes had been hustling odd jobs about San Luis Obispo. With nothing better on offer, he reluctantly returned to San Simeon and, protected by a new construction superintendent, George Loorz, stayed "25 straight months on the hill with nothing but Hollywood stars." Baldwin had to re-hire Hayes but not at his previous position. Hayes worked in various lowly capacities around San Simeon until April of 1933.

Near the beginning of those 25 straight months sequestered at San Simeon, Hayes received news that CT Studd had died on July 16, 1931, at Ibambi, south of Niangara in the Belgian Congo. Studd's "Don't Care a Damn" oath had eventually split the mission in twain: twenty-two of Studd's missionaries, twenty of them American, refused to swear the oath and left the Heart of Africa to establish their own evangelical station.

According to Hayes, Studd died "so deeply in the clutches of opium and morphine he dares not return home." After all the years gone by, Hayes tried (and failed) to muster a good word for his missionary boss. "The best I can say of CT Studd is, he was a selfish, obstinate charlatan who did the world a good turn by dying out of it."

As the months of the Depression ticked by at San Simeon, not even Hearst's prodigious fortune could withstand four years of Depression and his spendthrift ways. As wages became short and men were laid off at San Simeon, the jockeying for sinecures became increasingly rough. George Loorz came to Hayes in March of 1933 (the year US unemployment reached 25%) with "a hang-dog look and a silly grin," announcing a two-month layoff for Hayes. In fact, Hayes had it on good authority that Willicombe, above Loorz in the hierarchy at the Enchanted Castle, had ordered Loorz to "make a place for an old convivial of Hearst's, who is burned out completely with booze and fast living."

Hayes knew he had no chance against even a burned-out drunk if that wastrel was a member of the Masons. Willicombe was a fanatic of that fraternity. Assuming Loorz had softened the wording of an actual firing, Hayes said goodbye to the famed Irish playwright George Bernard Shaw, who happened to be visiting San Simeon at that moment, and trudged down the hill proud of the work he had done on the castle, its zoo, and the grounds about San Simeon.

During his five years in residence at San Simeon, Hayes had invested every cent he saved in what he called life insurance, some kind of annuity that would pay out after a fixed term. As banks failed and Hayes became increasingly wary of insurance scams, he sought advice from Frank Preston, the glass engineer with whom Hayes had maintained correspondence since their meeting on the *Vedic* in 1925. Preston steered Hayes to John Krisko, a reputable businessman in Butler, Pennsylvania. Following Krisko's investment advice, barring inflation, Hayes' "competence" would see him safely through his last years. Unfortunately, this thrift against the future left Hayes, now unemployed, with no ready cash.

In search of work, Hayes went from San Luis Obispo to San Francisco by bus, then to Portland, then to Bandon, then back to San Francisco. Nothing turned up anywhere. At

Fleishhacker Zoo in San Francisco, Hayes came across an Afrikaner named Bistany who had an interesting proposal: find ten people to pay $5,000 each for a hunting trip up the Nile. Bistany would take five up the Blue Nile; Hayes would lead the other five up the White Nile north from Khartoum. "It sounds too good to be true, but we'll see." (Bistany wrote six months later to say that no one had signed up for an

expensive African hunting trip during the height of the Depression.)

When not looking for work, Hayes hung around the San Francisco library most days, reading, thinking. Quite unexpectedly, one day a letter arrived from George Loorz, sent General Delivery. All those hangdog faces and grins Loorz had made when "firing" Hayes had been attempts at a wink and a nod. Loorz and a partner, F. C. Stolte, had formed a general contracting company. With Loorz' connections, Stolte and Company had signed a lucrative deal to build at Hearst's Wyntoon property up north near McCloud, California, in the shadow of Mt. Shasta. Loorz wondered if Hayes needed work.

Julia Morgan, the architect for San Simeon, had, according to Hayes, also drafted an initial design for Wyntoon during Hearst's easy money days. Her extravagant first set of plans called for reconfiguring a Cistercian monastery (one a Hearst agent had purchased, then illegally deconstructed, crated, and shipped stone by stone from Spain) together with the great tithe barn from Bradenstoke Priory in England (then lying around in crates at San Simeon) into Wyntoon Castle.

However, by the time Stolte and Company had been hired in 1933, Hearst's financial realities in the Depression forced a re-evaluation of Morgan's original plan for the grand hybrid castle. Tight times forced Hearst to settle for a more modest "Bavarian Village." (Hearst would declare bankruptcy in 1937 but held onto both San Simeon and Wyntoon. He and Marion Davies lived at Wyntoon through much of the Second World War.)

Contract work at Wyntoon required such physical stamina Hayes asked Loorz to be paid off the job after his first week moving thousand-pound stones with a crew of sturdy Italian men. Instead Loorz transferred Hayes to lighter work, painting and building.

Hayes hung on at the lighter work until October when a letter came from John Krisko urging Hayes to come to Butler, Pennsylvania. Krisko would arrange speaking engagements for eager crowds hungry for vicarious adventure. Hayes was reluctant to pursue public speaking but when work on Wyntoon shut down for the winter, Hayes eventually rode a wildcat bus east in January 1934. Writing from an unheated car between Chicago and Pittsburgh, Hayes described the entire eastern United States: "No beauty, no comfort, a drear, bitter waste."

Krisko came through on his promise. Hayes had quite a few speaking engagements: at schools, ladies clubs, philanthropic organizations, occasionally a theatre. He found public speaking not much to his liking, harder work than lifting stones at Wyntoon. And the weather! Thirty below zero with the cold wind off Lake Erie. By March Hayes was back in San Francisco.

With no job to be had in the City by the Bay, Hayes drifted north to see if he could get back on with Loorz and Stolte at Wyntoon. Now 56-years-old, the demanding physical work - digging deep pits in frozen ground with the same crew from the previous summer - nearly broke Hayes again. When even these big workmates nearly collapsed with rheumatism, working in the icy pits, Stolte declared a holiday. They could all take a couple of days at quarry work instead of the ice pits.

In December 1934, when the work season ended for winter at Wyntoon, Hayes rode back down to San Francisco in search of a new typewriter. To see if the new noiseless model he found would compare favorably to his standby of the previous eleven years, Hayes spent three months pecking away in a rooming house putting his diaries in order. At the outset, he mused: "I wonder if it will be of interest to anyone." He worried that tales of adventure were probably passé with "too much competition" from an adventurer behind every tree in 1934. But surely, later, someone would care? "At any other stage of history a resume [sic] of an adventurer's life would be of surpassing interest."

After three months typing, Hayes returned to Wyntoon in May of 1935, joining "forty-seven carpenters to say nothing of the brick layers, plumbers, masons, painters, artists – or mural decorators and the army of labor required to keep these going." To get back into work shape, Hayes was assigned to spray a couple of two-inch fire hoses over six-foot snow drifts to make an ice track for vehicles coming and going. Two weeks holding a hose in the cold and wet nearly crippled him.

Hayes' work at Wyntoon included laying fires in the assembly hall. One chilly July evening while he performed that duty, unnoticed by a crowd that included Clark Gable and Louis B. Mayer, Marion Davies swept in followed by "her anti-social dachshund, who will bite anybody who comes near her." As Marion positioned herself beside the fire, a "well knit, compact man carefully groomed, getting grey around his ears" emerged from Hearst's den. From where Hayes squatted by the fire alongside Marion Davies and her dachshund, he heard Louis B. Mayer announce the entry of (former) President Herbert Hoover. In the ensuing excitement, Marion's dog, Gandhi, went for the nearest leg. Hayes did not cry out, even though little Gandhi had "encompassed a fair mouthful of meat in his capacious jaws, and it stung sharply." Hayes managed to shake off "the beast" discretely without dropping his armload of wood. Only Hearst noticed Gandhi's attack, shooting Hayes a sly grin.

On most days at Wyntoon, Hearst paced the grounds accompanied by only his own small dachshund and three "muscle men" for protection. "The great man" often spoke genially to staff he encountered while walking. Hayes wrote, "It is said all things come to him who waits, but sometimes I wonder if it is not well to help them along." One morning, as Hearst approached, Hayes rose to dust off the knees of his pants and "asked Hearst point blank about going to Africa for him." In his diary Hayes didn't specify the errand he had in mind in Africa, probably a proposal to extend the zoo. Hearst listened attentively, "courteous as he always is to any man, great or small," and said he would give the matter his full consideration and promised he and Hayes would speak again soon. Hearst and all the parties left Wyntoon three months later, in October 1935, with no further mention of a trip to Africa for Hayes.

Laid off once again in the general culling of staff for the winter, Hayes decided he would return to dreary Butler, Pennsylvania. John Krisko had arranged more speaking engagements, a re-commencement of the "false friendliness" Hayes found so tiring. Hayes encapsulated the entire winter of 1935 in two pages of his diary. He wrote that he made decent money speaking but spent whatever he earned in company with this sophisticated crowd. He couldn't wait to get back to Wyntoon in March.

The diary entries for the next seven months at Wyntoon are nearly as sparse as those written in Butler. Why write when nothing new happens? Hayes had a bout of influenza; strained his side from the punishing work; and registered Republican so he could vote against Roosevelt.

By October, Hearst had come and gone again. The layoffs in the wake of his departure were so severe in 1936, Hayes knew his time there had come to an end. Even his benefactor, George Loorz, partner in Stolte and Co., got the sack.

The eight-year chapter of Hayes' life working for William Randolph Hearst deserves its own book. In fact, Hayes himself wrote one. Sometime in the 1950s he wrote a 113-page manuscript titled, *The Last of the Feudal Barons or My Life with William Randolph Hearst*. The manuscript has never been published or distributed even as widely as Hayes' diaries.

Hayes (guided by his collaborator and friend Frank Preston who assisted and encouraged everything Hayes wrote) trod very carefully with regard to libel. Hayes wanted his experiences and impressions recorded for history but feared losing his small competence to a suit alleging slander.

On the (presumed) last page of the fifth 400-page volume of his diary (in the edition I hold) Hayes wrote that he would reluctantly return to Butler for the winter of 1936. Winters in Pennsylvania were unbearably cold but unemployment remained above 15%. The laboratory Preston had been constructing for glass research was nearly complete. Hayes could live above the lab, do some groundskeeping, possibly establish an exotic animal park there. His diary ends abruptly there.

Sixteen years later, in 1952, Hayes would add a coda to his diary. Much of what I know of Hayes between 1936 and 1952 comes from some twenty letters Hayes wrote to a younger cousin, John Perkins, between April and December 1942. Johnny aspired to adventure and sought advice from his broadly experienced relative. After arranging for delivery to a false address, under a false name - lest his sisters learn of his whereabouts - Hayes consented to advise Johnny. A little of the detail of Hayes' life between 1936 and 1942 leaks around the edges of the advice given Johnny – which consisted mostly of: if you want to be an adventurer never marry.

Hayes remained in Butler through 1938 living in the "penthouse" above Preston's glass laboratory. The planned exotic animal park never got off the ground. Hayes did construction work and estimated he planted 1,600 trees, mostly pines, in his year and a half there.

In 2008 Jane Preston, Frank Preston's wife, donated the grounds of Preston Labs for a park maintained by the city of Butler. A visitor to Preston Park today can see the skeleton of "Perkins bridge," almost certainly built by Hayes while employed at the Butler Labs.

Hayes left Preston Labs in 1938. In a newspaper account written later, Hayes cited cold weather as his reason for leaving Butler. But in his letters to Johnny, Hayes mentions a falling out with Frank Preston. He doesn't give details, only that Preston had been exhorting him to return but he would not because, "[h]e did not treat me square when he had me, so I will not give him my confidence again." Both Jane and Frank Preston had written letters to Hayes inviting their friend and handyman to their forthcoming wedding. Hayes steamed open both letters, read and resealed them, then had his landlady re-address them to Redlands, California, where, after a time, they would be returned to Butler, apparently undeliverable. Johnny, not much interested in the intrigues between Hayes and his former employer, asked Hayes how to steam a letter open. Hayes replied with detailed instructions.

Hayes' letters to Johnny are return-addressed 671 Ocean View Boulevard, Pacific Grove, California. In the same newspaper article citing cold as Hayes' reason for leaving Butler, the writer says Hayes chose to settle in Pacific Grove because it wasn't cluttered up with bars. Doubtless Hayes would have been drawn to a dry town, but sometime in the previous four years George Loorz had also landed in Pacific Grove. Hayes doesn't mention his work for Stolte and Co. to Johnny, but one of the handwritten letters scribbled on company letterhead bears Stolte's and Loorz' names.

If Hayes Perkins is remembered today, it is for the other work he did at Pacific Grove, California, between 1942 and his retirement in 1957. During that time, he lived in an 8'x16' converted shower-house out near Lovers Point. From his front window, Hayes could look across the road at a small strip of land owned by the city onto a fine view of the ocean. As a kindness to the local youth who played on the strip between the road and the beach, Hayes rooted out the poison ivy growing there. The pocked ground looked a little unkempt so, in a gesture toward enhancing his view, as he had done the world over, Hayes planted a garden.

Most of the gardens Hayes planted in various locales across Africa, Australia, New Guinea, etc., had centered fruit trees, gifts to those who followed after he moved on. At Pacific Grove, Hayes planted flowers. With little civic support (and some opposition) Hayes single-handedly extended his plantings 1,500 feet along the coastline between 1942 and 1947, carrying five-gallon buckets to water its entire length twice a week. In a letter to Evelyn, Johnny's sister, dated 1948, Hayes says his garden stretched a quarter mile by then.

The Winter 2019 issue of *Eden*, the journal of the California Garden and Landscape History Society, has a beautifully illustrated article by David Laws on that small planting that grew over the years into Perkins Park (so designated by the city in 1950). Hayes knew the non-invasive succulent he'd encountered in South Africa as mesembryanthemum. Laws updates the identification to Dosanthemum floribundum. By either name the ground cover forms "a dazzling carpet of lilac purple blooms in spring." Laws says that in 1961 the garden also included "Aloe orborescensp … achilla, arctotis, calla lilies, cannas, century plants, dracaena palms, and veronica." Today, many of the local residents of Pacific Grove refer to Hayes Perkins Park as The Magic Carpet, and to its founder as The Magic Carpet Man.

Despite squabbling with what he considered an unappreciative town, and the constant plundering of vandals, bicycles, and dogs, Hayes kept at his work on the gardens with only two significant interruptions – his last African adventure in 1952 and a cruise around South America in 1955 – until he retired to Forest Hill Manor at Pacific Grove in 1957 at age 79.

16. Across the Sahara Desert, 1952

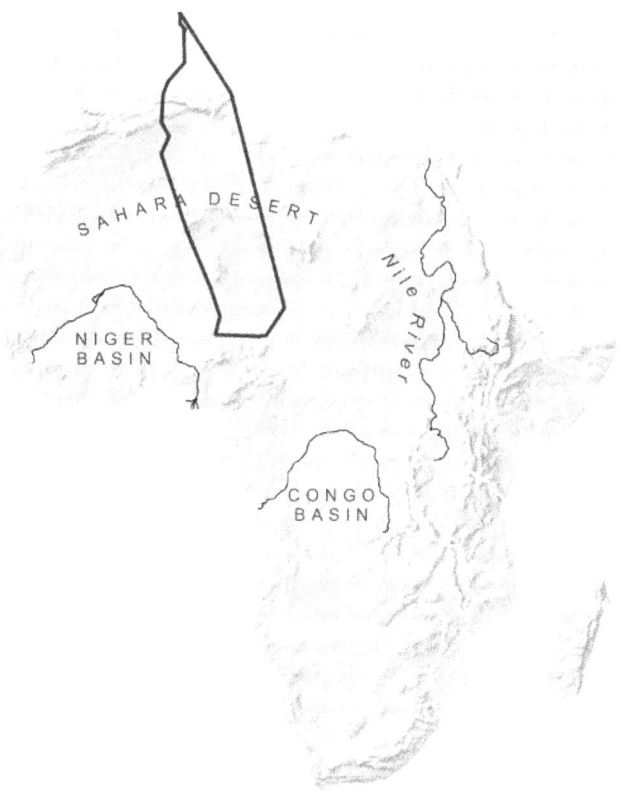

Between 1928 and 1952 Hayes had worked eight years at the Hearst properties in California, two years in Butler, Pennsylvania, then fourteen years planting and tending the gardens at Pacific Grove, California. During those long years continent-bound, the travel bug nibbled at Hayes sporadically – talk of that elephant hunt up the Nile with the San Francisco zookeeper at the height of the Depression; petitioning Hearst to send him out collecting for the San Simeon zoo; a note to Johnny saying Hayes had tried to enlist during WWII as a translator in the African theatre – but the bug never bit hard enough to move his aging body from the comforts of an established residence. Hayes lived quietly in the beach house at Pacific Grove until sometime in the early 1950s. Then, well past 70, a magazine advertisement caused that recurrent Africa fever to flair one last time.

Weariness with Pacific Grove partly explains Hayes' final African trip: "I fail to fit in with the people of this town. They regard me as a teller of tall tales." He thought he would come back to Pacific Grove when he had once more "had my fill of wandering." A few months among new people, living some more tall tales, would do him good. But, more importantly, he had unfinished business in Africa. To date he'd been: logging in Nigeria, down the Nile to the mission in Northern Congo, prospecting in Tanganyika, gold mining in the Southern Congo, up through South Africa by rail, and through the Ituri Forest then down the Aruwimi River by canoe with a toothache. Any experienced African adventurer would immediately spot the section of the continent Hayes had missed

At 74, Hayes reflected: "As a child I pored over such maps as a backwoods school afforded, tracing lines, trying to fill in the blank space bearing legends 'Unknown desert,' 'Unexplored,' or 'Waterless Desert,' that scattered themselves about the little-known spaces of the Sahara." True, he'd seen the sands of the Sahara sliding past the deck of a steamship chugging up the Nile but that wasn't the waterless desert. He meant the western Sahara Desert, below Algeria, with all the romance of the French Foreign Legion and veiled Tuareg raiders on swift camels. Hayes wrote that he'd been looking for a chance to "cross the sands" for more than fifty years.

In 1951, as Hayes was planning the trip, he knew he no longer had the stamina to trot off alone on a camel or even to find some punishing physical labor that would finance a trip down through the Sahara. Lucky then that he chanced across a magazine advertisement offering a softer trip. Right there in black and white, the French Government Tourist Bureau was peddling conveyance by bus from Algiers "across the desert to Lake Chad, the Niger, on to the Oubangi [sic]." Why, Hayes thought, at the Ubangi River he would be "almost at home." The Uele (to Hayes the Welle) River joins the Ubangi at Yakoma, just downstream (500 miles) from where Hayes had worked under CT Studd at the Heart of Africa Mission at Niangara.

Hayes made a quick trip up to San Francisco to follow up on the ad. He spoke to a representative of the French Travel Bureau whose "knowledge of the oases, the desert, Lake Chad and beyond was even less than mine." Characteristically undaunted by lack of information about where he was going, Hayes next (completely uncharacteristically) sought a traveling companion. He sent an invitation by mail to the "noted travel-writer" Harry Franck.

By 1951, Harry A. Franck, 71, only three years younger than Hayes, had published some two-dozen travelogues detailing his various adventures about Europe, South and Central America, China, the Middle East, and the West Indies – but nothing on Africa. In his letter to Franck, Hayes pointed out that he and Harry had a similar gap: the book Harry might write about an African ramble "would round out his career."

Harry's reply came swiftly. Great! Harry would be delighted to join Hayes. In fact, why stop at Lake Chad? Harry proposed they traverse the entire continent north to south, from Algiers to Cape Town. Harry's wife Rachel would eagerly join them as well! Rachel, only 60 in 1952, author of *I Married a Vagabond*, had accompanied Harry on a number of his international rambles and collaborated on several of his books.

Harry Franck wrote a 300 page draft called *Down Through Africa* detailing his travels through Northern Africa in company with "old bachelor Hayes." Information about

Hayes' last African adventure and most of the quotes below come almost entirely from Franck; Hayes gave the journey only two pages in his diary.

The bus Hayes boarded leaving San Francisco August 29, 1952, rolled through the night to Reno, Nevada, "'Greatest little city in the world!' they so proudly boast, but their prosperity is founded on wide open gambling, on handing out quick divorces, on open prostitution and whatever is forbidden in the other 47 states."

At Butler, Pennsylvania, the forests Hayes had planted at Preston Labs surprised him; how quickly they had become so tall. The lab staff gave him an enthusiastic tour of the grounds during which Hayes must have at least shaken hands with Frank Preston, who appeared, "heavier and more mature."

The French travel company from the magazine rerouted Hayes from his original booking on the *Georgic* to Le Havre onto the *Queen Elizabeth* to Cherbourg. The change caused Hayes no real concern; the Francks would not be able to join him in Algiers until November. The delay only meant "I will have to kill off six weeks or more in Paris and Algiers." The change of ships also meant an opportunity to ride on the *Queen Elizabeth*, the "biggest thing on the seas in history." His cabby to Pier Ten from 50th Street, "a typical New Deal Gimme artist," cursed the entire Perkins' ancestry when Hayes flipped him a 10¢ tip.

Hayes killed the six weeks waiting for Harry and Rachel in Algiers, rather than Paris. He spent no more than a day crossing the length of France from Cherbourg to Marseilles rolling through "the green hills of Normandy" still showing scars from WWII near Bayeux and Caen. At "fabulous Paris," Hayes stayed only long enough for a taxi ride to the station on the way to catch the late train to the south coast.

Room and board, $250 until November 6 (double the advertised price), at the Central Agha Hotel in Algiers included meals: "One can exist on the food served but not become obese." Somewhat rested and sufficiently fed, Hayes took a few days to recover his verve sitting on the benches of the "delightful little parks" lining the Rue Michelet. In his diary Hayes made detailed remarks about the beauty of the French women passing by his Algerian park bench.

Harry and Rachel Franck joined Hayes in Algiers just in time to catch the first of six yearly busses departing Algiers on November 6 for points south across the Sahara. The three would be traveling with the French-Algerian company Societé Africaine des Transports Topicaux (S.A.T.T.) Busses ran only in the winter months when the roads were cool enough not to melt rubber tires.

The small S.A.T.T. bus, a Renault, with an air-cooled diesel engine, "gleaming in aluminum paint and rather resembling in shape and size those milkwagons in which the driver stands up" far exceeded the "asthmatic, limping, worn-out vehicle we had visualized." The "camion," their little Renault bus, bore the "breath-taking legend MEDITERRANEÉ – NIGER – CHAD" lettered in blue the length of one side. Of the eight seats inside, four to the rear accommodated the only two passengers riding first class, Rachel and Harry. The four forward seats, separated from first class by a sliding, plate-glass barrier, had backs slightly more upright to seat the two second class passengers, Hayes and an Englishman, Wrey Gardiner, who had made half this trip once before. Harry and Rachel immediately dubbed their fine, small bus the Coccinelle, the ladybug.

While Franck wrote at length about lavish lunches, hotel accommodations, and the exotic sights of the first four days of their journey, Hayes concentrated on the local desert people, the Tuaregs. "Who the Tuaregs are, or from whence they came, has never been satisfactorily explained." He asserted that the singular name, Tarqui, translates from Arabic as "raider." (Harry records the same etymology - perhaps quoting Hayes.) The Tuareg had "ruled the desert" from the Atlantic, east into present day Niger; from the Mediterranean, south to Timbuktu on the Niger River. They lived a free, nomadic life trading salt and enslaved persons, squabbling among various "tribes, or clans." Hayes believed that had these warlike people united, "they might have created a great empire." Even divided as they were, the Tuareg clans "were able to take care of themselves" in the early days of European colonial incursion: "Many were the defeats the French received at the hands of the rulers of the Sahara before they learned to meet the latter on equal terms."

Upon return to the hotel their fifth night out from Algiers, Hayes, not eating, appeared noticeably weak. He thought he might be able to keep down a bit of milk if any could be located. At the "hole-in-the-wall grocery store" where Harry and Rachel finally found canned condensed milk, the proprietor apologized, telling them, no, he could only sell milk for babies or sick people. Did the Francks have a prescription? Two hours later, Harry and Rachel returned bearing a prescription for milk for Hayes obtained from a military physician at the nearby French base.

Even in his weakened state, the salt manufactory at Tiguidda M'Tiem fascinated Hayes. Wearing his amateur engineer hat, he wrote a close description on the method of salt refining: a brine spring diverted into permanent molds in the clay soil then evaporated in the sun. But his lecture immediately gave way to a more romantic reverie. Imagine the history of these desert salt mines worked by myriad enslaved men, "even captured Europeans," brought here century after century only to work – then die. The precious salt mined with their lives transported by caravans numbering 15,000 camels trudging across the desert sands to far-away Tripoli. Here was a slice of the old Africa Hayes had known must be hidden in these "uncharted, waterless deserts."

Later that afternoon, cruising along a savannah of golden grass like wheat stubble, Harry saw real ponds, with islands, and birds wheeling overhead. Here both he and Rachel began taking a "chloriguane (paludrine) pill" daily against malaria. They had only seen one mosquito but with the open water and

Hayes unable to eat, wasting away by the day, the couple would take no chances.

Harry laughed at the extensive paperwork required to leave Niger in French West Africa and enter Nigeria in British Africa: "the recording of our mother-in-laws' names and similar information." Bureaucratic red tape filled most of a day in Zinder, the only bright moment a chance to shake hands with the current Sultan. His majesty happened to be at the administrative offices for a semi-yearly military recruitment ceremony. His impressive royal air and costume contrasted with drab outfits of a mob of reluctant-faced recruits.

Speeding on through the night on the good British roads in Nigeria, Harry could immediately sense the change from a French to a British colony. "Traffic on the left was the least of the changes between French and British colonies that were oddly evident even at night." For one thing, more cars and trucks passed by than they'd seen in all the Sahara. But more than that, even at night, Nigeria teemed with life, more people, more villages, markets, "an indefinable sense of more prosperity, even more energy; in short, a perceptible difference in atmosphere, between French and British."

Nor was Hayes blind to political realities of Africa in 1952. He could see that African independence movements would throw off direct European colonial rule sooner rather than later. At Kano he spoke with a group of Southern Nigerian immigrants, some educated in mission schools, some at the finest universities of the United States. All cried, "'Freedom!'"

Outside Nguru, their driver, Louis Gardrat, and his assistant, Kiki, pulled a spare axel from beneath the bus and began repairs in the deep sand beside the rock on which one wheel had sheared completely off following Louis Gardrat's swerve around a slow-moving truck. At midmorning, Hayes and Harry, becoming increasingly fidgety, walked some distance along the dusty road to discover a side-path leading to a village. Crying babies greeted their arrival with screams "at sight of our ghastly white faces." Undeterred by screaming babies, Hayes haggled with their parents for a few small eggs. Harry says Hayes examined a chicken, but rejected it as too scrawny and too expensive, "besides, he could hardly eat it raw."

In the heat of the afternoon, Harry, Rachel and Hayes accepted a ride with a jolly young Frenchman, a plantation owner and Dunlop tire seller, who happened by driving a Dodge 'kit car.' Louis Gardrat and Kiki remained behind, sweating under the bus "as if they really thought they could patch Coccinelle up into running again."

Later that evening, as their passengers sat drinking limeade at Gashua with American missionaries, Mr. and Mrs. George Worling, what small bus rolled smoothly onto the mission grounds, "running as smoothly as if it had never tried to pass a truck?" Louis Gardrat waved for the Americans to climb aboard; they would drive through the night to arrive at Maiduguri by morning, making up a day on his ruined schedule.

At Maiduguri, Louis Gardrat decided he hadn't the strength to face "frontier formalities" crossing the border from British Nigeria into the panhandle of French Camerouns [sic] at the end of a long afternoon on the road. The hotel at Maiduguri had hot water, towels and plenty of pillows. For Harry, "[s]omehow the Englishness of it all was restful."

On Sunday, Nov. 23, 1952, 17 days and some 4,500 km out from Algiers, Hayes, Harry, and Rachel stepped, for the last time, out the Coccinelle's door. The customs house in Ft. Lamy, Chad, marked the end of the line for the S.A.T.T. leg of their journey.

Made comfortable at the Sudan United Mission by Walther Landolt and his wife, both from Switzerland, Hayes appeared, "obviously ill." A noncommittal French doctor, summoned to the mission on short notice, looked the patient over and suggested perhaps a touch of malaria, though Hayes had no fever. The doctor recommended rest and a soft diet with something of a suggestion that "it was really nothing."

Hayes had been losing about a pound a day during the two-and-a-half weeks traveling 4,500 km from Algiers to Ft. Lamy. Completing the trip as originally planned by Harry called for another 7,000 km of uncertain roads, rivers, and rails between Ft. Lamy and Cape Town. Hayes couldn't stand to lose that many more pounds. He and the Francks reluctantly decided the only prescription that would give Hayes real rest and a soft diet would begin with a plane ticket from Ft. Lamy to Paris, then another from Paris to California. Harry and Rachel would have to continue south toward the Cape without Hayes Perkins.

Though Mme. Landolt was an excellent cook, four days at the Sudan United Mission wore on all three Americans, especially as they had arrived on a Sunday. But every day at the mission might as well have been Sunday, as each was "punctuated with large doses of prayers and sermons." Some of the prayers implied Hayes would be departing imminently, "and not for California." How annoying to have one's death anticipated with unctuous missionary prayers.

On Tuesday, the three travelers returned to S.A.T.T. offices to bid Kiki and Louis Gardrat farewell. The Coccinelle, with no further repair, had a full load of six for the return trip to Algiers. Harry wrote of his resentment seeing others occupying "our" seats in the bus and of the "lumps in our throats," as the little bus chugged raucously off toward the river, the swamps, the desert, and eventually Algiers in another 17 days.

Rachel and Harry knew they must reach the Congo River system while the water remained high enough for navigation; no steamers ran east from Bangui, in French Ubangi-Chari (Central African Republic) after mid-December. Riding a bicycle on loan from the Landolts, Harry began enquiring about trucks running south across Chad. Yes, a freight company called Uniroute occasionally took on a passenger or two: $237 for 800 miles from Ft. Lamy to the Chad border. Expensive and dodgy, but what choice had the Francks?

As it happened, the Francks departed Ft. Lamy for Bangui the same day Hayes flew out for Paris: November 27, 1952, Thanksgiving. Harry reported after the fact that Hayes arrived in Paris eight hours after leaving Ft. Lamy and caught a Holland-America steamer to New York. Aboard ship the Dutch ship's doctor took him in hand "and long before we left Africa Perkins was again cultivating his famous Pacific Grove flower garden."

(Harry's account of the rest of the Franck's trip across Africa from its northern to southern tip continues for another 160 pages beyond the 140 he wrote about the portion of the trip Hayes shared with them. They made it all the way to Cape Town, but Harry's account breaks off abruptly with Harry and Rachel at Albert Park (Virunga National Park) on the eastern border of the Belgian Congo (Democratic Republic of the Congo) with Rwanda. Harry's manuscript was never completed or published. I am deeply grateful that his surviving family shared the unpublished manuscript with me.

17. Final Years, 1952-1964

Twenty-five pounds off his normal 180, Hayes flew Air France from Ft. Lamy to Paris with a two-hour layover in Tunis. At Le Havre, he tottered aboard the Holland-America steamer *Ryndhan*. Already somewhat restored by the doctor's care across the Atlantic, at New York Harbor, Hayes eschewed another winter bus ride across a dreary American continent and went instead directly to New York Municipal Airport (LaGuardia) and paid airfare to San Francisco. How glad he must have been to return, for the first time in his life, to his own home, his little cottage by the sea at Pacific Grove, its magnificent garden promising to cheer him with the riot of color due in a few short months.

At 74, Hayes' recuperative powers do not seem to have abandoned him entirely. In a photograph taken in 1953, less than a year after ill-health had chased him yet again out of Africa, Hayes stands hale and heathy holding a large axe alongside Andy Jacobson (for whom a second park in Pacific Grove is named) with whom he had volunteered to fight the Bryson-Hesperia fire in south Monterey County.

When not called to volunteer firefighting, Hayes did return to tending his garden at Pacific Grove, though no longer alone; by 1953, the city had hired him a competent assistant. The tasks of planting, watering, and weeding no longer fell solely to Hayes – though he still took on most of the policing himself. Some who came to vandalize his park acted purely from malice; some came to dig samples of his rare species; and, worst of all, others rode bicycles off the path. Hayes didn't object to his image as the local madman in the shack overlooking the garden, the one storming out, shouting and gesticulating across the road. City officials neither aided nor constrained him.

During 1953 and '54, Hayes must have spent many hours looking across his garden, gazing out to sea, fingers pecking at the keys of his typewriter. Though he rarely dated his manuscripts, a note with his receipts and correspondence with Frank Preston says he wrote *The African Experiences of H. Hayes Perkins, 1906-1953* in 1953. He compiled *Alaska and the Yukon, Fifty Years Ago* in 1954, much of it taken nearly verbatim from his diaries. Employees of Preston Laboratories typed both manuscripts in quintuplicate.

In March of 1955, Hayes, restless again, renewed his passport and paid $1,275 for his last sea voyage. Though he had passed through the Panama Canal many times and sailed around Cape Horn twice as a younger man, he had never really gotten a first-hand feel for the South American continent. Too old for a long walk across a continent or for seeking work, Hayes would tour the continent as he had Japan and China: on a freight liner hopping from port to port down the West Coast and up the East.

Together with ten other passengers, Hayes boarded the *Falkanger* at San Pedro, California. At 77, Hayes judged that he was probably senior among the passengers but all the others, six of them women, appeared similarly "past the prime of life." For a working freighter, the *Falkanger* boasted "most luxuries, even pretty white-clad girls for stewardesses, and despite being overladen, is far more comfortable than the giant *Queen Elizabeth*." A crewmember told Hayes not to worry about the towering load, assuring the elderly passenger they sailed on a favored ship; the *Falkanger* never saw a storm.

Hayes resumed his diary on this last trip, writing brief observations very much as he had always written when adventuring. Rain fell at Buenaventura, Columbia. All the shops were closed for Good Friday at a steamy, tropical Guayaquil, Ecuador. He could see only scorching desert sailing past Paita, Peru. At a stopover in Lima, Peru, a visit to the mummified remains of Francisco Pizarro prompted his long, familiar diatribe concerning the perfidy of the Catholic Church. The flyer he received at Antofagasta, Chile, telling him a girl cost $2.50 for the entire night, touched off his tirade concerning the evils of prostitution.

At Valvida, Chile, the *Falkanger* stopped a little longer to take on a load of lumber and a pilot to guide the ship through the rough weather round the Horn. The albatrosses that began to appear in these southern latitudes reminded Hayes of sailing hungry through these waters more than 50 years previously. Thankfully, in 1955, he didn't need to eat any albatross; food on the *Falkanger* was plentiful and good. Hayes ate well when not stricken with the old gastric trouble familiar from his last trip through the Sahara.

The boasts the crewman had made about a weather charm on the *Falkanger* proved false. Off the Evangelista Islands near Cape Horn, seas 30 to 40 feet high casually tossed then dropped "the sturdy Falkanger, manned by her crack Norse crew." Hayes wasn't worried, writing the *Falkanger* "takes it well, and asks for more." And he admired the skipper's acuity. The experienced seaman had tacked far out to sea then back toward land, gaining as much as 32 hours following this canny path.

The skipper must have anticipated these high seas; at Antofagasta, where crewmen had off-loaded the lumber from Valvida, their captain had ordered only a comparatively light cargo loaded, 750 tons of salt. Now the captain stood on a buoyant ship bobbing on tall seas, his legs braced on the bridge, supervising the load and his crack Norsemen. Maybe the sagacity of this man was the *Falkanger's* real weather charm.

Sailing north up the east coast of Argentina, passengers sighted a flock of geese far out to sea, surely from the Falkland Islands. At an enforced layover in Buenos Aires, Argentina, Hayes recorded his understanding of Eva Perón's rise to power. A country girl, she became a "ham actress" and discovered "she had a power over men." She exercised that power to marry "an undistinguished army colonel named Juan Dominguez Peron" and guided him into military dictatorship with herself "equal co-partner in almost complete control of the country." Then, in 1952, at the height of her power, Eva Perón, Argentina's Evita, age 33, died of cancer.

Natural beauty could still move Hayes to exultation at age 77: "There are no words in any tongue to adequately describe the magnificence of the approach to the harbor of Rio de Janeiro." The city had its points too, but "all that man can do is cheap and tawdry when compared to the sublime grandeur of the setting of land and sea."

Off Curacao, hardworking boobies plunged into the sea catching fish. When Hayes saw some of the boobies harassed into dropping their prey by piratical frigate birds, Hayes couldn't resist making his misanthropic comparison: "in this the greedy frigate resembles the human species."

At Colon, Panama, the eastern entrance to the canal appeared little changed since the last time Hayes had come through: lovely when seen from the bay; squalid at street level. Dogs and buzzards prowled the streets alongside prostitutes of every nationality. In contrast to a slovenly Panamanian city, efficient US administration of the canal itself sparkled for Hayes as a model of human ingenuity: "an example of what the genus homo might do over all the earth if he only would."

The *Falkanger's* skilled and thoughtful skipper drew the ship up close to the shore of Acapulco, Mexico, so those aboard could glimpse "what it has to offer as an attraction to those who have the means and leisure to travel." To Hayes, Acapulco seemed not a particularly pretty place, its main attraction the highway connecting it to the US. As far as Hayes was concerned, Mexico's first widely-advertised resort town couldn't hold a candle to Rio de Janeiro, Copacabana, or Angra Dos Reis. And, for the traveler willing to really break loose, he recommended an Australian city: "All round, I like Sydney better than any of them."

At the end of Hayes' four month cruise around South America, from March 23 to July 23, 1955, Hayes wrote: "Thus ends my 130th sea voyage. I am seventy-seven years old and feel splendid." This excursion ended as long sea voyages typically ended: "Booze parties every evening, [with] all the inanities of good will toasts that are insincere …" Always the odd man out, Hayes did not imbibe, instead he saved plenty of room for the ice cream served at the captain's farewell dinner their final night at sea. Hayes had seen some hardships of weather and ill-health on this journey but, as had always been the case, he accounted the hardships worth the cost to have checked the last box on his travel card. The last sentence of his diary from 1955 reads: "I have no plans for further travel, there are no lands to explore, and I don't care to go over old ground."

His garden at Pacific Grove must have been beautiful when Hayes returned home in late July 1955. By now he had only a casual hand in its maintenance and further let go its care in 1957 when he moved to Forest Hills Manor, an independent-living care facility about six blocks up the street from his previous seaside residence in Pacific Grove.

He complained off and on over the next seven years about the food at Forest Hills, about the elderly women with whom he lived, and about the absurdity of making monthly payments for the roof over one's head. He tried to address the last complaint by arranging to work on the grounds of the manor in return for reduced rent but soon let that arrangement lapse as so much unappreciated work. Most days he took a walk through his garden, down to the beach to stroll along the wrack line.

His travels finished, Hayes took to writing. In 1957, again with the help of Frank Preston and his staff, Hayes finished his manuscript *The Last of the Feudal Barons or My Life with William Randolph Hearst*, a 112 page tell-all about his time in Hearst's employ drawn heavily from Hayes' diaries. Hayes knew that his frank accounting of the violations of

Prohibition, Hearst's open affair with Marion Davies, the wild parties with movie stars and gaggles of would-be starlets at San Simeon ran perilously close to the lines of legality, morality, and respectability of the times. Hayes and Frank Preston discussed the real possibility of suit for libel should they seek publication and decided not to publish. In a letter dated February 1964, Hayes offered his Hearst manuscript to my grandfather John with the admonition: "If you say and promise to hold it safe, I might let you and Mary [John's sister] have … it. But remember it is in the raw. I held back nothing. Maybe your wife, but not your children or step-children, it is too strong meat for them until adults."

Nowhere in his diaries, or in surviving letters to family members, or in the correspondence with Preston or Franck that I have read, does Hayes mention writing a novel. Nevertheless, Hayes' novel, *The Rearguard,* came to light just a few years ago in a parcel received from the caretakers cleaning up Preston Laboratories. As with most of the other manuscripts, no date appears on any of the several copies. From its look, uniform in binding to his other shorter manuscripts, it appears to have been compiled sometime in the late 1950s or early 1960s at Preston Labs. Hayes almost certainly wrote it after the 1952 trip to the Sahara; much of the action takes place in the Hoggar Mountains of southern Algeria and one of the central characters, Alifa, is a Tuareg Prince. To what genre would "Old Bachelor Hayes" be most unsuited as an author? Yes, *The Rearguard* is a romance featuring Zeitoun, "Pearl of the Desert."

Sometime in 1955 or 1956, Hayes had been diagnosed with diabetes. In April of 1964, Frank Preston wrote to the manager of Forest Hills Manor inquiring about why Hayes might not have responded to Preston's most recent letter. The last Preston had heard from Hayes, the adventurer said he was feeling "by no means well." Could the manager update Preston on his old friend's condition?

In late April 1964, Floyd Marchant, administrator at Forest Hills, wrote to inform Preston that Hayes had fallen while walking on the beach two weeks previously. Marchant went on to worry that Hayes' tumble had been "no doubt, due to a light stroke." Hayes had been mostly unresponsive during the two weeks since Preston had written except to request that "a friend" from Oregon be called to visit.

That friend was Hayes' first cousin once removed, John Donaldson, my grandfather. John and his wife, Rae, rushed south, arriving on April 29th. In a couple of visits with Hayes that day, Hayes pressed two bound copies of his diary into John's hands, perhaps those of the closest living relative with which Hayes was on any kind of speaking terms. Hayes had already given one copy of his diary to the Pacific Grove Library. (Frank or Jane Preston donated the other two copies to the Royal Geographical Society and to the library at Cal Poly San Luis Obispo.)

Hayes died quietly at 7:00 AM April 30, 1964. An extremely brief will stipulated Hayes' body should be cremated with "no services whatever." Any remaining money was to be donated to the Pacific Grove Library, interest accrued, but never the principal, to be spent for the purchase of new books according to the following guidelines:

"Nothing political or religious. Nothing in the way of history written since 1900. [The previous line is crossed out.] Only the best nonfiction, specialize on engineering, mechanical training, nothing pertaining to war. Farming, geology, flying, any branch of useful science for men or boys. As for women and girls, use your own judgment."

Acknowledgements

I would like to thank the following for their contributions and support of this project:

My aunt Ruth Engelbart and my mother Mary Martin provided me a copy of Hayes' diaries *Here and There*. Ruth's dedication to tracking Hayes' wanderings through pre-digital atlases sparked my initial interest in our common cousin's travels.

Most of the other firsthand source material came to me through Dr. Michael Gimigliano who rescued a dozen manuscripts typed on onion-skin paper from a cleanup at Preston Laboratories in Butler, Pennsylvania. Without Michael the only copy of Hayes' novel *The Rearguard* and Hayes' hatchet(!) would have been lost.

The family of Rachel and Harry Franck graciously provided me a copy of *Down Through Africa* without which I would have known next to nothing about Hayes' final trip with Rachel and Harry through North Africa.

The Library at Cal Poly San Luis Obispo sent me copies of a number of Hayes' personal correspondences.

Itinerant cartographer Brian Timoney created the maps of Hayes' travels in Africa.

The beautiful photograph of Perkins Park in Pacific Grove, California, on the back cover was taken by David Laws a founding member of Friends of Perkins Park. See: https://www.friendsofperkinspark.com/

Joyce Krieg edited the final manuscript and created the book cover.

The support of the working members of Stonebridge Farm for my long project has been invaluable. Peter Butler, Hal Huntsman, and Mike Lane have been particularly persistent. The insightful comments of Rick Griffith precipitated two years of much needed thought, research, and introspection.

The Word Wednesday writers were also unstintingly supportive. Andrea Pontiers has thrown down various inspirational gauntlets.

Carolyn Morris, Paul Moeller, Gene Hayworth, and Patricia Appelfeller guided me through the publication process.

And to Kayann beside whom all my horizon lines beckon.

Author's Biography

John M. Martin earned his PhD in the philosophy of mathematics and, as an instructor at the University of Colorado, received a number of teaching awards for his innovative approaches to introductory calculus. His preoccupation with the mathematical infinite took a more practical turn with the establishment of Stonebridge Community Supported Agriculture Farm where he collaborates in the gardens and vineyards. First cousin thrice-removed to Hayes Perkins, Martin grew up reading the peripatetic traveler's diaries and remains fascinated with this complex adventurer whose intriguing world says so much about our own.